Responsible Leadership in Corporate Governance

Responsibly led boards of directors make it possible for modern companies to survive and prosper under conditions of change. Despite the importance of boards of directors, their activities are often lionised or vilified by shareholders and stakeholders, which obscures how boards enact responsible leadership. *Responsible Leadership in Corporate Governance* introduces an integrative model of responsible leadership in governance that positions the board as a nexus of all corporate participants. In this model, responsibly led boards seek to make decisions in the best interests of the modern company as an entity that operates in a dynamic business environment.

This book provides a timely focus on in-depth cases of board led responsible leadership. Examining boards of directors in listed companies, state-owned enterprises and private companies, the book connects insights from corporate governance and leadership to behaviours that affect boards' relationships with shareholders and stakeholders. In addition, these insights underscore key requirements and challenges of responsible leadership in governance, from the importance of purpose and the crucial role of value creation to the difficulties of ownership transition and accountability. Far-sighted and experienced-based, this book will not only help students connect to real-world situations but also will benefit those that interact with and support boards of directors.

Monique Cikaliuk is principal business consultant and founder, Wisdom Work Strategies, Victoria, Canada.

Ljiljana Eraković is an associate professor at the University of Auckland Business School, New Zealand.

Brad Jackson is a professor of leadership and governance at the Waikato Management School, University of Waikato, New Zealand.

Chris Noonan is an associate professor and associate dean postgraduate and international in the Faculty of Law, University of Auckland, New Zealand.

Susan Watson holds joint chairs in the University of Auckland Faculty of Law and the University of Auckland Faculty of Business and Economics, and is dean of the University of Auckland Business School, New Zealand.

Routledge Studies in Leadership Research

Digital Supply Chain Management
Reshaping Talent and Organizations
David B. Kurz and Muragan Anandarajan

Researching Leadership-As-Practice
The Reappearing Act of Leadership
Vasilisa Takoeva

Adaptive Leadership in a Global Economy
Perspective for Application and Scholarship
Edited by Mohammed Raei and Harriette Thurber Rasmussen

Women Business Leaders
Identity, Resistance, and Alternative Forms of Knowledge in Saudi Arabia
Liela A. Jamjoom

Responsible Leadership in Corporate Governance
An Integrative Approach
Monique Cikaliuk, Ljiljana Eraković, Brad Jackson, Chris Noonan and Susan Watson

Leadership and China
Philosophy, Place and Practice
Edited by Ralph J. Bathurst and Michelle Sitong Chen

Leadership and Narcissism in the Organization
Mateusz Grzesiak

Public Sector Leadership
A Human-Centred Approach
Petri Virtanen, Marika Tammeaid and Harri Jalonen

Toxic Leadership
Research and Cases
Steven Walker and Daryl Watkins

For more information about this series please visit: https://www.routledge.com/Routledge-Studies-in-Leadership-Research/book-series/RSLR.

Responsible Leadership in Corporate Governance

An Integrative Approach

Monique Cikaliuk, Ljiljana Eraković, Brad Jackson, Chris Noonan and Susan Watson

Routledge
Taylor & Francis Group
NEW YORK AND LONDON

First published 2023
by Routledge
605 Third Avenue, New York, NY 10158

and by Routledge
4 Park Square, Milton Park, Abingdon, Oxon OX14 4RN

Routledge is an imprint of the Taylor & Francis Group, an informa business

Library of Congress Cataloging-in-Publication Data
A catalog record for this title has been requested

ISBN: 978-0-367-48156-8 (hbk)
ISBN: 978-0-367-51512-6 (pbk)
ISBN: 978-1-003-05419-1 (ebk)

DOI: 10.4324/9781003054191

Typeset in Bembo
by Taylor & Francis Books

Contents

Author Biographies

Monique Cikaliuk is principal of Wisdom Work, a consulting practice in Canada. Prior to this role, she was a post-doctoral research fellow with the New Zealand Leadership Institute at the University of Auckland Business School. She received her doctorate in management learning from Lancaster University, UK. Monique has co-authored papers published in the *Journal of Management and Organization, New Zealand Business Law Quarterly* and *Leadership for Health Services*, and chapters in the *Research Handbook on Boards of Directors* and *More Women on Boards: An International Perspective*. She is co-author of the book *Corporate Governance and Leadership: The Board as the Nexus of Leadership-in-Governance* (Cambridge University Press, 2020).

Ljiljana Erakovič is associate professor at the University of Auckland Business School. Her research focuses on corporate governance and boards of directors. Ljiljana is particularly interested in exploring board-management relationships and the interface of governance and leadership processes in organizations with different ownership structures. Her research has been widely published in scholarly books and international academic journals, including *Corporate Governance: An International Review, Public Administration, British Journal of Management* and *Journal of Business Ethics*. Ljiljana co-authored two books: *Corporate Governance and Leadership: The Board as the Nexus of Leadership-in-Governance* (Cambridge University Press, 2020) and *Stepping through Transitions: Management, Leadership and Governance in Not-for-Profit Organisations* (CGO Transitions, 2013).

Brad Jackson is professor of leadership and governance and MBA director at the University of Waikato Management School. The author of seven leadership books and the editor of two others, Brad's current research explores the inter-relationship between leadership and governance practices in promoting and sustaining social and economic innovation and the application of place-based approaches to foster cross-sectoral leadership development and education.

Chris Noonan is an associate professor in the Faculty of Law at the University of Auckland. He researches in corporate law, competition law and policy, and international trade law. His publications include the monograph *The Emerging Principles of International Competition Law* (Oxford University Press, 2008) and the treatise *Competition Law in New Zealand* (Thomson Reuters, 2017)

Susan Watson holds joint chairs in the Faculty of Law, and the Faculty of Business and Economics at the University of Auckland. She is the dean of the University of Auckland Business School. Susan has a particular interest in the corporate form and in her research seeks to understand how the form evolved, why it is so successful, and the economic and societal impact of corporations. Her monograph *The Making of the Modern Company* focusses on these questions, in particular challenging the dominant contractual model and setting out an alternative model that conceives of the modern company as an artificial legal person based on a fund contributed by shareholders that becomes an entity as it operates in the world. Susan has edited and co-authored treatises and textbooks, edited collections, and numerous articles and book chapters in these and related areas. Her work has been cited and discussed by other scholars in the field and by courts at all levels including the NZ and UK Supreme Courts. She is a research member of the European Corporate Governance Institute.

Acknowledgements

We are grateful to the University of Auckland Business School for providing initial funding support when we formally began this project back in 2011, as well intermittent support through the entirety of the project. In particular, we wish to acknowledge the encouragement and support we received from our former dean, Professor Greg Whittred, and our former deputy dean, Professor Jilnaught Wong.

We want to acknowledge enthusiastic support and guidance of Professor Steve Kempster, the editor of the Routledge Studies in Leadership Research series. Steve has corralled and championed a remarkable collection of leadership books and we are proud to contribute to this series.

Warm thanks are due to Yiling Liu, who provided valuable assistance in the book submission phase, funded by the Waikato Management School.

We greatly appreciate the patience, persistence and professionalism of the Routledge team we have worked with on this book project, most especially Brianna Ascher, Mary Del Plato, Jessica Rech and Naomi Round Cahalin.

Finally, we gratefully acknowledge the vital contributions of research participants who generously shared their insights and experience into the practice of responsible leadership in corporate governance. Thanks especially to Roger France for encouraging us to change our tack early in the research project and for opening up the all-important first case study.

1 Introduction and Overview

Introduction

How corporations perform, how corporate directors behave and how shareholders and executives act have emerged from the background and into the spotlight in the past decade (Coulson-Thomas, 2019). Both successes and debacles have prompted a deeper questioning of issues such as whether traditional corporate governance practices are a good fit for the modern world, whose interests corporate leaders serve and promote, and what measures can be taken to ensure all involved live up to corporate values and responsibilities (Eliot, 2017).

Corporate governance and leadership are traditionally treated as separate topics studied by scholars and developed by practitioners who rarely interact (Yar Hamidi & Gabrielsson, 2014). Corporate governance is commonly defined and discussed from legal or regulatory perspectives, while leadership is approached from psychological, political science and cultural perspectives. In a sharp departure, this book argues that leadership is a core activity in governing an organisation. Leadership, regardless of whether it is good, mediocre or outright bad, is inherent to the governance of every organisation. Institutionalised structures and legal rules provide only a general definition of the director's principal roles. Within these customary prescribed roles directors, through the quality of their individual and collective leadership, significantly influence the effectiveness of corporate governance and the achievement of the organisation's purpose and goals.

Leadership extends beyond star performing organisations; it plays out in middle-of-the-road performers as well as corporate laggards. Leadership in governance concerns the leadership *of* directors and leadership *in* boardrooms. Decisions with far-reaching consequences for shareholders and other stakeholders are either undermined or strengthened by the leadership exercised at the pinnacle of the organisation.

The use, and sometimes misuse, of leadership raises governance issues (Helms, 2012). The performance of the board, even in the most complex of governance configurations, hinges on value creation and control decisions influenced by shareholders, directors, and managers. Ensuring

DOI: 10.4324/9781003054191-1

effective leadership needs to be part of every organisation's system of good governance to deter debilitating, value eroding practices. More crucially, effective leadership in governance promotes new governance practices guiding directors to move beyond a narrow focus on monitoring to adopt a broader, more generative and expansive view of their role in value creation (Huse et al., 2018).

We have written this book for leadership and corporate law researchers and postgraduate students as well directors, executives and other governance practitioners, in an effort to bring board leadership to the forefront of academic and professional discourse and to lay out the terrain for this topic for years to come. The book is neither about the psychology of leaders, nor does it recommend political or policy solutions. It certainly does not endeavour to provide a 'one-size-fits-all' approach to leadership in corporate governance. Instead it alerts the reader to real world situations encountered by directors where difficult decisions need to be made. The book prompts the reader to recognise that there are no clear-cut right answers and compels the reader to understand that certain behaviours align with governance processes to achieve different organisational objectives.

By presenting and discussing extensive case studies of real organisations and contemporary governance issues, the book provides a prism through which the reader is given an opportunity to contemplate how directors' beliefs and behaviours (leadership) and structural frameworks (governance), jointly interact and impact upon organisational practices and performance. In a nutshell, it considers *what* leadership in governance is, *why* it is important, and it offers practical approaches on *how* it can be developed and more widely practised.

Rationale for the Book

The primary objective of this book is to integrate and cross-fertilise research and practice of leadership and corporate governance. To achieve this, the book argues that leadership in the boardroom is core to governing an organisation and governing it well or poorly; thereby explaining why a change in how we understand leadership in governance is needed and showing how change can be achieved.

This book examines the key ideas that inform leadership in governance practices, arguing that their understanding, interpretation and application have consequences for 'everyday' governance. We focus our attention on the use, and sometimes, misuse of leadership to align or subvert systems of corporate governance. Accordingly, the book explores how the legal rules, which create the constraints, structures and environment within which governance happens, provide the boundaries to which leaders (have to) adjust or decide to challenge in some cases. We direct our empirical attention to the efforts of some large listed companies, private firms and state-owned enterprises from New Zealand that have international presence and international business strategies. In a series of field-research case studies, we explore the value creation and control decisions of directors, examining the central features of how leadership has been exercised among directors, with shareholders through management and across stakeholders. The decisions in this nexus of relationships focus on board functions which include formulating business strategies, developing corporate policies, appointing CEOs, monitoring management and being accountable to shareholders. We illustrate the wide range of expression in practice and consequences for directors to alleviate or avoid problems.

Informed by our leadership in governance framework, we show how desired organisational outcomes are affected by the nature of the leadership exercised by directors in relationship with the quality of the corporate governance processes. By demonstrating the contingent basis of our current understanding of leadership in corporate governance through contemporary cases, we believe we are well placed to help set the terms of the discussion and define the terrain on this topic.

We seek to encourage scholars to adopt a different approach to governance, proposing that corporate governance offers a specific and focused context within which to explore leadership impact. We also aim to support practitioners wanting to develop a leadership approach to governing informed by a deeper understanding of how different leadership and governance interactions influence board effectiveness and enterprise performance.

This book is different from existing texts on governance because of its integration with leadership to generate a new framework, the scope of its leadership, governance, and regulatory thematic focus, and its use of in-depth cases to illuminate the actual behaviours and decisions undertaken by directors entrusted with the performance and control of organisations. The number of governance books has grown substantially in recent years. However, the idea of 'leadership in corporate governance' is not an approach that other scholars have made central to their work. Chait et al. (2005) provided a 'governance leadership model' that highlighted the fiduciary, strategic and generative modes of governance that was developed for non-profit boards. This model greatly influenced our early thinking. Steger and Amann (2008) examined corporate governance through a contingency approach but did not examine board leadership for value creation or name the actual organisations in most case studies. Zinkin (2014) examined the board's oversight role for rogue CEOs within the banking industry. Several journal articles have also examined leadership and decision making of board chairs (e.g. Banerjee et al., 2020; Harrison & Murray, 2012; Levrau & Van den Berghe, 2013). However, we contend that our findings offer a considerably more detailed and integrated analysis than existing accounts, address a wider range of themes in more depth and examine a greater range of ownership structures. Given the potency of our findings to change the way corporate governance is theorised, studied and practised, we remain puzzled that other scholars have not placed the leadership of directors under greater scrutiny.

In an earlier volume in the Routledge Studies in Leadership Research series, Wilson et al. (2019) argued that leadership studies is in urgent need of revitalisation as it has become an isolated, abstract and 'special' phenomenon that is de-contextualised from the work streams within the organisation. The authors proposed that the field could be significantly revitalised by returning to the theorisation and the empirical exploration of '*leading*' activities within clusters of work activities such as '*leading in*' supervisory management, human resource management, innovation and entrepreneurship and governance. Among other tasks, this book responds directly to this challenge by directly examining leadership in the context of governance activities. It aims to show the benefits of conducting 'leadership-practice-in-context' research that reinforces the idea that leadership is only of value if it is shaped by, and responds to, the needs of a particular context, in this case the governance context (Wilson et al., 2019).

Finally, the book also aims to make an important contribution to the burgeoning responsible leadership literature (Jackson et al., 2022; Maak, 2007; Pless, 2007; Waldman & Balven, 2014). In this regard the present book builds on two edited collections that have also been featured in the Routledge Studies in Leadership Research series: *Responsible Leadership: Realism and Romanticism* (Kempster & Carroll, 2016) and *Good Dividends: Responsible Leadership of Business Purpose* (Kemspter et al., 2019). To date, with the exception of Zindler (2019) (featured in the second of these books), the primary focus of both the theoretical and empirical research of responsible leadership has been on the behaviours of individual senior executives (most especially the CEOs), owner-managers and founders and middle managers. Moreover, there has been a central pre-occupation with leadership processes and practices with very little consideration given to the intersection between leadership and governance processes and practices.

The Research Process

In 2011, the University of Auckland Business School introduced the research theme of leadership and governance as an area it wanted to promote as a core research area by bringing together scholars in the Business School who researched these areas from their own disciplinary perspectives. The theme brought together Susan and Chris who had been writing about corporate governance from a legal perspective for some time with Ljiljana and Brad who had already identified intersectionalities in their two fields of corporate governance and leadership. In our conversations we were fascinated by how with each of us drawing on the well of our knowledge of our respective fields, we deepened and enriched our shared understanding of the relationship between leadership and governance. In light of this we decided and were supported to work on a series of projects where we applied an integrated multidisciplinary perspective to boards of directors.

Our team was greatly bolstered by Monique's appointment after a worldwide search as a Post-Doctoral Fellow. Monique had recently completed her doctorate at Lancaster University and was responsible for conducting most of the empirical research with Ljiljana as well as analysing the data and writing up of our case studies. Thankfully Monique has stayed with our team even after returning to her hometown of Victoria in British Columbia, Canada, where she runs her business consultancy.

We collectively recognised how difficult it was to open up the 'black box' of the boards of directors to acquire data on corporate governance practices (Eraković & Overall, 2010). Like a jury, we can find out the decisions made by boards of directors but not the process by which they are reached. And so our initial line of thinking hinged on accessing and analysing publicly available legal records as a means of accessing corporate governance practices. In 2012, we applied for and received some internal seed money for a research project which was somewhat melodramatically entitled, 'Opening Up the Black Box: Exploring the Crucial Interface Between Poor Leadership and Bad Governance in Australasian Organisations'. This project sought to understand what drives organisational failure at the board room level through what Helms (2012) describes as a combination of 'poor leadership' and 'bad governance'. Poor leadership was broken down into ineffective, inefficient, unethical or illegal behaviour on the part of the board members. Bad governance was construed as a combination of bad policies and plans (i.e. ill-conceived and/or poorly implemented) and bad outcomes for the organisation. We identified a rich source of data for studying governance and leadership processes that had hitherto not been used but was publicly available and relatively ubiquitous. When companies fail, part of the fall-out is often litigation or even Royal Commissions of Inquiry. The interrogative powers of Courts and Commissions override any actual or desired confidentiality obligations of directors. Judgements, Royal Commission Reports and their ilk contain painstaking chronologies of the deliberations and decisions that led to particular corporate failures. They are an untapped source that allow us to open the black box and explore the crucial interface between leadership and governance process.

While we drew on court records as data sources for some cases, these data still remain largely untapped because our project took a 180-degree turn thanks to the intercession of Roger France, one of New Zealand's highly experienced and very well-respected board director. He spoke with our group and strongly encouraged us to conduct research on good rather than bad governance that was inspired by enlightened rather than poor leadership. He argued that this work was most needed in order to promote better and more enlightened corporate governance practice. Most especially he thought it was vitally important to produce top-notch case studies for current and aspiring directors. Moreover, he offered to negotiate access on our behalf to Air New Zealand directors who had been engaged in the most significant corporate governance challenge in the past decade in the country, saving and turning around the nation's airline in spectacular fashion. Because of this engagement we produced our first case study, 'Board Leadership and Governance for Clear-Sighted CEO Succession at Air New Zealand' which is featured in an abridged format in Chapter 7 and was published in full in the *Journal of Management and Organization* (Cikaliuk et al., 2018). The highly favourable feedback that we received for this case study when we launched it to a packed Master Class held at the University of Auckland provided us with the impetus and the credibility to conduct further governance research with other prominent boards of directors including the Bank of New Zealand (featured in Chapter 8) and the Auckland International Airport (featured in Chapters 6 and 7) and Solid Energy (featured in Chapter 3). These cases have been used extensively in teaching, most especially in the University of Auckland and the University MBA programmes and have been refined based on the input we received from our students.

For the empirical part of our research project we conducted in-depth interviews with 67 non-executive and executive board members from seven companies who conducted business internationally and domestically in New Zealand. All of those who were interviewed participated in an ethical research oversight process. Members of the team interviewed nine current and former chairs, 34 directors and three managing directors/founders. We also interviewed 5 CEOs and 16 executives/managers. Some companies generated so much data that we were able to produce multiple cases over an expanded time frame that included key events for the boards including a change of ownership. Consequently, Auckland International Airport, one of the country's most celebrated boards is featured in three cases. Another company, Diligent Board Member Services, and the Aldridge Energy company are featured in two cases. In the Diligent Board Member Services cases and the Lombard Financial Services case we relied exclusively on public sources. The companies and directors we interviewed are identified in all of the cases except for two companies which we have concealed the identities of as well as the board members.

This book acts as an effective companion piece to the first book that we published from this project, *Corporate Governance and Leadership: The Board as the Nexus of Leadership-in-Goverance* (Cikaliuk et al., 2020). In this book, we endeavoured to expand our understanding of board leadership by focusing on the modern company as a legal person comprised of a capital fund and the relationships among directors, shareholders, management and stakeholders. We argued that seeing the company with its corporate fund and dynamic set of relationships had important implications for current conceptualisations of how boards enact leadership in governance. We proposed a model which integrated insights from the fields of leadership and corporate governance. Our theoretical conception was illustrated by empirical findings at three intersections: team leadership on the board, the chair's leadership of the board, and strategic leadership by the board. We argued that this integrative model provided a powerful means to further an understanding of the board as the nexus of leadership and governance. The current book provides further empirical elucidation and theoretical refinement of this model by focusing on a wide range of governance themes and providing rich, albeit compressed illustrative case studies. Our previous book was published in the Cambridge University Press's Elements in Corporate Governance series. This book is featured in the Routledge Studies in Leadership Research Series. We hope that in contributing to these well-established book series we can reach the all-important cross-over audience of corporate governance and leadership scholars and practitioners.

Before we provide an overview of the each of the chapters' key arguments, themes and content within this book, we will briefly describe and discuss the distinctive nature of the New Zealand corporate landscape and why we believe it to be especially pertinent and instructive to governance leadership researchers based elsewhere.

The New Zealand Governance Context

Given that New Zealand was colonised by the British, it is not surprising to learn that corporate governance is generally underpinned by the Anglo-Saxon governance model (Ahmad & Omar, 2016). This model has tended to emphasise the maximisation of shareholder wealth; the separation of ownership of control from ownership; shareholder control and a one-tier board in which appointments are administered by an independent audit committee. In common with many jurisdictions, these tendencies have been substantially ameliorated as many New Zealand companies are now actively seeking to balance shareholder interests with other stakeholder interests and have placed a growing emphasis on their responsive engagement with a growing array of stakeholders (Institute of Directors, 2021).

The corporate governance landscape in New Zealand is guided by a variety of sources, including separate legislation that governs companies, limited partnerships, incorporated societies and Crown entities (Institute of Directors, 2021). Since colonisation began in the early nineteenth century, there has been a strong tradition of either state or family ownership of organisations. A distinctive feature of the New Zealand economy is the scope and scale of state-owned enterprises (SOEs) in which the government has either full, majority or at least a substantial minority interest. Three of the case studies that are featured in this book are SOEs. Approximately 97 per cent of companies within New Zealand are small and mid-sized enterprises (SMEs) (employing 29 per cent of all employees) with little or no formal governance mechanisms in place. For those SMEs where governance arrangements are in place, the most common governance model is an advisory board rather than a statutory board. Family businesses are a prominent feature of the New Zealand economy. Many family companies have either a controlling shareholder or a significant minority of large shareholders.

A second distinctive feature of the New Zealand corporate governance landscape is its international track record in ethical practice. In the 2021 Corruption Perceptions index released by Transparency International, New Zealand ranked first equal with Denmark and Finland with a score of 88 out of 100 (Transparency International, 2021). It is a point of honour for many New Zealanders that the country continues to maintain this important distinction. It has provided an important platform in the country's export and foreign investment strategy and its cherished role as an 'honest broker' in brokering free trade agreements. Legislation is in process to maintain this standing. The Companies (Directors Duties) Amendment Bill outlines that a director, in acting as the mind and will of the company, may take actions based on considerations that go beyond the financial bottom line. In the Bill these considerations are open-ended but will likely include matters such as the principles of Te Tiriti o Waitangi (New Zealand's founding document), environmental impacts, good corporate ethics, being a good employer, and acting in the interests of the wider community (New Zealand Parliament, 2022). The Institute of Directors identified the following five issues as being the most critical for boards to address in 2022: 'climate crossroads; reconnecting globally; talent shortage; board character; and active regulators' (Institute of Directors, 2022).

A third distinctive feature of New Zealand governance has been the prevalence and rapid growth of Māori organisations which are governed and led by the Tanagata Whenua of Aotearoa, the original inhabitants, pre-colonisation. In Māori organisations (e.g. companies, partnerships, Māori trust boards, Māori reservations and Māori incorporations), the objectives of governance take into account the way in which Māori relate to the assets and what they are used for (Te Puni Kokiri, 2022). In some instances, although the organisation operates commercially, commercial objectives need to balance with the need to safeguard the assets for future generations. Kawa (i.e. policy), Tikanga (i.e. procedures) and values are also put into practice on the board of Māori organisations often alongside Western governance principles in order to meet the aspirations of *iwi* (nation), *hapū* (community) and *whānau* (family). Māori organisations, therefore, tend to have to blend multiple purposes. Many have to balance being financially viable with the social and cultural aspirations of the collective owners as their core purpose. Māori organisations also tend to hold a comparatively long-term view of the future.

While the authors are primarily based in New Zealand and the cases that are presented feature New Zealand-based companies, the focus of this book is on the theory and practice of responsible leadership by boards of modern companies in general. Companies are incorporated through general incorporation statutes that are in place in almost every jurisdiction across the world. Boards are collective decisionmakers. Their decisions determine the direction of the company. Decisions are made in a corporate context with different ownership structures which may create challenges for directors to discern to whom they owe obligations (or duties).

Recently the New Zealand Supreme Court, in Debut Homes summarised, obiter, the three theories of the company:

> It is the duty of directors to act in the best interests of the company. The traditional view is that this requirement is fulfilled by directors acting in the best interests of the shareholders as a whole. This is known as the shareholder primacy model. The main competing model of corporate governance is the stakeholder model, whereby the interests of those with some stake in the company and its business (such as employees, creditors and the wider public) should be taken into account by the directors, alongside the interests of shareholders. Wider considerations beyond maximising profits might therefore be acceptable for directors under the stakeholder model. A third view is that the concentration should be on the company itself. This approach arguably allows other interests to be taken into account more explicitly than under the traditional approach, as long as it is in the best interests of the company to do so.
>
> (*Debut Homes Ltd (in liq) v Cooper* [2019] NZSC 59, 28–30)

In this book we adopt the third view which we term the 'entity' model of the company. The entity model of the company emerges from an extensive study that Susan has conducted of the evolution of the modern company (Watson, 2015, 2019, 2022). This approach will be fully elucidated in Chapter 2. The entity model serves to unleash the potential of the corporate form to generate value over time. It also provides a way for boards to balance the interests of shareholders as owners of shares in the company, with the interests of stakeholders of the company. By requiring a focus on the company itself, the entity model also legitimises boards adopting a long term perspective that extends beyond current shareholders. In short, the entity model allows for a broader conceptualisation and more sophisticated approach of how boards of directors realise their obligations than other models, such as the shareholder primacy model. The shareholder primacy model is based on a contractual understanding of the company. In this model current shareholders are akin to principals with directors their agents. The shareholder primacy model therefore may make it difficult for boards to justify decisions that may not favour the current interests of existing shareholders even though they are in the long-term interests of the company. These decisions may also favour current stakeholder interests and mean that the board is acting responsibly. In line with the historical analysis, boards exercising responsible leadership with a focus on the long-term can benefit the company in the long term and therefore shareholders as the owners of shares in the company. The success stories set out in this book demonstrate the boards of New Zealand companies adopting a long-term perspective and making decisions as responsible leaders in the interests of the company.

Structure of the Book

The book is comprised of nine chapters. Chapters 1 and 2 provide the conceptual platform for the book. Chapters 3–8 are dedicated to examining the leadership in governance dynamics of an important contemporary corporate governance challenge, from value creation to corporate control transition to CEO succession to diversity and inclusion. In each of these chapters we feature case studies that provide rich empirical insights from those who were directly engaged in tackling these issues supplemented by factual material provided in organisational documents.

In Chapter 2 we outline our distinctive leadership in governance approach. Our research has revealed that boards behave responsibly when the directors are intrinsically motivated to contribute their knowledge and skills to the well-being of the company and its stakeholders; their value system and personal identity correspond with the purpose and goals of the company; directors have high belief in their own self-efficacy and ability to mobilise the efforts of others; and they are willing to self-evaluate their actions. The entity model opens up the possibility for the board to enact agency (leadership) for decisions about the direction and management of the company. We argue that an agentic view of boards of directors, based on social cognitive theory, compels us to broaden our conceptualisation of *why* and *how* directors behave and do what they do to shape relationships (social systems). In so doing, directors, individually and collectively, may enact responsible leadership acting as agentic fiduciaries rather than as constrained agents. We believe that structural and behavioural characteristics in analysing boards of directors should not be considered in isolation but in an integrative manner. Structures (i.e. internal/corporate and external/systemic policies and procedures) and actions (i.e. individual and collective behaviours) work in a constantly interdependent manner. Structural conditions can serve to both regulate and enable boards to act in a certain manner. Therefore, boards can be instructively conceived of as 'products' of a particular configuration of structures which continuously evolve. At the same time, driven by motivations, capabilities and a sense of efficacy, directors can collectively undertake actions through which they can actively influence and shape (that is, *lead*) the current structural context. More importantly, we argue that directors can behave agentically (not in the way that was traditionally conceived by agency theorists) to create new structures in order to create dynamic companies. They can and should be both proactive and transformational shapers (or 'producers') in their governance fields.

Companies with a near to optimal capital structure operate effectively in a dynamic business environment with access to financial resources to pursue opportunities and respond to change. Although the performance effects of different capital arrangements have been examined in relation to investments, survival, growth and solvency, few accounts explore the role of the responsibly led board and shareholders as shaped by the legal nature of the company. In Chapter 3, we focus on the board's roles and responsibilities in relation to shareholders as the board makes decisions that affect the company's capital structure. We examine the leadership role of the board through the lens of shareholder diversity, board-shareholder relationships and accountability. We use these lenses to illustrate the ways in which boards' behaviours aid or hinder its relationships with different shareholders with diverse objectives and time horizons in three case studies. The different lenses allow us to juxtapose insights from the boards of a publicly listed international software company, a state-owned coal mining enterprise and a privately-held construction management consultancy company, and to link these different capital structures and shareholders to boards' behaviour as they seek to enact responsible leadership in governance.

One of the essential governance roles is oversight or monitoring. Shareholders and other key stakeholders can use different sources of internal and external oversight to control the functioning of the company. In Chapter 4 we employ the leadership in governance framework to problematise the monitoring role of the board, illustrating the need for multiple, diverse sets of governance systems and arguing that formal regulations alone will not prevent bad behaviour and corporate collapse. We provide a broader accountability approach that complements corporate governance and responsibly led board oversight. We analyse and derive insights from the boards' conduct of oversight tasks from two company case studies in the financial and software industry. By focusing on formal and informal accountability in the conduct of board oversight, our cases provide evidence that boards can shape a specific combination of governance practices that either *are or are not* in the company's best interests.

In Chapter 5 we draw on an entity conception of the corporation to propose a framework that integrates a finer grained understanding of board led responsible leadership in governance and establishes a link between these constructs and value creation. Value creation by companies has long been associated with economic relationships exclusively between management and shareholders. Most accounts focus on a specific conception of the corporation that is strongly associated with shareholder value creation which fosters an impoverished view of board leadership in corporate governance. We use the leadership in governance framework to show how both instrumental and integrative orientations of responsibly led boards of directors and stakeholder and purpose driven corporate governance affect value creation across stakeholders, including shareholders. The framework allows us to compare insights from four cases of large, listed companies and to distil theoretical and practical implications for boards of directors and those who support and interact with them. The clear implication of this approach is that without considering how responsibly led boards of directors purposefully create value across stakeholders, discussion of value creation remains in the abstract, removed from the actual practice of governing large, listed companies.

Companies commonly use acquisitions and initial public offerings to gain new resources to grow and achieve sustained performance. While the effects on performance outcomes are well documented following these changes, few accounts explore responsible board leadership to affect changes in ownership structure. In Chapter 6, we focus on the board's roles, responsibilities and board characteristics as the board interacts with stakeholders to reconfigure a company's share ownership. We use the lens of the board's roles and responsibilities, composition, reputation and capabilities as well as interactions to illustrate the ways in which board led responsible leadership can either enable or hinder strategic change in two cases that feature an acquisition of a large, listed company and an initial public offering by a state-owned enterprise. The different lenses allow us to compare the cases and connect board led responsible leadership insights that warrant attention for scholars and those who interact with and support boards of directors.

The succession and selection of CEOs is frequently singled out as the most important task performed by boards of directors for large, listed companies to achieve its purpose or improve its capability to achieve its purpose. Despite the prevalence and frequency of this task, boards vary widely in their capability to be successful. In Chapter 7, we present two complementary pathways to understand how responsibly led boards of directors mobilise processes for CEO succession and selection that engage stakeholders who are both internal and external to the company. Combining psychological and knowledge-based pathways underpins the dynamic process that boards of directors can mobilise to bring about shared benefits in the conduct of CEO succession and selection. The links between board led responsible leadership and CEO succession and selection are illustrated in a case study of a widely celebrated international airline company that shows how that independently-led boards can shape a specific combination of governance practices to contribute to successful CEO transitions.

Understanding how a company fits its dynamic external environment is essential to making beneficial strategic changes to its products, services and processes. One of the ways that companies align with the emerging environment is through diversity initiatives. In Chapter 8, the final empirical chapter, we look at how boards promote diversity and inclusion to improve their companies' economic and social performance. We focus on three areas that prior research has shown to be critical in diversity and inclusion: board attitudes and composition, corporate strategy and role modelling. We analyse and derive insights from the series of decisions that a responsibly led board made in the process of effecting a strategic transformation of a bank through a diversity strategy that has been internationally recognised for its progressive nature.

In the concluding chapter of the book (Chapter 9) we review the key learnings from developing the leadership in governance conceptual framework and applying it to the case studies featured in this book. The main features and benefits of our integrative approach to research are highlighted in the hope that it will encourage other researchers to explore and further refine this approach. Fundamentally, this integrative approach promotes greater engagement and cross-fertilisation within multi-disciplinary teams, and between researchers and practitioners.

Looking ahead to how leadership in corporate governance research can profitably develop in the future, we advocate that *diversification* is a key imperative. This imperative encompasses diversification in research methods; diversification in theorisation; diversification in knowledge sources; diversification of governance concern and issues; diversification in governance leadership; diversification in stakeholder engagement; and diversification in governance technologies.

References

Ahmad, S., & Omar, R. (2016). Basic corporate governance models: A systematic review, *International Journal of Law and Management*, 58(10), 73–107.

Banerjee, A., Nordqvist, M., & Hellerstedt, K. (2020). The role of the board chair—A literature review and suggestions for future research. *Corporate Governance: An International Review*, 28(6), 372–405.

Bower, J. L., & Paine, L. S. (2017). The error at the heart of corporate leadership. *Harvard Business Review*, 95(3), 50–60.

Chait, R. P., Ryan, W. P., & Taylor, B. E. (2005). *Governance as leadership: Reframing the work of nonprofit boards.* John Wiley & Sons.

Cikaliuk, M., Eraković, L., Jackson, B., Noonan, C., & Watson, S. (2018). Board leadership and governance for clear-sighted CEO succession at Air New Zealand, *Journal of Management & Organization*, 26(5), 774–797.

Cikaliuk, M., Eraković, L., Jackson, B., Noonan, C., & Watson, S. (2020). *Corporate governance and leadership: The board as the nexus of leadership-in-governance.* Elements in Corporate Governance Series. Cambridge University Press.

Clarke, T., & Branson, D. (eds). (2012). *The Sage handbook of corporate governance.* Sage.

Coulson-Thomas, C. (2019). Board leadership, crisis governance and governance in crisis. *Effective Executive*, 22(3), 42–58.

Debut Homes Ltd (in liq) v Cooper [2019] NZSC 59. www.courtsofnz.govt.nz/assets/cases/SC-29-2019-Debut-Homes-v-Cooper.pdf.

Eliot, H. (2017). *Board shorts: Effective governance for the next generation of directors.* Milford.

Eraković, L., & Jackson, B. (2012). Promoting leadership in governance and governance in leadership. In A. Davila, M. Elvira, J. Ramirez & L. Zapata-Cantu (eds), *Understanding organizations in complex, emergent and uncertain environments* (pp. 68–83). Palgrave Macmillan.

Eraković, L., Jackson, B., & Kudumula-Arora, S. (2011). *Leadership-in-governance in the professional services context: The case of an architecture firm.* Paper presented at European Group for Organisational Studies (EGOS), Stockholm, 7–9 July.

Eraković, L., & Overall, J. (2010). Opening the 'black box': Challenging traditional governance theorems. *Journal of Management & Organization*, 16(2), 250–265.

Filatotchev, I., & Boyd, B. K. (2009). Taking stock of corporate governance research while looking to the future. *Corporate Governance: An International Review*, 17(3), 257–265.

Gabrielsson, J., Khlif, W., & Yamak, S. (eds). (2019). *Research handbook on boards of directors.* Edward Elgar.

Harrison, Y. D., & Murray, V. (2012). Perspectives on the leadership of chairs of nonprofit organization boards of directors: A grounded theory mixed-method study. *Nonprofit Management and Leadership*, 22(4), 411–437.

Helms, L. (ed.). (2012). *Poor leadership and bad governance.* Edward Elgar.

Hoppmann, J., Naegele, F., & Girod, B. (2019). Boards as a source of inertia: Examining the internal challenges and dynamics of boards of directors in times of environmental discontinuities. *Academy of Management Journal*, 62(2), 437–468.

Huse, M. (2018). *Value-creating boards: Challenges for future research and practice.* Cambridge Elements in Corporate Governance Series. Cambridge University Press.

Institute of Directors. (2021). *The four pillars of governance best practice for New Zealand Directors.* The Governance Leadership Centre.

Institute of Directors. (2022). The top five issues for directors in 2022. www.iod.org.nz/news/boardroom/boardroom-magazine-summer-2021/the-top-five-issues-for-directors-in-2022/#.

Jackson, B., Kempster, S., Liyanage, C., Shang, S., & Sun, P. (2022). Responsible leadership: From theory building to impact mobilisation? In D. Schedlitzki, M. Larsson, B. Carroll & M. Bligh (eds), *Sage handbook of leadership* (2nd edition, pp. 240–262). Sage.

Kay, J., & Silberston, A. (1995). Corporate governance. *National Institute Economic Review*, 153, 84–97.

Kellerman, B. (2005). *Bad leadership: What it is, how it happens, why it matters.* Harvard Business School Press.

Kempster, S., & Carroll, B. (eds). (2016). *Responsible leadership: Realism and romanticism.* Routledge.

Kempster, S., & Jackson, B. (2021). Leadership for what, why, for whom and where?: A responsibility perspective. *Journal of Change Management*, 21(1), 45–65.

Kempster, S., Maak, T., & Parry, K. (eds). (2019). *Good dividends: Responsible leadership of business purpose.* Routledge.

Leblanc, R. (2005). Assessing board leadership. *Corporate Governance: An International Review*, 13(5), 654–666.

Levrau, A., & Van den Berghe, L. (2013). Perspectives on the decision-making style of the board chair. *International Journal of Disclosure and Governance*, 10(2), 105–121.

Lipman-Blumen, J. (2005). *The allure of toxic leaders.* Oxford University Press.

Maak, T. (2007). Responsible leadership, stakeholder engagement, and the emergence of social capital. *Journal of Business Ethics*, 74(4), 329–343.

Machold, S., Huse, M., Minichilli, A., & Nordqvist, M. (2011). Board leadership and strategy involvement in small firms: A team production approach. *Corporate Governance: An International Review*, 19(4), 368–383.

Morais, F., Kakabadse, A., & Kakabadse, N. K. (2019). Dealing with strategic tensions on the board: The role of the chair in fostering engagement and debate. In J. Gabrielsson, W. Khlif & S. Yamak (eds), *Research handbook on boards of directors* (pp. 31–48). Edward Elgar.

New Zealand Parliament. (2022). Companies (Director Duties) Amendment Bill. www.parliament.nz/en/pb/bills-and-laws/bills-proposed-laws/document/BILL_115958/companies-directors-duties-amendment-bill.

Nolan, R. (2015). *Executive team leadership in the global economic and competitive environment.* Routledge.

Pless, N. M. (2007). Understanding responsible leadership: Roles identity and motivational drivers. *Journal of Business Ethics*, 74(4), 437–456.

Steger, U., & Amann, W. (2008). *Corporate governance: How to add value.* John Wiley & Sons.

Te Puni Kokiri. (2022). What is governance? www.tpk.govt.nz/en/whakamahia/effective-governance/what-is-governance.

Transparency International. (2021). 2021 anti-corruption index. www.transparency.org/en/cpi/2021.

Tricker, R. I. (1994). *International corporate governance: Text, readings and cases.* Prentice Hall.

Waldman, D., & Balven, R. M. (2014). Responsible leadership: Theoretical issues and research directions. *Academy of Management Perspectives*, 28(3), 224–234.

Watson, S. (2015). How the company became an entity: A new understanding of corporate law. *Journal of Business Law*, 120(2), 1–24.

Watson, S. (2019). The corporate legal person. *Journal of Corporate Law Studies*, 19 (1), 137–166.

Watson, S. (2022). *The making of the modern company.* Bloomsbury.

Wilson, S., Cummings, S., Jackson, B., & Proctor-Thompson, S. (2019). *Revitalising leadership: Putting theory and practice into context.* Routledge.

Yar Hamidi, D., & Gabrielsson, J. (2014). Developments and trends in research on board leadership: A systematic literature review. *International Journal of Business Governance and Ethics*, 9(3), 243–268.

Zindler, R. (2019). The good dividends and governance: A leadership perspective. In S. Kempster, T. Maak & K. Parry (eds), *Good dividends: Responsible leadership of business purpose* (pp. 177–194). Routledge.

Zinkin, J. (2014). *Rebuilding trust in banks: The role of leadership and governance.* John Wiley & Sons.

2 A Leadership in Governance Approach

Introduction

In this book, we apply interdisciplinary lenses to consider what the corporation is and, consequently, how the boards that govern the corporation make sense of their purpose and carry out their responsibilities. The entity model of the corporation (Watson, 2015, 2019), we employ, facilitates and legitimises boards in their decision-making, actively considering the interests of stakeholders beyond shareholders to capture and enhance forms of value. Our own understanding of corporate governance has been informed by combining corporate law, business history, and organisation studies scholarship. This intersectional understanding of corporate governance draws a more complex and nuanced picture of the role of the board. We argue that directors themselves are *agentic*. As opposed to economic and legal understanding of directors as corporate agents of shareholders as principals, we argue that directors are fiduciaries who act on behalf of the corporation. They act *agentically*. That is, they should be seen to operate proactively, not only reactively. Boards are more than a structural product of the current (legal) corporate governance framework (i.e. the reactive position). They have the resources, opportunity and legitimacy to shape more 'democratic' and value-creating governance structures (i.e. the proactive position). As such, board directors may enact responsible leadership through agentic behaviour as fiduciaries of the corporation.

Board Leadership in the Entity Model

We approach board leadership from the perspective of the entity model, as we argue that the nature of the corporation defines 'the corporate governance problem' (Learmount, 2003) and the purpose and functioning of the board of directors. The entity model departs from a simplistic focus on the shareholders (principal)—managers/directors (agent) relationship where the board is just one of the mechanisms of corporate control; the mechanism which is supposed to protect the interests of the owners of capital. According to our view, the corporation can have multiple 'owners' and

DOI: 10.4324/9781003054191-2

these owners may contribute in various ways to its formation, development, continuation (Veldman & Willmott, 2013) and dismissal. The corporation may, therefore, be responsible 'to a range of constituents—to shareholders, but also to employees, customers, creditors, and the general public' (Ciepley, 2013, p. 147). Consequently, directors and managers' legal duty is to the corporation as well as to shareholders. If the corporation is independent (i.e. separated) from the shareholders and, if the right to direct the corporation is vested in a board of directors, then, as argued by Bower and Paine (2017), directors are not agents but *fiduciaries* for the corporation and shareholders. As fiduciaries, as opposed to agents, they are supposed to exercise their independent opinion and make discretionary decisions on behalf of those who entrusted them with these powers.

This broader conceptualisation of the accountability of the corporation, the scope of the corporate governance problem, and the duty of directors indicates that directors and managers do not necessarily or inevitably promote their self-interested agendas (as proposed by agency theory). Organisational life is more generally complex than is acknowledged by economic models. What these models often ignore is that companies are indeed controlled and managed by human beings who might have different interests and motivations in their corporate quests. The reality (see for example Serafeim, 2014), supported also by our own research (see Cikaliuk et al., 2019, 2020), has demonstrated that directors and managers are 'capable of taking into consideration the interests of others alongside their own [and those of shareholders] in making decisions and taking action, and are not solely motivated by incentives, monitoring and fiat' (Learmount, 2003, p. 169). They can consciously and actively consider needs and concerns of other stakeholders and explore and challenge the existing corporate governance arrangements. In contrast to the traditional economic and legal understanding of what directors actually do, we suggest that in practice directors can undertake activities and make decisions over what they can exert their individual and collective influence (or exercise leadership). That is, directors can and should behave agentically. This conclusion leads to the following consideration as to how we might begin to best understand what boards really do.

Social Cognitive Theory Perspective on 'What Boards Really Do'

A behavioural perspective on boards of directors places director-actors as the locus of attention. This actor-centric approach focuses on relationships between the board members and management (see Roberts & Stiles, 1999; Westphal, 1999), the role of the chair (see Leblanc, 2005; Morais et al., 2019), board internal dynamics (see Bezemer et al., 2018; Brundin & Nordqvist, 2008), cognitive aspects of board's behaviour (see Rindova, 1999; Westphal & Shani, 2016), board's leadership (see Machold et al.,

2011; Yar Hamidi & Gabrielsson, 2014); to mention just some examples of behavioural studies.[1] Although there is an increasing number of theoretical discussions exploring links between the nature of the corporation and role of the board, and a wealth of empirical studies investigating various behavioural aspects of the board's work, researchers have not yet paid sufficient attention to investigate whether (and under what conditions) board members behave as *agents* or as *fiduciaries*. Of course, it is likely that directors tend to act in either role at particular points in time.

We propose that social cognitive theory (Bandura, 1986, 1989, 2001; Wood & Bandura, 1989) might provide a particularly pertinent approach to exploring this line of inquiry. In analysing relationships between people or person's individual behaviour in a group or organisational setting, the theory emphasises complex and co-evolutionary interactions between a person's cognitive attributes, behaviours and the environment. The main predisposition of the theory is that people's actions are the 'interplay of self-produced and external sources of influence' (Bandura, 1989, p. 1179). By employing their interests, knowledge, past experience and self-belief in their own competencies, people can through their actions change their environments. Simultaneously, by engaging in self-reflection processes (i.e. self-evaluating their goals and the personal efficacy of their current actions) 'people can generate novel ideas and innovative actions that transcend their past experiences' (Bandura, 1989, p. 1182).

In organisational settings, social cognitive theory provides a theoretical framework that explains how individuals align their personal beliefs (and actions) with an organisational mission and goals. In this vein, the theory may become an important and useful framework in understanding why (and how) directors behave in a particular way and why (and how) they take (or do not take) actions in 'managing' relationships with various stakeholders.

To fulfil their role at the apex of the corporation (as ultimate decision-makers), directors need to have good judgement of their cognitive capabilities (i.e. how well informed they are about and experienced in certain aspects of the business or what their value positions are); they need to anticipate the possible direct effects of their actions (i.e. how their decision would affect the value of the corporation in the short and long run); and they need to estimate the environmental opportunities and threats (i.e. how the community/customers/employees/creditors would react to their actions). These factors guide and regulate directors' behaviour—to behave and act as agents or fiduciaries or, in terms of social cognitive theory, to be 'products' or 'producers' of social systems (Bandura, 2001).

Corporate governance arrangements in a formal framework are defined in a company constitution and board's charter. How directors operate in or 'functionally use' (Bandura, 2001) the existing corporate governance arrangements is a matter of their beliefs, aspirations and motivations. It is also the subject of context—the prescribed demands and expectations of those who vested them with the director mandate as well as their fellow directors and executives.

The traditional assumption is that directors are agents, loyal to shareholders. Their main prescribed task is to control and monitor managers (other agents) of the corporation on behalf of shareholders (principals). Their personal goals, which may be related to prestige, monetary award or an intrinsic aspiration to create value (Hoppmann et al., 2019) are in line with the purpose of the corporation—the maximisation of shareholders' wealth. Directors' capabilities, primarily informed by financial and commercial expertise and experience drive their actions towards projected (often short-term) financial goals. As loyal agents, directors are accountable to shareholders and need to behave with the prescribed governance rules and norms. As such they are a product of the specific social system (i.e. existing corporate governance framework). Their behaviour is reactive, adaptive and transactional.

In the entity model of the corporation, directors are fiduciaries as they act in the best interest of the corporation. The board of directors is the trustee of corporate assets. Directors as fiduciaries, in opposition to acting as agents, base their actions on a sense of duty and identification with the organisation (Learmount, 2003). In this context, directors are expected to be intrinsically motivated, to be engaged, to act proactively and reformatively. Their task is not only to sustain the corporate assets overall, but also to 'balance fairly the various claims to the returns which these assets generate' (Kay & Silberston, 1995, p. 91). Thus, directors' accountability is not to a specific stakeholder but to a collective; that is, the corporation. Consistent with social cognitive theory, the following section presents and integrates insights that relate agentic behaviour and leadership constructs with board directors in the modern company.

Directors Behaving Agentically and Exercising Responsible Leadership

Bandura (2001) argues that changes in human behaviour are 'socially interdependent, richly contextualised, and conditionally orchestrated' (p. 5). In other words, an interplay of personal characteristics and sociocultural factors influence a person's behaviour and actions within a given situation. People are agentic when they are aware of their own capabilities and they intentionally control their goals and have a high sense of their self-efficacy. In organisational settings, agentic decision makers will find effective ways to mobilise collective efforts and undertake actions which promote changes in social structures (Bandura, 1989).

In taking this agentic view of board directors we have foregrounded the important leadership role that directors can play within a corporation. That is, we want to duly recognise their contribution to creating a common purpose, identity and direction for the corporation (Jackson & Parry, 2018).

This is often ignored as the conventional view assumes that board directors *do* governance while senior executives, most especially the CEO, *do* leadership. Taking a collective perspective of leadership, we recognise that the responsibility for creating leadership is and should not be confined to one person. Collective leadership represents an emerging theoretical umbrella that captures diverse scholarship on the shared, distributed, pooled, and relational aspects of leadership, its emergence and relation to hierarchical leadership, as well as its impact on work and performance (Bryman et al., 2011; Denis et al., 2012; Uhl-Bien & Ospina, 2012; Yammarino et al., 2012). Moreover, if we recognise the fiduciary responsibility that directors have for ensuring that this leadership is responsibly carried out, then we can begin to appreciate the central role that board directors play in promulgating responsible leadership (Waldman & Balven, 2014).

Companies are increasingly incorporating environmental, social and governance issues into their core strategies due to increased stakeholder activism and scrutiny (Berns et al., 2009; Waldman & Galvin, 2008). The type of leadership that recognises the importance of committing to the common good has become the focus of increasing attention from leadership researchers committed to promoting a normative theory of leadership that is most commonly described as 'responsible leadership' (Kempster & Carroll, 2016; Kempster et al., 2019). Pless (2007) defines responsible leadership as a 'values-based and thorough ethical principles-driven relationship between leaders and stakeholders who are connected through a shared sense of meaning and purpose through which they raise one another to higher levels of motivation and commitment for achieving sustainable values creation and social change' (p. 438). The primary task of responsible leaders, therefore, is to build and cultivate 'sustainable relationships with stakeholders … to achieve mutually shared objectives based on a vision of business as a force of good for the many, and not just a few (i.e. shareholders, managers)' (Maak, 2007, p. 331). We note that directors can play a very important role in building, cultivating and sustaining trustful relationships. By the same token, they can play a powerful and immediate role in challenging and destroying these relationships. In a number of important respects, responsible leadership closely aligns with the four features of agentic behaviour—intentionality, forethought, self-reactiveness and self-reflection (Bandura, 2001).

In considering how directors practise responsible leadership through agentic behaviour as fiduciaries rather than agents, we note the following normative behaviours. First, directors are not merely reactive and adaptive in their governance roles. They have their personal goals when accepting positions on corporate boards, and these goals are often embedded in their intrinsic motivation to employ their talents and knowledge in building relationships with the corporate key stakeholders or developing innovative capabilities within the corporation or crafting sustainable corporate strategy. Second, to achieve these goals directors may opt to adjust and change the current practices in specific situations or explore new ways to influence and control corporate affairs. Hoppmann et al. (2019), in examining the boards internal challenges during the environmental discontinuities, argue that boards must engage in their own self-evaluation and self-reconfiguration in order to be able to judge strategic issues and shape strategic changes. The lack of independent self-evaluation and capability renewal processes contributes to boards becoming a source of organisational inertia and leads to decline in organisational performance (Hoppmann et al., 2019).

Many directors work actively and intentionally to change the current hierarchical context of corporate governance. They make things happen by considering demands of the key stakeholders, their personal goals and motivations and by estimating the effectiveness of their actions. Consequently, they carefully plan and execute their actions towards a broader engagement of internal and external stakeholders in the process of corporate strategic decision-making. In that vein, Cikaliuk et al. (2019) found evidence that directors, might decide to 'protect' interests, or reduce risks, of a certain group of key stakeholders even if such a decision may result in marginally reduced profitability (see Aldridge Energy case study in Chapter 5). With this intention directors may initiate the actions, carefully shape the process of engagement and actively participate in finding solutions to various problems with stakeholders. Such actions are usually led by directors' personal beliefs in the broader company's responsibility as well as their anticipation of actions that are likely to create strategic value for the company. In his discussion on keeping action in line with one's personal standards (value system) Bandura (2001) stresses that an 'individual with a strong communal ethic will act to further the welfare of others even at costs to their self-interest' (p. 9). In the case mentioned above, the action was designed and led by the board chair, whose clarity of strategic vision, political acumen, personal moral judgement and willingness to engage with a demanding stakeholder promoted the interests and values of all parties - community (stakeholder), corporation and chair herself.

The ability to mobilise efforts of others is one of the key capabilities of agentic and responsibly led boards. Board leadership which enables mobilisation eschews spot-checking at random or designated points in favour of continuous engagement which limits negative surprises and promotes deeper, more nuanced insights for long-term growth. A board enables this by building new relationships and maintaining existing ones with senior management, stakeholders and among directors. By expressing a sincere interest in their opinions and seeking out similarities with others, board leadership fosters a shared purpose and a supportive climate. Often, among directors the major challenge is as much about gaining an understanding of (and strengthening) the relationships that shape a company's assets and processes, as it is one of letting go of outmoded processes and policies that impede growth. It is essential that a board frequently evaluate and challenge the established system and conventional approaches and also anticipate the rewards which would be satisfying in helping a company grow. Directors should repeatedly self-examine what they are seeking to accomplish and what is at stake. If a board is to work as a strategic group, then all members' actions need to be intentional, coordinated and invested in building collective capability of the company.

Furthermore, directors and, in particular, the chair's belief in their personal efficacy is likely to result in a successful realisation of organisational goals in relation to corporate stakeholders. Sometimes these actions require bold and brave moves which remove current normative barriers and build new relationship bridges. In our research on responsible board leadership, we have come across a board having encountered a serious conflict with an important stakeholder. The chair and other directors had a sense of responsibility towards this specific group of stakeholders ('moral judgement') but did not have structural and cognitive capabilities to resolve the issue effectively. Through processes of self-evaluation and self-reflectiveness, the board came up with a 'novel' idea and deliberately re-configured the board by appointing a prominent representative of this stakeholder to the board. Although considered as an unprecedent action by a corporate board in the current corporate governance practice, this appointment proved to be an effective enabler of the conflict resolution (see Air New Zealand case study in Chapter 7).

Concluding Points

Our research suggests that boards behave responsibly when directors are intrinsically motivated to contribute their knowledge and skills to the well-being of the company and its stakeholders; their value system and personal identity correspond with the purpose and goals of the company; directors have high belief in their own self-efficacy and ability to mobilise the efforts of others; and they are willing to self-evaluate their actions. The entity model opens up the possibility for the board to enact agency (leadership) for decisions about the direction and management of the company. We argue that an agentic view of boards of directors, based on social cognitive theory, compels us to broaden our conceptualisation of why and how directors behave and do what they do to shape relationships (social systems). In so doing, directors, individually and collectively, may enact responsible leadership acting as agentic fiduciaries rather constrained agents.

We believe that structural and behavioural characteristics in analysing boards of directors should not be considered separately. Structures (i.e. internal/corporate and external/systemic) and actions (i.e. individual and collective behaviours) are in a constant interdependent relationship. Structural characteristics can both regulate and enable boards acting in a certain manner. Therefore, boards can be productively viewed as 'products' of a set of structures. At the same time, driven by motivations, capabilities and sense of efficacy, directors can undertake actions through which they can actively influence (that is, *lead*) the current structural context. More importantly, we argue—directors can behave agentically to create new structures. They can be both proactive and transformational shapers (or 'producers') in their governance fields realm.

Note

1 For an overview of behavioural studies on corporate governance see Westphal and Zajac (2013) and on boards of directors see Huse (2018).

References

Bandura, A. (1986). *Social foundations of thought and action: A social cognitive theory.* Prentice-Hall.

Bandura, A. (1989). Human agency in social cognitive theory. *American Psychologist,* 44(9), 1175–1184.

Bandura, A. (2001). Social cognitive theory: An agentic perspective. *Annual Review of Psychology*, 52(1), 1–26.

Bandura, A., & Wood, R. (1989). Effect of perceived controllability and performance standards on self-regulation of complex decision making. *Journal of Personality and Social Psychology*, 56(5), 805–814.

Berns, M., Towned, A., Khayat, Z., Balagopal, B., Reeves, H., Hopkins, & Kruschwitz, M. (2009). The business of sustainability: What it means to managers now, *MIT Sloan Management Review*, 51(1), 20–26.

Bezemer, P. J., Nicholson, G., & Pugliese, A. (2018). The influence of board chairs on director engagement: A case-based exploration of boardroom decision-making. *Corporate Governance: An International Review*, 26(3), 219–234.

Bower, J. L., & Paine, L. S. (2017). The error at the heart of corporate leadership. *Harvard Business Review*, 95(3), 50–60.

Brundin, E., & Nordqvist, M. (2008). Beyond facts and figures: The role of emotions in boardroom dynamics. *Corporate Governance: An International Review*, 16 (4), 326–341.

Bryman, A., Collinson, D., Grint, K., Jackson, B., & Uhl-Bien, M. (2011). *The Sage handbook of leadership*. Sage.

Ciepley, D. (2013). Beyond public and private: Toward a political theory of the corporation. *American Political Science Review*, 107(1), 139–158.

Cikaliuk, M., Eraković, L., Jackson, B., Noonan, C., & Watson, S. (2019). Board of directors: Building relationships with non-shareholder stakeholders. In J. Gabrielsson, W. Khlif & S. Yamak (eds), *Research handbook on boards of directors* (pp. 209–228). Edward Elgar.

Cikaliuk, M., Eraković, L., Jackson, B., Noonan, C., & Watson, S. (2020). Board leadership and governance for clear-sighted CEO succession at Air New Zealand, *Journal of Management & Organization*, 26(5), 774–797.

Denis J. L., Langley, A., & Sergi, V. (2012). Leadership in the plural. *The Academy of Management Annals* 6(1), 211–283.

Hoppmann, J., Naegele, F., & Girod, B. (2019). Boards as a source of inertia: Examining the internal challenges and dynamics of boards of directors in times of environmental discontinuities. *Academy of Management Journal*, 62(2), 437–468.

Huse, M. (2018). *Value-creating boards: Challenges for future research and practice*. Cambridge Elements in Corporate Governance (series editor T. Clarke). Cambridge University Press.

Jackson, B. & Parry, K. (2018). *A very short, fairly interesting and quite cheap book about studying leadership*. Sage.

Kay, J., & Silberston, A. (1995). Corporate governance. *National Institute Economic Review*, 153, 84–97.

Kempster, S., & Carroll, B. (eds). (2016). *Responsible leadership: Realism and romanticism*. Routledge.

Kempster, S., Maak, T., & Parry, K. (2019). *Good dividends: Responsible leadership of business purpose*. Routledge.

Learmount, S. (2003). Theorizing corporate governance: organizational alternatives. *Journal of Interdisciplinary Economics*, 14(2), 159–173.

Leblanc, R. (2005). Assessing board leadership. *Corporate Governance: An International Review*, 13(5), 654–666.

Maak, T. (2007). Responsible leadership, stakeholder engagement, and the emergence of social capital. *Journal of Business Ethics*, 74(4), 329–343.

Machold, S., Huse, M., Minichilli, A., & Nordqvist, M. (2011). Board leadership and strategy involvement in small firms: A team production approach. *Corporate Governance: An International Review*, 19(4), 368–383.

Morais, F., Kakabadse, A., & Kakabadse, N. K. (2019). Dealing with strategic tensions on the board: The role of the chair in fostering engagement and debate. In J. Gabrielsson, W. Khlif & S. Yamak (eds), *Research handbook on boards of directors* (pp. 31–48). Edward Elgar.

Pless, N. M. (2007). Understanding responsible leadership: Roles identity and motivational drivers. *Journal of Business Ethics*, 74(4), 437–456.

Pugliese, A., Bezemer, P-J., Zattoni, A., Huse, M., Van den Bosch, F. A. J., & Volberda, H. W. (2009). Boards of directors' contribution to strategy: A literature review and research agenda. *Corporate Governance: An International Review*, 17 (3), 292–306.

Rindova, V. P. (1999). What corporate boards have to do with strategy: A cognitive perspective. *Journal of Management Studies*, 36(7), 953–975.

Roberts, J., & Stiles, P. (1999). The relationship between chairmen and chief executives: Competitive or complementary roles? *Long Range Planning*, 32(1), 36–48.

Serafeim, G. (2014). *The role of the corporation in society: An alternative view and opportunities for future research*. Working paper 14-110, May. Harvard Business School. https://dash.harvard.edu/bitstream/handle/1/13506440/14-110.pdf?sequence=1.

Uhl-Bien, M., & Ospina, S. M. (eds). (2012). *Advancing relational leadership theory: A dialogue among perspectives*. Information Age Publishing.

Veldman, J., & Willmott, H. (2013). What is the corporation and why does it matter? *M@n@gement* 16(5), 605–620.

Waldman, D., & Balven, R. M. (2014). Responsible leadership: Theoretical issues and research directions. *Academy of Management Perspectives*, 28(3), 224–234.

Waldman, D. A., & Galvin, B. M. (2008). Alternative perspectives of responsible leadership. *Organizational Dynamics*, 37(4), 327–341.

Watson, S. (2015). How the company became an entity: A new understanding of corporate law. *Journal of Business Law*, 120(2), 1–24.

Watson, S. (2019). The corporate legal person. *Journal of Corporate Law Studies*, 19 (1), 137–166.

Westphal, J. D. (1999). Collaboration in the boardroom: Behavioural and performance consequences of CEO-board social ties. *Academy of Management Journal*, 42 (1), 7–24.

Westphal, J. D., & Shani, G. (2016). Psyched-up to suck-up: Self-regulated cognition, interpersonal influence, and recommendations for board appointments in the corporate elite. *Academy of Management Journal*, 59(2), 479–509.

Westphal, J. D., & Zajac, E. J. (2013). A behavioural theory of corporate governance: Explicating the mechanisms of socially situated and socially constituted agency. *The Academy of Management Annals*, 7(1), 607–661.

Wood, R., & Bandura, A. (1989). Social cognitive theory of organizational management. *Academy of Management Review*, 14(3), 361–384.

Yammarino, F. J., Salas, E., Serban, A., Shirreffs, K., & Shuffler, M. L. (2012). Collectivistic leadership approaches: Putting the we in leadership science and practice. *Industrial and Organizational Psychology* 5(4), 382–402.

Yar Hamidi, D., & Gabrielsson, J. (2014). Developments and trends in research on board leadership: A systematic literature review. *International Journal of Business Governance and Ethics*, 9(3), 243–268.

3 Shareholder Capital and Other Investor Strategies

Introduction

Companies rely on two main sources of finance: equity finance provided by the owners of the company in their capacity as shareholders; and debt finance provided by way of loan or credit from creditors. Creditors may or may not be shareholders. The main difference between equity and debt finance is that should the company become insolvent and wound-up creditors have a right to be paid in full before shareholders receive any of their capital. There are a variety of types of creditors, and some have priority in being repaid over others. Creditors will normally be entitled to interest on their debts, which will be due even if the company has made no profits. Shareholders are entitled to the residual profits of the company after the payment of creditors. During the life of the company, shareholders may realise their investments through the sale of shares, dividends, or the buy-back of shares.

Through its capital structure a company can minimise the cost of capital and enhance the shareholder value. Financial markets press boards to prioritise these objectives in their decision-making. Even so, the trade-offs between debt and equity capital may be complex and there is no magic debt to equity ratio for all firms. The optimal capital structure for a corporation, and the choice of method of raising capital, will depend on a host of factors not in company spreadsheets. These are continuous decisions. Corporations often have a strategic or philosophical view of their ideal structure, which may be related to corporate control. The choice of capital structure and accountability for those choices is core to corporate governance and directly engages the need for board leadership. An examination of board led responsible leadership in governance would be incomplete if it did not address this function.

We begin this chapter with an analysis of what economic theory does and does not tell us about boards of directors and the capital arrangement function they perform. We then examine the leadership role of the board through the lens of shareholder diversity, board–shareholder relationships, and accountability. We present three case studies of capital arrangements by

DOI: 10.4324/9781003054191-3

boards of directors that involve issues around an initial public offering of an international software company, an unsuccessful partial privatisation of a state-owned coal mining enterprise, and an emergence of a governance structure in a closely held management consultancy. We discuss the most important learning points from the cases followed by a conclusion.

Corporate Governance of Capital Structure

In a famous paper Modigliani and Miller postulated that the capital structure of a company does not affect its overall value (Modigliani & Miller, 1958). Subsequent research has suggested a range of factors, including taxes, bankruptcy or distress costs, asymmetric information, and agency costs, have qualified that initial view. However, corporate governance and finance research has failed to build models that can explain the observed capital structures in the real world (Graham & Leary, 2011) or through empirical work identify the determinants of capital structure (Frank & Goyal, 2009). Some of existing research speaks to areas where board leadership is important, such as exemplary corporate governance practices. More importantly, the factors that the research has not adequately accounted for, and which it may be unable to address with existing methodologies, reveals why board leadership is important.

The capital structure and debt finance can be utilised to maximise the return on shareholder's equity. Company debt can increase the returns on shareholder equity where the return on capital is greater than the cost of debt. The tax deductibility of interest provides an incentive to use more debt (Miller, 1977; Modigliani & Miller, 1963). Using debt will, however, require the corporation assume a level of financial risk. Some risks are unavoidable. Managers may increase the risk of default after debt is issued. The costs of financial risk are ultimately borne by the shareholders, which increases as the level of debt increase (Jensen & Meckling, 1976). On the other hand, debt has been conjured to mitigate the agency costs that arise between managers and shareholders (Jensen, 1986), but does not receive support from empirical evidence. These models ignore the investment decisions and do not capture the reality that financial decisions cannot be divorced from investment decisions. The connection between borrowing spikes and investment has been established (DeAngelo, 2022).

Another stream in the literature focuses on the information asymmetries between management and investors—the so-called pecking order model. Rather than target some flexible leverage ratio, managers prefer internal over external financing (Frank & Goyal, 2008; Frank & Goyal, 2009; Myers, 1984; Myers & Majluf, 1984). The empirical literature supports the conclusion that managers often behave as the pecking order theory predicts (Alves et al., 2015; Lemmon & Zender, 2010). A more diversified and independent board may be able to decrease information asymmetries and build trust with potential investors, and see companies rely more on long-term debt and new equity (Alves et al., 2015). An alternative interpretation of the evidence is not so much a preference for one form of funding over another per se, but a board and management preference for ensuring access to funding and possessing sufficient untapped debt and cash balances for future investments (DeAngelo, 2022).

Neither the optimal trade-off nor pecking order theories can explain all situations encountered in real life. Their inability to explain why firms with low debt would issue equity is well-known (Denis & McKeon, 2021). A body of empirical literature has shown that a company's choice of capital structures is impacted by the economic and business environment, culture, and the legal environment, including corporate and banking laws and tax systems (Aggarwal & Goodell, 2010, 2011, 2014b; Antonczyk & Salzmann, 2014; Antoniou et al., 2008; Arosa et al., 2014). More importantly for present purposes, models of capital structure, including those based on agencies costs or asymmetric information, that ignore the governance and leadership of the board are incomplete. This conclusion is evident when we move beyond the highly stylised corporate structure of those models. It is also supported by extensive empirical evidence. Access to finance is positively associated with better investor protection (Aggarwal & Goodell, 2014a). A higher quality board with greater capacity to monitor management can contribute to the reduction of agency costs of debt financing (Fields et al., 2012; Lorca et al., 2011). Corporate governance has been shown to affect the use of equity versus debt financing (Jiraporn et al., 2012; John & Litov, 2010). Stronger boards (Harford et al., 2008) are associated with higher leverage, but CEO entrenchment with lower (Ghosh et al., 2011).

The financial risks and cash flow constraints of debt need to be weighed against the impact that increasing share capital may have on corporate control. There is evidence that companies with equity blocks and family-controlled firms tend to have higher leverage (Brailsforda et al., 2002; Céspedes et al., 2010; King & Santor, 2008; Setia-Atmaja et al., 2009). The incumbent board and key shareholders may or may not share similar concerns with potential changes in corporate control from the issue or sale of shares. The directors' duty to act on the best interest of the corporation or for a proper purpose may not align with the aspirations of controlling shareholders. Newer corporations and corporations with difficult to value assets may be more constrained in their ability to raise debt.

The corporate governance literature identifies some factors that influence capital structures. The theories explain some tendencies but not the decisions and processes in individual cases. The scope for leadership in capital structures is more obvious once freed from the overly stylised image of the company in the corporate governance and finance literature. One study documents the different financial policies at Ford and GM, despite the similarities of the business, as articulated and implemented by Alfred Sloan and Henry Ford (DeAngelo, 2021). Evidence shows the identity of managers is a determinant of financial policy (Bertrand & Schoar, 2003; Fee et al., 2013). Recent research has recognised the limits of full-knowledge optimisation models for situations where the company board and management will necessarily have imperfect knowledge (DeAngelo, 2022). The idea that financial decision-making involves uncertainty is not new (Kay & King, 2020; Knight, 1921). Preserving options for future investment means that decisions on equity and debt frequently have a strategic dimension. While a big step forward, board and management decision-making is not simply by fiat but involves others also with imperfect knowledge and often heterogeneous and mixed objectives. This is where a leadership in governance perspective has much to contribute.

Shareholder Diversity and the Corporate Entity

The role of the board in corporate capital structures and shareholder relations is necessarily shaped by the legal nature of a company. As discussed in chapter two and elsewhere in this book, a company is not simply an association of shareholder-investors that combine together to achieve corporate status, with directors and management as their agents. While private ordering matters a great deal, the company is not simply a nexus of contracts. Consequently, shareholder wealth maximisation cannot be—in fact or in law—the exclusive objective of all companies. On the other hand, the objective of a company is not to simply balance the interests of diverse groups of stakeholders. To do so ignores the essential nature of company as an entity and a fund. That does not mean that boards do not need to engage with and take account of the demands of competing stakeholders. Nor does the broad discretion the law gives the board to direct or manage the business of the company preclude consideration of the interests of relevant stakeholders.

If the corporate governance and finance literature has adopted an overly reductionist view of company managers and shareholders, at its apogee in the Fisher Separation Theorem, the legal literature dwells on the actual and potential disputes between shareholders and managers and among shareholders. This manifests in lawsuits as well as contractual or constitutional provisions aiming at avoiding or managing dissent. Legal involvement is, at root, grounded in the assumption that shareholder preferences will diverge and there may be no obvious way to reconcile those preferences. The board's role will be shaped by the heterogeneous and evolving interests of individual shareholders. Apart from wealth maximisation, shareholders may at times be motivated by a desire to build an enterprise, to gain or retain control, or environmental and social values. These objectives may sometimes conflict with the interests of management and directors.

The diversity among stakeholders extends to the structure of shareholding in companies. The notion of that the shareholding of large companies is widely distributed with no single shareholder able to exercise significant influence was always part myth (Greenspon, 2019; La Porta et al., 1999). In many markets, large blocks of shares in many companies are controlled by individuals or families. Institutional investors control a controlling portion of all shares around the world (Fichtner et al., 2017; Moreolo, 2021). Many billion-dollar tech companies have seen founders with large blocks of shares seeking to retain lasting control through the issue of multiple classes of shares (see below).

The concentration of shareholding makes more visible and salient the role shareholders have when they are acting collectively. Recognition of the influence of shareholders on key corporate decisions, and the shadow they cast over others, is missing from stakeholder theories, which struggle to explain the centrality of shareholders and their funds to the corporation. The board is at the nexus of the corporate participants, balancing the interests of different stakeholders, and subject to the corporate constitution managing or directing the management of the corporation. The legal structure of the corporation and allocation of power elevates the importance of the relationship between the board and key shareholders and shareholders as a group over other stakeholders. The legal structure is one of the determinants of how divergent shareholder preferences manifest in practice.

Many companies are sitting on large amounts of cash. Rather than reinvesting in the business, many companies are returning money to shareholders via large dividend payments and share buyback schemes. There is evidence that many companies are increasing debt to finance share buybacks (Farre-Mensa et al., 2020). The concentration of ownership, however, creates a greater risk of the board inappropriately agreeing to or endorsing pay outs to shareholders. In some cases, company boards have agreed to large dividend payments that have benefited controlling shareholders leaving the company financially vulnerable. The demise of BHS saw the 'owner' Philip Green extract over US$745 million (rounded figures) from the company during his tenure only to sell the company in 2015 for US$1.50. In 2005, his wife, who legally owned all the shares in the parent company, received a huge US$600 million dividend payment amounting to more than the year's profit (UK House of Commons, 2016; see also Butler, 2016; Butler & Ruddick, 2016). BHS's auditors PWC were fined nearly US$10 million for signing off accounts that were 'incomplete, inaccurate and misleading' (*The Executive Counsel to the Financial Reporting Council v Denison and PriceWaterhouseCoopers LLP*, Particulars of Fact and Acts of Misconduct, 10 August 2018).

In most companies, as noted above, each shareholder is entitled to dividends and votes at a company meeting in proportion to the number of shares owned. An increasing number of listed companies have introduced classes of stock with superior voting rights, which typically allow company founders and top executives to maintain control even as their shareholding declines. Dual-class companies include some of the most successful and highly valued companies in the world, such as corporate giants Facebook Inc., Alphabet Inc. (parent of Google), Berkshire Hathaway Inc., and News

Corp. From a corporate governance perspective, dual-class companies are claimed to reduce accountability, entrench management, and skew incentives (Bebchuk & Kastiel, 2017, 2019; Papadopoulos, 2019). Dual-class companies are more likely not to have independent board chairs or leadership, engage in related-party transactions, and have less gender diversity on the board. Having a class of shares with superior voting rights, which is predictably opposed by many institutional investors, may free a company from short-term market pressures and allow a greater to focus on growth and long-term strategy. Alternative approaches are available to encourage longer-term strategic planning. French companies bestow double voting rights on those who hold shares beyond two years. This, of course, rewards past behaviour as opposed to future commitment (Mayer, 2013).

Shareholders have a number of relationships with the company. As well as shares giving individual rights to shareholders to act through the general meeting as an organ of the company, shareholders are also investors. Accumulation of blocks of shares by major shareholders, the rise of socially responsible investment and increasingly active institutional investors like BlackRock mean that boards meet with investor groups (McNulty & Nordberg, 2016). Indeed, every guide to good governance emphasises the importance of board-investor relations.

Shareholder–Board Relationships

The differing legal rights, interests, and ability of shareholders to, individually and collectively, participate in and influence company decisions reinforces the information uncertainty faced by boards and means board decisions affecting capital structure are often 'political' and not just technical. The relationship between the board and shareholders is an organic and defining element of a corporation. The classic image of the founding shareholders bringing their capital and skills together to form the company is incomplete. On incorporation, a separate legal entity is created that owns or controls the corporate fund. The founding shareholders agree to, in the constitution, articles of incorporation or equivalent, the procedures which will be followed to operate the company. The existence of a statutory default constitution or equivalent solves the problem of incomplete contracting for shareholders as initial participants. In return, shareholders are issued shares. The shareholders own shares, not a share of the corporate fund. Most companies also will have limited liability, so the debts of the company will not ordinarily become debts of the shareholders if the company cannot pay.

Shares have legal rights attached to them. The rights may typically include *in personam* rights for shareholders, such as the right to receive notice of and participate in shareholder meetings as part of one of the decision-making organs of the company. Rights also attach to the shares that might be called capital rights. Examples of capital rights are entitlements to pro rata shares of dividends and residual rights on dissolution. Those rights affect shareholders as investors. Shareholders also usually have voting rights on the election of board members. It is now common for voting rights to be attached to shares rather than persons. In practice, this right affects the number of votes each shareholder has (and a shareholder may be required to vote all of their shares in the same way on a particular issue).

While the shareholders can in theory appoint and remove directors, information and collective action problems mean that shareholders will only sometimes be able to control appointments. The ability to control appointments usually coincides with a shareholder acquiring a significant parcel of shares. Individual shareholders with small parcels of shares have little or no influence. With the presence of substantial and institutional shareholders, collective action becomes more credible. The influence of shareholders is further diluted if the board has power to appointment replacement directors between shareholder meetings.

Like all stakeholder groups, some shareholders individually or in groups will seek to influence decision-making by boards. The potential for shareholders through participation in the corporate organ of the company, the shareholders meeting, or the voting to appoint or remove directors from the board means that the influence of shareholders with big voting blocks may be great. Influence can be scaled up through proxy votes and shareholders or directors may compete for other shareholders proxy votes. Through the voting rights attached to their shares, they have the potential to influence or even control the board. The shareholders meeting has some decision-making rights, but influence is not circumscribed by formal processes. Boards and shareholders interact through formal and informal processes. The possibility that a shareholder, either alone or together with like-minded shareholders, will exercise their formal rights on an issue or another issue of importance of the directors (e.g. remuneration) or other stakeholders will provide influence and motivate both shareholders and boards to engage.

The board needs to communicate with and 'manage' the relationship with the shareholders. Where the board has power to appoint directors between shareholder meetings, the power will rarely be exercised without engagement with influential shareholders. The extent to which the board and shareholders are active, or passive, will vary with influence and information flowing both ways. The information advantages possessed by the board (often through management) and power derived from being at the nexus of corporate relationships will sometimes give the board the upper hand in the relationship, upturning the notion that the board is the agent of the shareholders.

Accountability Structure Preserves Leadership

The shareholders as a group have formal powers to elect directors and select corporate decisions but the power to manage and direct the company lies with the board and management. The board owes duties to the company, which are intended to protect the interests of shareholders. Nonetheless, company law rules protect the space for the board to act as leaders. The need for an independent but accountable board goes to the heart of company law. The topic has generated considerable discussion in the United States (Bebchuk, 2013; Strine, 2014). Corporate law debates question claims that insulating or shielding boards from shareholder pressure by limiting their rights and powers serves the long-term interests of publicly traded companies and their long-term shareholders. The centre of gravity within the discussion differs from the usual position under Anglo-Australasian law where shareholders have generally had greater control, de jure or de facto, over corporate boards. The listing requirements now provide for a minimum number of independent directors. The rules also recognise that directors may (at least initially) be appointed by other directors. The board has influence over the future constitution of the board.

Agency theory has been the dominant paradigm in the practice and study of corporate governance. Within this paradigm, the directors and senior management on the board are seen as agents of the shareholders. Corporate law and governance practices are intended to align the incentives of managerial agents with the interest of shareholders as the principal also deterring opportunistic behaviour by the board and management. A basic account of the agency perspective is important because it frames the decision-making of many directors, managers, and shareholders, and brings into relief the leadership in governance perspective. While shareholders are the residual risk bearers (at least while the corporation remains solvent) and collectively have the power to appoint the directors, contractarianism does not expect shareholders to be active participants in corporate governance (Easterbrook & Fischel, 1996). Indeed, ironically, the contractarians are generally suspicious of any exercises of shareholder voting power.

The theory, however, ignores the leadership role of the board, which is preserved by corporate law, as well as the diverse shareholder goals and the imperfect information of the board, management, shareholders and creditors. The informational and collective action impediments to the effective functioning of the shareholder franchise within large public corporations with widely dispersed shareholdings are significant. If shareholders were actually the simple rational maximisers that they are assumed to be, there would be limited need for active board engagement with shareholders. If a diversified portfolio is the only practical option open to shareholders to protect their interests, due to informational and collective action problems, there would be no scope or need for the board to exercise leadership in relation to shareholders.

Despite the formal authority that shareholders may possess, and the legitimate concerns about lax or opportunistic behaviour of management, some boards are able to exercise leadership in their relations with shareholders. Statutorily mandated communication between the board and the shareholders, such as annual meetings and reports, are not simply compliance activities, nor perhaps even primarily a means of ensuring board accountability to shareholders. Two-way communication between the board and shareholders can help tame shareholder activism, garner additional resources for the company, and more generally build greater trust between the company and its longer-term shareholders.

Enhanced levels of shareholder communication and engagement have been witnessed in a number of jurisdictions, notably the UK and the United States, and has become an established part of conventional good governance recommendations (Aguilar, 2015). Several reasons for increased shareholder engagement have been suggested, including say-on-pay legislation, influence of proxy advisory firms and concentration of share ownership, in particular in the hands of institutional investors.

The powers of the board are balanced by duties to prevent the direct harm to shareholders and creditors. The duties are crafted as general principles that provide significant discretion to the board in directing and managing the company. While the primary duty of board may be formally obliged to act in what it believes to be the best interests of the company as a whole and as an entity, the best interests of the company cannot be identified objectively but are the outcome of engagement with management and key stakeholders. With limited exceptions, nominee directors have a duty to act in the interests of the company and not their appointor and a duty not to fetter their discretion. A behavioural perspective (van Ees et al., 2009) on goal formation would not assume the goals of the corporate constituents would inevitably align around the maximisation of shareholder value through maximisation of the financial capital in the fund. If the determination of the best interests of the company is indeed a political exercise, new light is shed on the duty to act in good faith and in the best interests of the company. Without an objective function, a director's assessment of the best interests of the company will involve an element of subjective judgement. This might provide an alternative, perhaps better, explanation for the subjective nature of the duty of each director than concerns about intruding into the decision-making power of directors and the 'moral' nature of the duty.

Other commentators have observed that the duty of good faith is more a duty not to act in bad faith (Summers, 1968). This usually involves the director acting for a collateral purpose or acting in circumstances where the director could reasonably be thought to have a collateral purpose. Hence the rules on conflict of interest and account of profits. Traditionalists have objected to the (occasional) judicial objectification of the duty. These cases have typically involved a failure of a director to consider a decision independently or the failure of a director (or the whole board) to consider the interests of a member of a corporate group. These 'slips' are perhaps best not seen as 'slips' into objectification, but a concern to ensure that the director is actually considering all relevant interests and balancing them. The directors acting collectively need to assess and balance all relevant interests—a political task.

The risk of financial consequences from a breach of the duty of care, particularly by non-executive directors, is virtually non-existent in the

United States (Armour et al., 2009; Black et al., 2006). Well-known Australian decisions demonstrate a real risk of liability for executive and non-executive directors that fail to exercise reasonable care to understand the business and implications of all decisions of the board (*ASIC v Hellicar*, 286 ALR 501 (2012)). The risk of liability will push the board towards taking a more active role and towards exercising leadership over management. The limited ability of a bankrupt firm to indemnify directors may also limit the appetite for leverage and intra-group transactions that leave some entities with the liabilities and few assets (e.g. *Yan v Mainzeal Property and Construction Ltd (in liq)* [2021] NZCA 99).

The unfair prejudice remedy and the shareholder derivative action protect the board from being subject to the demands of majority shareholders. The deference to the board's business decisions is also reflected in the nature of the obligations imposed on directors. For example, the unfair prejudice remedy has been interpreted to preclude complaints about decisions that can be attributed to business judgement. The fiduciary duties of directors are intended to ensure directors work zealously for the company, but strict rules dealing with conflicts of interest and accounts of profits do invite the courts to make business judgements, including on whether a company could have taken advantage of a business opportunity (*Fhr European Ventures Llp v Cedar Capital Partners LLC* [2014] UKSC 45). It appears that shareholders—even acting unanimously—do not have the power to usurp the decision-making role allocated to directors in the corporate constitution. Furthermore, the business decisions of the board are not subject to review by the courts (*Howard Smith Ltd v Ampol Petroleum Ltd* [1974] AC 821).

Case Studies

The following three case studies help to illustrate how different capital structures and shareholders influence board leadership in governance.

Case Study 3.1 Due Diligence of the Diligent Board[1]

David Liptak, non-executive director and chair of Diligent Board Member Services, considered shareholders' response to the allegations of stock market manipulation. Allegations alone had eroded more than US$12.5 million from the software's company's value. With a trial pending for a former CEO/director and block shareholder, board led responsible leadership would be needed to prevent further shareholder harm of the New York-based, New Zealand-listed company.

Diligent's Founding History

In the late 1990s, a small group of consultants in Manhattan, New York had developed database-driven software for companies before shifting focus to corporate governance service delivery software. An early client relationship with a mutual funds company led to the development of an online software package called Boardbooks designed to speed and simplify access to board material for directors, management, and administrative staff. With further refinements, the company became a pioneer of a commercially viable secure, web-based portal for boards to compile, update and examine materials before, during and after board meetings.

Company Operations and Management

In 2003, the company began to market and sell subscriptions to a core group of blue-chip clients which included AIG SunAmerica Funds, Investors Bankers Trust, and Motorola. The annual renewable subscriptions provided access to the virtual boardroom system hosted on its servers. The subscription approach or software-as-a-service (Saas) model allowed for a predictable and recurring revenue stream with relatively fixed operating costs.

Brian Henry, CEO, took a major step when he relocated the software research and development arm of the company from New York to his hometown, Christchurch New Zealand, following the attacks of 11 September 2001. The head office remained in New York with Alessandro Sodi. He had been the executive vice president of the company's predecessor company where he led the development of Boardbooks from 2001 to 2003. In 2003, the predecessor company was renamed Diligent Board Member Services (hereafter referred to as Diligent) and Sodi was appointed president.

Sharon Daniels, chief marketing officer, was responsible for the creation and maintenance of the company's brand and market position. Prior to her involvement with Diligent, she had consulted to international technology and finance service companies. Kiri Borg was responsible for management and operations as one of the founding members including Diligent's predecessor along with Henry (spouse). Previously, Borg had been a vice-president of sales and marketing for a United States based construction company.

Diligent Prepares for IPO (2007)

In 2007, Henry and the other founders recognised that external capital investment was the next major step for the company. Listing Diligent would provide access to additional resources for the international growth envisioned and the sales force needed to drive increased market share and revenue.

Mark Weldon, CEO of the New Zealand Exchange, was keen to increase the number of companies that joined New Zealand's public market. Alerted to Diligent's interest in an IPO by Sodi,[2] the founding group shareholders agreed to become the first United States-based, New Zealand-listed company. Over several months, Henry and a team, which included a New Zealand brokering firm and legal counsel, prepared for the IPO.

BOARD OF DIRECTORS

Listing the company required a board of directors. Henry, Sodi and Daniels were appointed as executive directors along with Kevin Lawler (CFO, New Zealand). Borg served as corporate secretary. Edward Charlton, board chair, was appointed as an independent director. Charlton brought more than 30 years of experience in international banking where he held a range of executive positions. Previously, he served as a solicitor of the Supreme Court in the United Kingdom. He served as a director of HSBC Private Bank (UK) and held several non-executive directorships.

Three independent directors were appointed: Rick Bettle, Mark Russell and Guy Saxton. Bettle, an experienced board director was chair of Dominion Finance, Civil Aviation Authority of New Zealand, and Aviation Tourism and Travel Training organisation. He served as director on Goodman New Zealand, a global industrial real estate group, and Revera, an IT infrastructure services company, among others. He brought financial and legal skills to the board.

Russell, senior commercial partner in a New Zealand law firm, brought his experience in corporate finance and structuring, banking and insolvency to the board. Guy Saxton brought his experience as a CEO of a merchant banking business based in the United Kingdom and the United States. Prior to this role, he was CEO at a venture capital company specialised in early-stage equity finance for high growth companies. He served as a non-executive director of several private companies. Peter Huljich, a non-executive director from New Zealand, was a managing director of a New Zealand-based wealth management company founded in 2007 by his family. He brought 10 years of investment experience to the board.

The board aimed to raise US$18.6 million (rounded figures) through the IPO. A distinctive feature was the warranted offer by company founders. They were prepared to forfeit up to 20 per cent of their shareholding should sales target projections outlined in the prospectus not be met. Anticipated proceeds from the IPO were expected to fund the sales and marketing strategy. Although Diligent had not yet marketed its Boardbooks product within New Zealand, its initial client was the New Zealand Exchange. Over the next two years, the international sales force was expected to grow to more than 75 employees.

The envisioned ownership structure of Diligent post-IPO assumed full subscription of the 24 million shares on offer, which would translate to more than 20 per cent of shares to be held by new shareholders. The remainder of shares were allocated as follows: nearly 4 per cent for employees and directors, almost 6 per cent for converting debt holders, and nearly 68 per cent would remain with the founding group members. In short, the company would continue to be closely held after listing.

In December 2007, Diligent's closing share price was 5 per cent lower than its listing share price. It raised US$16.4 million net of listing costs, falling short of its projected US$18.6 million.

Fallout from the IPO: Founder's Past and Present Collide (2007–2008)

Prospective shareholder interest had not translated into share ownership. Controversy concerning Henry's past role as a director for Energycorp and its bankruptcy in 1988 had not been publicly disclosed in the IPO prospectus. Although the New Zealand Exchange had no legal requirement for Diligent or any company to disclose that a director had discharged a bankruptcy outside of the past five years, online share trading forums and mainstream media pointed to a lack of full disclosure.

Energycorp had been founded by Henry's brother, Gerald Henry, who became the company's executive deputy chair. The company had featured wood fuel burning equipment invented by the father of brothers Gerald and Brian Henry. Within 6 months of listing, the company collapsed. New Zealand's then richest individual had a 30 per cent share ownership of Energycorp. Gerald declared bankruptcy owing nearly US$33 million to shareholders (Stuff, 2009a).[3] In the 1990s, Gerald Henry was found guilty of fraud charges related to other business activity in the United States and was imprisoned.

Some directors were aware of Henry's involvement with the bankrupt company. Mark Russell was involved with the wind down of Energycorp's affairs on behalf of the Bank of New Zealand. Russell explained: 'We have gone through a very rigorous process in relation to Brian [Henry] and his history and we are proud to have our brand associated with Diligent and with Brian in particular. We have no concerns whatsoever' (Ninness, 2009).

The lead manager from the New Zealand brokering firm for the IPO, Andrew McDouall concurred, 'In my opinion, it is not really relevant and the important thing here is that Brian [Henry] has a clean record, has never been on the wrong side of the law and was a director of a company that went under. I think that is as far as the story needs to go' (Stuff, 2009a). The Shareholders Association chair explained that Gerald Henry's convictions bore no relevance to Diligent's shareholders: 'Brian Henry was not his brother's keeper, and his chair should have defended him' (Stuff, 2009b).

The Board Responds to the Controversy

Diligent's board met to discuss how integral Henry was to the future of the company. As far back as 2003, when the company had three clients, Henry featured prominently in the print marketing materials. With more than 70 clients by 2007, he had successfully used video and DVD as a medium to personally explain the IPO opportunity for Diligent investors. He had devoted months traveling to meet with prospective investors in the United States, England, and New Zealand. In 2007, Henry was one of the company's founders, block shareholder, and 'face' of Diligent.

The board decided the company could not operate without him and crafted a compromise. Charlton, board chair, accepted Henry's resignation as chief executive officer but retained him as a board director. The board further invited Henry to take on the role of global sales director where his sales skills could benefit shareholders. He stepped down the next day, having set a record as the shortest-lived listed company chief executive officer in New Zealand—a 24-hour appointment. The board appointed Alessandro Sodi as CEO.

Promises Come Due amid the Global Financial Crisis (2008–2009)

The global financial crisis created an uncertain economic outlook for many of the companies targeted as Diligent's prospective customers. They were not interested at the time, and it led to a sharp decline in sales. Failure to meet stated targets warranted in the IPO prospectus resulted in the forfeiture of 14 million shares by the company's founding shareholders. The net effect was an increase in the pro rata share holdings of all other shareholders of 16 per cent.

Bettle and Sodi reaffirmed in the 2008 Annual General Report that, 'Diligent is 100 per cent focused on driving shareholder value—our core objective is to create and increase wealth for our shareholders'. Despite that objective, the company reported a loss of nearly US$18 million. Amid liquidity concerns, the company scaled back operations. The sales force, which peaked at 23 in September 2008, shrank to 10 employees by December 2008. The company also brought group legal counsel in-house which reduced legal costs. They also cut R&D expenses. Salaries for some of the higher compensated personnel were reduced, and the New York—New Jersey offices merged to reduce overhead expense.

THE BOARD RESTRUCTURES

By the end of 2008, Diligent announced that the size of the board had decreased from nine to five to reduce operating expenses. Charlton, board chair, and Saxton stepped down. Board resignations offered by executive directors, Henry and Lawler, were accepted.

Following Charlton's resignation from the board, Bettle, who had served as interim chair, became formally appointed as chair at the May 2008 annual general meeting. Huljich became an independent director. Russell, Daniels and Sodi remained as directors.

New Investors

As of December 2008, the company's principal sources of liquidity were cash and cash equivalents along with term deposits that totalled approximately US$1.3 million (with accounts receivable of US$0.4 million). Amid liquidity concerns, the company sought additional sources of financing. In March 2009, Diligent secured US$3 million of financing from two US-based private investment companies: Spring Street Partners (US$2 million) and existing shareholder Carroll Capital Holdings (US$1 million).

They collectively purchased 30 million shares of newly created Series A Preferred Stock for US$0.10 per share. The Preferred shares carried a fixed, cumulative dividend of 11 per cent per annum to be paid either in cash or in kind for additional Preferred shares. The shares also came with preferred annual dividend payment over common shares and were convertible at any time to common shares at US$.10 per share.

Analysts pointed out that Spring Street's 20 million preference shares were effectively an 18 per cent stake in Diligent, purchased at a fraction of the amount paid by New Zealand investors for 24 million shares just over a year earlier with the company's IPO. However, share prices had dropped to around US$0.09 by January 2009 from its 2007 IPO share price of US $0.77. A shareholders meeting was held in March 2009 in which resolutions passed with 98 per cent approval for the transaction.

NEW BOARD CHAIR

David Liptak, CEO of Spring Street Partners, became the largest shareholder of Diligent's preferred stock. As part of the share purchase agreement, Liptak was appointed to the board as a non-executive director. In consideration of the special provisions for that type of share ownership, Liptak was ineligible for election at the annual general meeting. In 2010, Liptak was elected by the other holders of the preferred shares as board chair, replacing Bettle. Liptak brought a track record of corporate restructuring and reorganisation experience, knowledge of the finance industry along with strategic and analytical skills to his role as chair.

Diligent Makes a Profit (2010)

In 2010, the company rebounded. For the first time as a listed company, it achieved positive operating cash flow of nearly US$18,000 net compared with a net negative cash flow of US$2.5 million in the previous year. Growth was attributed to a full sales pipeline, its recent expansion into Asia with the opening of a subsidiary in Singapore, and the introduction of an iPad compatible version of its Boardbooks software. In its 2010 Annual General Report, Liptak and Sodi congratulated management for 'its ability to drive substantial growth with increased efficiency'. Meanwhile, Henry decided to take a different course of action.

Secret Trades Exposed

Although Henry resigned from the board in 2008, he and Borg were trustees and beneficiaries of the B Henry & K Borg Living Trust which continued to hold shares in Diligent. Henry and his wife were substantial security holders of Diligent shares.

In the months of April, May, and June 2010, Henry created an impression of trade activity and lifted share prices. Known as 'wash trades' by effectively trading in Diligent shares with himself, Henry moved the share price upwards and set the market closing price in early April 2010. Two weeks later, he was again active in trading Diligent shares with himself and set the market price higher on the first trade of the day.

Henry's actions appeared suspicious. In late April, he was warned about market manipulation during a telephone conversation with the bank manager of ASB. The bank closed the trust's share trading account. Henry then telephoned and emailed New Zealand's financial regulator about a mistaken amendment to his existing sell order. He advised the officer that, 'I don't think it's a big deal … I spoke with the ASB and basically, they said "back luck—be more careful"'. He pointed out, 'The mistake cost me about US$325. Lesson learnt, be super careful when trading online'.[4] His explanation to the financial regulator at the time related to a specific portion of his trade activities in mid-April rather than all his activities at the time.

Henry then gained access to another online trading platform. On four occasions in April, May, and June 2010, Henry placed several buy and sell orders and traded in Diligent shares. He then withdrew his buy orders once the market moved in his favour and other buyers had traded with his sell orders. Overall, the trading gave an artificial inflated impression of interest in Diligent shares and forced other buyers to bid at higher prices.

Following a referral from the New Zealand Exchange about suspicious trade activity, Henry's actions came under scrutiny by the Financial Markets Authority of New Zealand (FMA).[5] The FMA's role was to regulate New Zealand's financial markets. Their responsibility was to oversee securities, financial reporting, and company laws as they applied to financial services and markets. In 2013, three years after the FMA initiated its investigation, six charges were laid against Henry. Each charge carried a fine of up to US$0.84 million with the maximum penalty of more than US $5 million.

Initially, Henry acknowledged he made errors in trading. He argued that the trading had a minimal effect on the market, inadvertently lowering then raising the prices of stock by a matter of cents. The net effect of these trades, Henry explained, was about US$1,000 at the time.

Plea Deal

In August 2014, the day prior to the start of the trial in the New Zealand High Court, Henry entered a guilty plea on all six charges that he breached the Securities Market Act 1988. Although Henry did not gain materially out of the trading at issue, and his actions in themselves were deliberate, Justice Venning did not find that Henry deliberately set out to breach the New Zealand Securities Market Act. Henry's defence submitted that he acted as he did to provide support and liquidity for Diligent's stock because he considered the true value of the stock was suppressed by the media publicity that had surrounded his resignation.

But what started out as Henry's consideration of himself 'as an amateur "market maker" by providing support and liquidity for Diligent's stock',[6] evolved into the first case of market manipulation brought in New Zealand. Justice Venning explained, 'Mr Henry was in a position of dominance and control over the trading in Diligent shares'.[7] He stated, 'The conduct that Mr Henry engaged in undermines the development of a fair, efficient, and transparent financial market. Such market manipulation is likely to undermine the integrity of the NZX and jeopardise the confidence of both overseas and domestic investors in the NZ security markets. A pecuniary penalty is appropriate'.[8] Henry was fined more than US$125,000.

Belinda Moffat, Director of Enforcement, Financial Markets Authority, stated, 'The public want and deserve to invest in the markets with confidence that any trading activity reflects genuine supply and demand for shares in the market. There is a strong public interest in deterring share trading that is false and misleading' (New Zealand Exchange, 2014). She elaborated, 'Where there is a case that meets the standard of evidence required and where court action satisfies the public interest, then FMA will take proceedings to ensure confidence in the development of fair, efficient and transparent markets'.

The Board's Next Steps

Liptak and the directors looked to put the court case and conviction in the rear-view mirror. They had recently completed a board led remediation of the company's oversight role of the New York based, New Zealand listed company. The press coverage did not seem to have any adverse consequence for the share price, which hit a seven-week high in mid-August 2014. For Liptak, stakeholder confidence in Diligent warranted the continued pursuit of best options for the company.

Case Study 3.2 Solid Energy: Board Accountability[9]

In May 2013, former chair of Solid Energy, John Palmer, adjusted the microphone before he responded to the question posed to him at the hearing convened by the New Zealand Parliamentary Select Commerce Committee into the near collapse of the coal mining enterprise. Palmer answered, 'This was not being run to prepare it for partial privatisation, it was being run because it was the right thing to do' (Small & Rutherford, 2013). Under further questioning, Palmer elaborated, 'I am willing to acknowledge that we made some mistakes. But it is very important for New Zealand that we have a risk culture that says taking risk in business is crucially important'. He explained, 'For someone who has been in business, and volatile businesses, for a lifetime, you take risks and they do not always work. But I have no regrets with the path and the strategy we set out and some regrets that we did not perform as well as we could have' (Smellie, 2013).

In an earlier statement, Tony Ryall, Minister for State-Owned Enterprise, pointed out that the government accepted responsibility 'in as far as its role and responsibilities are under the state-owned enterprises act. But the law is very clear, it is the responsibility of the board to manage debt, dividend and investments' (Small & Rutherford, 2013).

Palmer had gained recognition as an outstanding chair who tackled some of New Zealand's most difficult governance leadership roles. Twice named 'Chairperson of the Year' in 2007 and 2009[10], his role as board chair for the troubled energy company appeared to raise more questions about the Solid Energy board and its relationship with its shareholding ministers.

With Palmer's closing remarks, both critics and advocates of the privatisation of state-owned enterprises (SOEs), who anticipated a simple explanation for the company's performance over the past three years, left puzzled. Questions about the shareholding ministers' decision to delay listing the company on the New Zealand Exchange lingered.

History of Solid Energy as a State-Owned Enterprise

Coal mining was among the oldest industries in New Zealand. Coal was a primary means of generating energy and essential for steel production. Despite the industry's importance, it did not readily translate into a profitable one. By the mid-1980s, mining operations owned by the government operated at a loss.

In 1988, State Coal Mines was incorporate as part of New Zealand's economic reform. Established by the State-Owned Enterprise Act (1986), the Minister of Finance and the Minister for State-Owned Enterprise each held 50 per cent of the company's shares. The coal company entered a new relationship with government. It adopted policy and structural reforms. Its board of directors were appointed from business. By the end of its first year of operation as a state-owned enterprise, the coal producer enjoyed its status as a profitable company. It had turned 20 years of losses, including a nearly US$40 million (rounded figures) loss the previous year, into a profit.

HARDSHIP ENCOUNTERED

Rebranded as Solid Energy New Zealand in 1996, the company's performance suffered following the Asian Economic Crisis (1997–1998). The shareholding ministers' response was to replace the board. In December 1998, Tim Saunders, an experienced corporate director, accepted an appointment as board chair. He promptly initiated a strategic review and restructuring. Neither the strategic review nor the plan to restructure stopped the erosion of Solid Energy's value. By 2000, the board appointed Don Elder as chief executive officer to wind down the company over the next three years.

TURNAROUND

While investigating Solid Energy's options, a key discovery was made. Southland's vast lignite and conventional coal sources were identified. The company also expanded its export market. Rather than the company being wound down, it soon grew to become the second largest producer of locally sourced energy (excluding oil) after Shell.

In 2004, Solid Energy diversified into two development streams: Renewable Energy with wood pellets and New Energy with lignite conversion into higher value products. By the end of its 2006 fiscal year, the company earned record breaking revenue of US$3.5 million, up 40 per cent from the previous year's US$2.5 million. Its improved performance was driven by high export prices with strong market demand for steel and energy coming from China and the rest of Asia as well as strong domestic sales.

Solid Energy Board in 2007–2008

In 2007, John Palmer, an independent non-executive director, accepted an appointment as the new chair to replace Saunders. Palmer served as chair of Air New Zealand and as a director of AMP Life, Rabobank Australia, and Saxton Fruit. He was recognised as *Deloitte/New Zealand Management* magazine as Chairperson of the Year in 2007. In 1999, Palmer received an Officer of the New Zealand Order of Merit for services to the New Zealand kiwifruit industry. Palmer brought his proven track record of transforming companies in difficult situations, extensive leadership experience, and strategic insight to the role of board chair. Palmer, like all other directors, was appointed by the shareholding ministers.

The board had expertise in fields ranging from natural resources to law. Directors who had been with Solid Energy prior to Palmer's appointment included Tony Williams (stepped down April 2007), Adrienne Young-Cooper, Helen Cull, John Spencer and Alan Broome. Directors who joined the board over the next 18 months following Palmer's appointment included John Fletcher, John McDonald and Simon Marsters. As deputy chair, Fletcher brought experience with the energy sector having served as managing director of Shell New Zealand and previously held senior positions with Royal Dutch Shell. McDonald, also appointed to the board of Air New Zealand and public companies including HY-Fi Securities and Dairy Equities, had experience with the Fletcher Challenge group of companies which was the country's largest multinational corporation in the 1980s. He added general management experience. Educated as a chemical engineer, Marsters had several executive positions in the ceramics industry and was experienced as a business broker.

Board and Shareholders' Reporting Relationships

The board reported quarterly to its shareholding ministers, the Minister for State-Owned Enterprise and the Minister of Finance, through the Crown Company Monitoring Advisory Unit.[11] It provided interim and annual reports, financial statements as well as a statement of corporate intent (SCI) and a business plan to shareholding ministers. It met reporting requirements under the Companies Act, 1993. Each year the shareholding ministers gave an account to Parliament of Solid Energy's performance.

Global Financial Crisis Affects Solid Energy

The global financial crisis (2008–2009) affected demand for coal as the manufacturing industry's need for steel made from New Zealand's high-quality coal had fallen, hurting volumes and prices. Although total revenue neared US$570 million for the first time in the company's history due, in part, to the sale of a coal mine and high coal prices in the first 5 months of the year, the year closed on a sharp downturn. The company's two diversification initiatives, Renewable Energy and New Energy, were affected. Palmer explained in his annual statement, '2009 has been a difficult year for staff as we cut back production and budgets, restructured operations and closed our two smallest mines'.

VALUE IN USE VERSUS COMMERCIAL VALUE

In 2008, the board reassessed the commercial value of the company at US $2.1 billion, up from US$340 million in the previous year. The new valuation triggered a query from the shareholding Ministries and Treasury. The board pointed out that the SCI valuation was a 'value in use' and, as such, it did not represent the value which would be reflected in a transaction for the company. A series of exchanges between the board, Treasury and the Ministry for State-Owned Enterprises unfolded. Ultimately, State-Owned Enterprises Minister, Simon Power, conceded that the responsibility to assess commercial value of the company resided with the board.

POLICY FOR PROFIT

In May 2009, Power issued a letter to Palmer in which he advised the board to increase the gearing and dividend yield. The initiative, issued to all SOEs, set out to standardise and simplify the dividend policy to ensure that a more consistent share of profits was returned to the Crown as shareholder. Over the past five years, dividends from Solid Energy had been variable. The dividend yield had averaged 1.9 per cent per annum.

Recovery

In late 2010, demand and sales rebounded. Major investments were made over the year, as planned, to increase productivity and production. This included a new coal processing plant, construction of a new pellet plant, and a biodiesel facility. Employee numbers increased from 815 to 1,223 largely owing to recruitment for the country's largest open cast coal mine operation.

The board approved and initiated an external borrowing program that increased its gearing ratio from 35 per cent to 40 per cent to finance its capital expenditure for changes over its three-year planning period. In response, Simon pointed out that external equity was inconsistent with current policy for SOEs.

Solid Energy: The Vision of a Natural Resources Company

Between 2009 and 2010 Palmer and the board worked with Elder and his management team to develop a bold new vision of Solid Energy as an integrated national resources company. They called it National Resources Ltd. The proposed new company would include its current coal operations, Renewable Energy and New Energy initiatives and it would be granted preferential access to all hydrocarbon and mineral rights.

Earnings would initially fund capital expenditure and over time, private interests would be able to buy into the business at the project level (e.g. through joint venture, project finance, or initial public offering) or at the parent level. The proposed business plan argued that the integration of energy-related activities into a single entity under New Zealand ownership would accelerate and capture maximum value and wealth creation for the country.

In May 2010, Palmer and Elder met with John Key, Prime Minister, and senior officials to discuss the National Resources company proposal. The meeting concluded with support, in principle, for the existing coal mining and diversification projects in Solid Energy's business plan. They agreed that further analysis by Treasury of the proposed development of a single National Resource company needed to be conducted over the next few months, and once completed, they would revisit the proposal.

The next day, Palmer and Elder met with Power to debrief the meeting, provide an update on the status of the SCI and business plan, and explain the approximate 60 per cent increase in commercial valuation of the company from US$1.7 billion to nearly US$2.8 billion when the long-term energy outlook had not changed. Palmer clarified that the change in valuation reflected the development-to-sales cash flow anticipated for New Energy projects, such as coal-to-fertiliser and briquetting, where value was added to low quality resources through technology. Palmer was advised by Power that the proposed suspension of dividend payments for nine years (2010 to 2019) was not supported in the absence of an approved business case for each project. Power confirmed that a 'no dividend payments' strategy to fund investment opportunities was inconsistent with the expectations of shareholding ministers. Subsequently, the board prepared and submitted a revised SCI and business plan.

In August 2010, Palmer and Elder met with Power to further discuss the National Resource Company proposal. Following that meeting, Power acknowledged the vision and effort in generating the proposal. The company's ambitious expansion plans—to spend more than US$1.4 billion over the next 10 years to expand and diversify its business into oil, gas, coal, and minerals and to gain the synergies from an integrated portfolio approach to energy—was not supported by the shareholding ministers. Palmer was advised to focus efforts on the company's core business.

Shareholder Announces Initial Public Offering of Energy SOEs

In December 2011, Solid Energy was confirmed as one of the four energy companies to be listed on the New Zealand Exchange as part of a planned reduction from 100 per cent to 51 per cent share ownership. Palmer, like other board chairs of energy related SOEs, received a letter from the shareholding minister, outlining the shareholder's expectations for the company. Palmer confirmed in the 2011 annual report, 'We will work constructively to identify the optimal equity structure and timing that would best benefit the company and the shareholder'.

UBS Report in Preparation for Initial Public Offering (2011)

The global investment bank, UBS, was commissioned by Treasury to provide an equity-analyst style valuation report of Solid Energy. The report was designed to identify and examine the main drivers of the company's performance and, ultimately, its value. UBS conducted its scoping study to provide a capital market perspective of Solid Energy and its readiness for an initial public offering (IPO). UBS presented its draft report to the Solid Energy board and management along with Treasury representatives in October 2011.

The UBS report identified product, client, and market features that would appeal to prospective investors. The strengths of Solid Energy, and one of the reasons for its strong performance, resided in its long-established exports from its West Coast mines of high-quality metallurgical coking coal to key international steelmaking clients such as SAIL, Mittal Steel, Tata, Baosteel and Mitsubishi. These were among the largest steel companies in India, China and Japan. The report also identified business issues that needed to be mitigated or resolved prior to any IPO.

The report presented recommendations in key categories: coal mining (operations), strategic business positioning (renewables and new developments), cost structure (overhead), along with board composition and capital structure. Its recommendations for the board itself included a reduction in board size from eight to six directors, which would be comparable to Australian coal mining counterparts. The report also called for changes to board composition. It recommended the appointment of two directors with direct coal mining experience and one international director with large scale oil and gas development experience as a minimum.

UBS recommended that Solid Energy have no debt at the time of the IPO. This contrasted with the company's gearing of 30 per cent in 2011, with a total debt of nearly US$170 million, compared with 33 per cent in 2010. The company was valued at US$970 million by UBS, considerably less than the company's own valuation. The report concluded that at least 12 months were needed to prepare Solid Energy for an IPO with the full support of the board and management as well as additional time to demonstrate the results of its shift in strategy to the market. This made 2014 a potential IPO date for the company.

After hearing from UBS and Treasury, the board made three requests of management. One, management should formally respond to Treasury on key elements of the report. Two, a proposal on Renewables should be brought by management to the next board meeting. Three, management should generally rationalise and refocus New Developments.

Treasury's Response to the UBS Report (2012)

Treasury noted that the board needed to restructure the operations of the core coal business and provide a more disciplined approach to the management of the Renewable Energy and New Development activities as identified in the UBS report. Importantly, the UBS report pointed to the contradiction between the company's valuation of coal prices and the rest of industry analysts that had a 'consensus view' of coal prices. Treasury stressed in its analysis that UBS sought but was unable to obtain documentation and analysis from Solid Energy to support management and the board's view on commodity price paths. In short, major differences existed between Solid Energy and the UBS report arising from assumptions for future coal prices. Solid Energy's figures were significantly higher than the 'consensus view' held by industry analysts which informed the UBS report. Of additional concern, Treasury's analysis pointed out that the UBS report:

> Highlighted the continuation of Solid Energy's ambitions to become a project based, multi-resource developer in order to maximise value for New Zealand through responsible custodianship and development of strategic natural resources. In part the high level of corporate overhead reflects resourcing of the company's ambition to be an integrated natural resources company. Moreover, expenditures incurred for these broader public or national interests are not valued by investors.
>
> (Treasury Report, 2011)

Treasury anticipated that the board's response to the UBS report would likely involve restructuring of governance, management, and operations. Finally, Treasury pointed out that the UBS report 'effectively expressed no confidence in Solid Energy's business strategy' (Treasury Report, 2012). The conclusion was that 'Treasury and Ministers needed to engage more intensively with Solid Energy over the next three to six months to ensure that the restructuring would contribute to the Mixed Ownership Model[12] objectives in a timely manner' (Treasury Report, 2011).

Board Responds to UBS Report: Different Visions and Strategies Become Clear

At a board meeting in February 2012, the directors convened to discuss the direction and plans for the next 12 to 18 months as part of the board's regular planning process. The board consolidated its recommendations into four primary strategic issues (business performance, capability, capital, and monetising assets) along with two others related to future value growth—global commodity outlook and the cost of carbon.

Following that board meeting, Palmer crafted a letter to Tony Ryall (who replaced Simon Powers as Minister of SOEs) that outlined several concerns. Palmer pointed out that Solid Energy's 'product mix, its exposure to world commodity markets and exchange rates, and its long-term growth strategy' made it 'unique amongst the nominated SOEs' (Palmer, 2012). He expressed concerned that the application of the Mixed Ownership Model objectives to Solid Energy 'had driven a series of recommendations that may not be in the best interest of the business nor its future shareholders, including the Crown'. Palmer stated, 'We are keen to work together with Treasury on delivering a capital plan that maximises value for Solid Energy while meeting the Crown's Mixed Ownership Model fiscal and political objectives'.

Treasury's Response to the Board's Strategy and Business Plan Update

Treasury responded to Solid Energy's 2012–2013 business plan by commissioning Deutsche Bank to conduct a new review. Although the board had agreed to divest its Renewable Energy commitments (e.g. wood pellets and biodiesel), it remained steadfast in the pursuit of New Energy developments. The Deutsche Bank report concluded that the coal price used by Solid Energy should be market based and informed by analysts' 'consensus view'. Overall, the Deutsche Bank report supported the initial analysis and recommendations provided by the UBS report. Although the company had incorporated some elements of pre-IPO actions into its business plan, there was too much uncertainty that it would be ready for an IPO.

In early March 2012, Treasury identified two options for the ministers: one, withdraw Solid Energy from the mixed ownership programme; or two, seek confirmation from the board and Palmer whether the board could support a significant shift in strategy as outlined in the UBS report. Meanwhile, coal prices dropped to 2004 levels which further complicated the decision to be made by the shareholders.

Board Presents a SCI and Business Plan to the Shareholders

In early May 2012, Palmer and Fletcher (deputy chair) attended a meeting with Ryall, Minister of SOEs, and Bill English, Minister of Finance. Ryall wanted to discuss the SCI and business plan informed by the UBS report. Palmer and Fletcher left that meeting disgruntled. The ministers and board did not see eye-to-eye on the future of Solid Energy and the role of the board. The findings of the two reports made the shareholders sceptical that the board was preparing the company for an IPO. The revised SCI and business plan submitted to the shareholding Ministries later in May 2012 were again rejected because they were not viewed as being responsive enough to changing market conditions.

Plan Rejected: Things Go Awry

By June 2012, the shareholders showed alarm. The shareholding ministers placed the board under intensive monitoring. Palmer received a letter from Ryall detailing the implications. Palmer was advised that he and the board were expected to revise and resubmit the SCI and business plan and present the updated business plan to Ryall in person. It was expected that Palmer would give his personal assurance to Ryall that the proposed actions would address the underlying challenges. In addition, Palmer was expected to report to the shareholding ministers monthly, and to meet monthly with Treasury to discuss each monthly report. Finally, Palmer was advised that Ryall had asked Treasury to increase its use of external advisers in its monitoring function of Solid Energy.

Following this, Palmer announced his decision to step down before his term expired. Palmer and the board expressed concerned about the minister's decision to put Solid Energy under intensive monitoring. They considered what message this decision would send to directors of other SOEs. Palmer also thought carefully about potential future investors' reactions given the desire for an IPO. Finally, Palmer considered that the different visions for Solid Energy could not be reconciled. Palmer decided to leave effectively at the end of August 2012 with 15 months remaining in his term.

Having announced his early departure, Palmer continued to work with the board to move forward with changes. The board created a restructuring plan to respond to the continued drop in coal prices. The plan called for the closure of a recently purchased mine, reduced production for another, and layoffs. Following a meeting with the ministers, the changes were announced. The company issued its Annual Report for 2011–2012 with a net loss of US$33 million. Write-downs worth US$90 million were included in the result.

Prior to his departure in August 2012, Palmer resubmitted the SCI and business plan. The shareholding ministers once again rejected both documents. They did not provide the confidence sought by the shareholding ministers that the company's strategy had sufficiently acknowledged and incorporated a changed market. The deadline for the revised SCI and business plan was extended until a new chair could be appointed to the board.

By the end of August, the Minister for Finance (Bill English) announced that Solid Energy's IPO had been deferred:

> We would only take any of these companies to the market if they were in good shape for investment and Solid Energy right now certainly is not. It has some fairly substantial issues that they have signalled. Whether it ends up being able to be floated would depend on whether they can get in suitable shape for public investors.

He pointed out:

> We would not be planning to float it any time soon. It is a tax-payer asset, it is experiencing the difficulties of the global economic crisis, and we have to act as good stewards and get that asset into good shape.
> (Hartevelt, 2012)

By October 2013, a new chair was appointed, and debts were restructured. John Key, Prime Minister of New Zealand, commented on the coal mining enterprise, 'My own personal view is if we would have had the mixed ownership model applied to Solid Energy, it may well not have gotten itself in the mess it did. That is because the external analysis would have rung a lot of bells and demanded a lot more accountability' (Kirk, 2013).

Case Study 3.3 Calibrating Board Leadership in Frequency Project Management[13]

Jonathan Barry, executive director and founding partner of Frequency Project Management, surveyed the site of the company's latest infrastructure project. The demand for the company's specialist project management and advisory services increased with the construction of transport services, ports, telecommunications, healthcare and education facilities throughout the country. Barry, along with shareholding and independent directors of the board, anticipated that the recommendations for employee shareholding options for the privately held company would soon be received.

Frequency's Founding History

In 2010, Jonathan Barry established a specialist project advisory consultancy, Frequency Project Management (hereafter referred to as Frequency) that filled a niche in the New Zealand construction industry. Previously, he had led award-winning high-profile projects from inception to construction over his 20-year career in international construction. In his new solo role, Barry and engineering consultants worked to plan, optimise and implement large, complex infrastructure projects vital to the economic and social growth of the country. Initial projects involved rail, road and transport.

In 2012, Barry sought out two shareholding directors who shared a vision of leading a premiere project management consultancy. After he met with several prospective partners, he brought in a colleague with whom he had worked with in the transportation sector and knew well. Like Barry, the new partner saw the potential for greater professional opportunities in a small, technically proficient practice than in a large company.

At the same time, Barry also brought Andrew Taylor into Frequency. Taylor had a long history of managing projects, having previously guided Air New Zealand's refurbishment of its domestic check in and the pier at its hub, Auckland International Airport. He had also built new stadiums and sports complexes in the United Kingdom. Having worked in large international firms, he was looking for the next challenge in his career and the opportunity to shape the growth of a start-up company into a leading professional consultancy had appeal. The three shareholders strove to bring alignment to a shared vision of Frequency, but it remained elusive. After 10 months, one partner realised his expertise resided in project management rather than in building a business. Barry bought out the 20 per cent share ownership of the third director in 2013.

Company Operations and Management

The company's operations supported the work of public and private sector clients in the design, development, construction and maintenance of facilities, services and systems. Initially focused on sectors with large, complex projects in airports, rail, road and transport, the company expanded to include education, ports, water, telecommunications and healthcare.

Purposefully structured as a flat organisation, the company pooled its collective employee expertise in response to clients' needs. Some clients, such as the rail sector, preferred to work with a specialist team whether it was based in Auckland, Christchurch or Wellington. Other clients were regionally focused, such as the three-year education project on the North Island.

The expectation was that each regional office generated its share of the overall revenue for the company, ensuring that each office was profitable. Employees were encouraged to develop enduring relationships with clients so they would be well positioned for repeat business opportunities as they arose. The relationships unfolded through each employee's own network of clients and industry contacts. The approach found traction in regional and national projects. Other projects came about through a competitive bidding process, which included the government's tender service.

Three professional levels within the company evolved over time. Barry and Taylor maintained a high level of engagement across projects, often acting as technical directors. The next broad band of professional leaders were regional managers whose responsibility included revenue generation. That level was followed by the senior project manager level, which gave some granularity to the talent pool along with a career pathway for junior project managers. The administrative staff provided day-to-day operational support with accounting and human resources contracted on a part time basis. Professional staff worked on specific projects because of their expertise in a sector or with a client or because they had successfully bid for the contract. Everyone accepted the fluid nature of the type of work they performed.

MANAGEMENT

While construction brought together people and materials, it also required planning, discipline and innovation. To help achieve this orientation within the company culture, Barry and Taylor strove to engage employees through the practices they adopted. In consideration of the geographic distance between offices throughout the country, they met regularly by conference call with regional managers. They also travelled to regional offices to meet with managers, project managers and clients.

Travel related directly to the nature of the projects and expertise required. Barry, acting as project director, travelled extensively to Queenstown to secure a large project with the Ministry of Education. As that project unfolded, his travel tapered off. Taylor typically travelled to regional offices at least once a month. Although travel equated time away from the corporate office and its demands, it also ensured that the partners had a good grasp of the projects along with the skills and specialist project management knowledge of the regional managers. In addition, they conducted regional management retreats two to three times per year which offered a different dynamic for interactions to unfold. They shared technical excellence and innovative solutions along with trouble-shooting client issues.

Barry and Taylor balanced recruitment of full-time employees with client commitments. Its employee profile diversified as the company expanded with new client sectors. Many held professional certifications and degrees within their technical fields (e.g. chartered civil engineer, chartered building surveyor, Master of Civil Engineering, or professional civil engineer). New talent was identified through existing networks and professional contacts. Collectively, the company's 19 employees brought expertise across the project management lifecycle, including consultant management, design management, contract administration, client liaison, value management, risk management and contract procurement.

They also believed that the company should play a role in supporting the community. Staff interacted with each other outside of work at charity events like bike races, mud runs and other sporting events. The company also sponsored the development of the next generation of young athletes. It also sponsored scholarships for aspiring students interested in property or construction credentials. The initiative provided funds, mentorship and work experience for three years.

Board Leadership and Governance for Shared Ownership Performance

In 2014, Barry and Taylor recognised that a board which provided outside, nonbinding strategic advice concerning long term company plans was the next major step. The board could provide guidance and connections for Frequency while Barry and Taylor retained control.

CHAIR APPOINTED

In 2014, Brett Murray accepted the invitation to become Frequency's first board chair. Murray had served as a director on three advisory boards for small to medium size enterprises (SMEs). He had entrepreneurial experience as a CEO of his own professional service company in management training for tourism. More recently, he had provided managerial consulting services to SMEs in Australia and New Zealand. Although he had not previously served as a chair, they agreed to embark on a corporate governance journey together.

Murray had initially worked with Barry as an executive coach in 2008. The established, trusted business and personal connection positioned Murray as the only potential candidate for the role of board chair from Barry's perspective. Like Barry, Taylor trusted Murray's neutral stance, appreciated his commitment to the business, and respected his facilitation and teambuilding skills. Murray had most recently worked with the original three shareholders, individually and collectively, to bring them together in a shared vision of the company and its growth. He knew Barry and Taylor well professionally and had gained some insight into Frequency's business.

At the first board meeting, Murray faced questions about his interest in share ownership. He pointed out that his motivation as chair was different and that he did not want a conflict of interest. He knew the tremendous amount of work required to build a successful company and respected the candour, loyalty and commitment of Barry and Taylor. They had consistently and repeatedly put the collective good of employees and clients at the centre of their decision-making, affecting strategic choices for the company in the short and long-term. Murray believed he could work with them to help achieve results greater than they had expected. The integration of coaching with the full scope of responsibly as a chair distinctively positioned him for his new role.

DEVELOPMENT OF BOARD LEADERSHIP AND GOVERNANCE PROCESSES

Over the next 10 months, Murray and the two executive directors developed governance processes that would meet the evolving needs of a young professional service company. The board met bi-monthly. In between each board meeting, Murray, in his role as a coach, met with each director. As an independent director and board chair with expertise outside of the construction industry, Murray found that these sessions gave him an insider's perspective of the challenges, opportunities and strengths of each director.

Board meetings were held in Auckland's head office. Murray prepared the agenda with input from Barry and Taylor. The discipline for reporting and compliance helped to keep the bigger picture of Frequency in focus. Taylor pointed out:

> The day-to-day management of the business and projects would overrun everything else if you let it. Having board meetings and putting together a board paper does force you to make time to look at where we are headed, look at the strategies and targets we set ourselves and focus on those.

Employees viewed Murray like a mentor and a steady hand on the ship when Barry and Taylor were finding the way at times. Others pointed out that Murray was quite adept at drawing them back to where they should be going.

Board Performance Health Check

After its first year, the board conducted its own performance review. Murray believed that self-evaluation provided an essential snapshot of how each director viewed the boards' performance to-date and to inform improvements. Murray reaffirmed his commitment as board chair: 'As long as I feel as if I am giving value, I am learning, and I am enjoying and having fun with it, then I will continue. They are good people so why would I not?'

The evaluation was, on balance, positive. It also revealed some growing pains. Collectively, they had anticipated that creating a board and developing governance processes would be more like a sprint than a marathon. They acknowledged it was a never-ending process and affirmed their commitment to the next phase of board development. Barry pointed out, 'I like the idea of a board that asks tough questions. I want the board to help grow the business into an ambitious, accountable and profitable entity'. Although the board had made great strides in gaining an understanding of their roles, three pressing issues remained: share ownership, board composition, and the board's strategic role.

New Ownership Model Considered

At a board meeting in 2014, the directors considered the share ownership structure of Frequency. They recalled that when Barry launched Frequency, he envisaged a diversified shareholding structure. Prompted by the exit of one of the founding directors, the ensuing share buy-back had led to Barry's disproportionate 80 per cent share ownership. Taylor's original 20 per cent ownership remained unchanged since 2012. They believed the time was right to revisit the ownership model on two fronts: share option and upfront share acquisition.

Barry wanted to instil a shared ownership model and mind-set among employees. He envisaged a company that would not restrict share ownership to five or six directors; it would allow for a wide distribution of shares. Barry imagined that over the next 10 years there would be a high level of participation in Frequency share ownership, ranging from one-half to five per cent among staff. He believed that the model would foster greater engagement to act in the best interests of the company while appealing to employees' own entrepreneurial orientation and need for autonomy.

Taylor supported an exploration of employee share incentive options. Upfront shareholding had, in part, brought Taylor to Frequency. The right for employees to acquire shares based on the achievement of specific performance targets also held appeal. The upfront share acquisition and share option arrangements were both used in other professional services firms to attract and retain talent. Used individually or in combination, they could allow employees to benefit from Frequency's success.

To move this issue forward, Murray recommend a legal firm with expertise in employee-owned firms. In generating their briefing, it became clear to Barry and Taylor that they needed multiple shareholding directors to join Frequency. While a substantial capital infusion would be useful, it was secondary to the real core asset they would bring—knowledge. An injection of specialist technical knowledge and the in-depth knowledge of industry clients would allow Frequency to accelerate its strategic growth plan.

Barry and Taylor could foresee three to five shareholding directors with each one responsible for an industry segment. They anticipated a combination of external appointments and internal promotions to fill the new sector lead positions. Barry and Taylor signed off on the briefing for the legal firm and pondered how to put this plan into action while waiting for the firm's recommendations. They turned their attention to the profile of a new ideal shareholding director.

New Shareholding Director Selected

An ideal external shareholding director, Barry and Taylor surmised, was someone who brought 10 years' experience from a large, top-tier engineer consulting or construction firm, accompanied by a robust network in a business segment like roads or rail with a genuine interest in growing the company. Despite the company's healthy revenue stream, they could ill afford to mentor team members for very long. Barry and Taylor envisioned an individual who would be at an earlier stage of their career or even mid-career. The prospective shareholding director would need to be self-financing or arrange for financing for share ownership, as Frequency did not provide that option.

The challenge in this scenario, as Barry and Taylor knew too well, would reside with the persuasion of a candidate to leave a large, well-known company with a firmly established brand, relative security, and a clear career path to join Frequency. Despite the rock-solid reputation of the company generally and Barry and Taylor specifically, identifying, attracting, securing and retaining top talent among a finite pool of candidates was a persistent concern. Having already experienced the repercussions of a choice that did not fit with the young company, both were keen to get the next move right.

Despite an attractive recruitment package, they encountered a competitive market. While they could offer many benefits, they simply could not match the larger salaries offered by bigger competitors. Undeterred, they took these setbacks in stride, pleased that a small company even attracted interest from some industry heavy weights. Their commitment to accelerating their growth plan did not give them pause in their pursuit of candidates, even to discuss this intended change in share ownership with Murray. They were resilient in their belief that a new shareholding director was on the near horizon.

In mid-2015, Frequency introduced its newest shareholder director, Shane Sutherland. Prior to joining Frequency, he had gained experience in the project management of major rail initiatives in Sydney and Melbourne Australia before returning to New Zealand to work with Auckland

Transport. The complexity and scope of the new projects in Auckland factored into Sutherland's decision to join Frequency. He wanted to work with a team committed to the delivery of projects on time, on budget while meeting high standards for design, quality and safety.

New Independent Director Appointed

CRITERIA FOR A NEW DIRECTOR

In late 2014, Murray had initiated a discussion for a second independent director to join the board. The idea landed well. To guide them in the search for a candidate, Murray introduced a process to identify the desired criteria. First, the directors discussed broadly what each one was seeking to achieve with the appointment, given the development of the company to-date. Their preference for an outside director with client-specific and industry knowledge became evident. Then each director completed a gap skill evaluation to winnow and isolate key criteria. Finally, the directors discussed their individual results and reached a consensus about the preferred knowledge, skills and experience of a new board member. With a clear profile in hand, they set out to identify someone from among their networks interested in the opportunity.

IDENTIFICATION AND SELECTION

Taylor recalled an individual he had met at a transportation industry event more than a year ago. He approached Claire Stewart. She worked with the region's largest transport services as the chief infrastructure officer. Following an exploratory discussion, Taylor and Barry learned that a directorship role with Frequency piqued her interest. Stewart, in turn, introduced Taylor and Barry to a colleague who provide insight on whether she would fit with their culture and the board. Meanwhile, Stewart conducted her own due diligence, which involved 'meeting with the usual suspects, including the accountant'. Following a separate meeting with Murray, the board collectively supported her appointment. Stewart negotiated and signed a declaration to prevent a conflict of interest with her employer.

In late 2015, Stewart was appointed as Frequency's second independent director. As a lawyer, she brought a commercial orientation to the board. She had practised corporate and commercial law prior to moving into the financial advisory sector. Stewart believed that she could contribute her commercial expertise, industry relationships and more formal discipline in the board's processes.

Stewart recalled her first impressions of the board meeting:

> It was well chaired. Brett Murray was well prepared and well in tune with the issues. They were quite direct conversations, as you would

expect with a SME. You are talking to two of the working directors—key employees. The meetings have to run to time. I know these things sound insignificant, but when everyone is busy and there is a lot to get through on an agenda, it is a good sign.

She observed, 'The inclusion of independent directors supports each of them in different ways, allowing them to put their directors' hats on more in board meetings'.

The Board's Next Steps

Barry and Taylor were mindful that the pending recommendations from the legal firm concerning employee share incentive arrangements could alter the company's competitive positioning, profitability and growth prospects. They were committed to retaining Frequency's ethos of doing well by doing good and working with companies that aligned with their cultural and environmental values. With a new shareholding director and an independent director recently appointed, the board continued its commitment to pursue the best options for the company.

Discussion

Although these case studies feature different issues in consideration of the different types of capital arrangements that range from an initial public offering for a private sector software firm, the unsuccessful pursuit of partial privatisation of a state-owned coal mining enterprise, and the emergence of director/employee ownership of a construction management consultancy, they emphasise shared challenges in realising directors' roles and responsibilities to shareholders in the context of serving the best interests of the company. Our discussion points are developed around these topics.

In this first point, we discuss how *a responsible board represents shareholders' interests*. Boards make decisions that affect the choice of a financial pathway to ideally provide the resources needed for that company to operate. The company's capital structure evolves with boards' decisions to adapt and exploit changes in the business environment. The decision to alter the company's capital structure involves factors that range from the size of the company and industry characteristics, profitability and growth opportunities as well as the nature of assets (tangible and intangible) as well as board characteristics (Hundal & Eskola, 2020; see Chapter 6). But change of this sort may be accompanied by new shareholders which, in turn, affects how board leadership in governance is enacted and the nature of what is considered to be in the best interests of the company.

In the Solid Energy case, the shareholding ministers and the board had different visions for the company and the strategy for its future development. These differences created tension about what was viewed to be in the best interests of the company which unfolded in the context of an unsuccessful attempt to alter the company's capital structure and ownership. The shareholding ministers' strategy was partial privatisation (divestment) of the coal mining company which was neither profitable (e.g. small and inconsistent dividends to shareholders) nor sustainable in the current business environment (e.g. volatile and uncertain international and domestic sales in an industry facing a prolonged downturn). Following the receipt of two independent reports which indicated the company would not be ready for privatisation for at least 2 years at a minimum, the government decided to remove Solid Energy from the mixed ownership programme. It was in the government's interest to partially privatise only market attractive energy companies to help achieve its economic and political objectives.

In contrast, the board argued that the transformation of the coal company into an energy company which included New Energy and conceded the divestiture of biofuels or Renewable Energy was in the best interests of the company. As this case illustrates, the board's continued pursuit of an energy diversification strategy kept the company on a developmental trajectory and would have required significant further financial investment, which was not in the interest of the shareholders. This case demonstrates the different interests of shareholders and an independent board in determining what is in the best interests of the company. It also raises questions: How can the board of a company in a declining industry protect the interests of the company? What is in the best interest of the company in this case? What can the board do if the company does not have a long-term future?

In the case of Diligent, the board decided to seek a new external block shareholder less than one year after the company's initial public offering in the interest of the company's survival. Faced with the prospect of financial distress, the board identified private equity as a strategy to introduce much needed cash to meet operational requirements amidst the turbulence of the global financial crisis. To bring about this financing, the board and shareholders agreed to a new class of shares that provided the new block shareholders with advantages such as a fixed, cumulative dividend, a conversion option to common shares at a favourable exchange, and an appointment to the board (and effectively as chair) at a substantially lower share price than available at the company's initial public offering. In this way the board realised its fiduciary duties to work zealously for the company and its survival.

In the second point, we discuss the ways in which *a responsibly led board represents internal shareholders' interests.* Boards adopt governance practices that support different capital arrangements and ownership models and adapt them as changes take place over time. Both the Frequency and Diligent cases feature small knowledge intensive firms with ownership closely held among a group of founders with new boards. Although there is a variety of employee ownership structures, majority employee ownership is often associated with a longer-term perspective (for a review see O'Boyle et al., 2016).

The board leadership challenges were similar in both cases—to implement new capital arrangements that expanded share ownership while retaining internal majority block shareholders as directors of the board. However, the boards faced differences due to prior decisions that had been made as well as the differing nature of shareholders' interests. As a privately held firm, the shareholding directors adapted the way in which decisions were made as they supported and challenged each other aided in part by a chair/coach. An employee share ownership programme was being developed as a strategy to improve the company's financial performance, create greater long-term commitment, and promote alignment of shareholder/board/employee interests in a company with a flattened hierarchy.

The case of Diligent required board changes consistent with its new status as a publicly listed company. The board's lack of transparency of the CEO/founders background for the IPO destroyed value and compelled his resignation in the interests of new and prospective shareholders as well as the company's reputation. Similarly, the internal/founding group shareholders were obligated to transfer their shares that had been held in escrow following the failure to achieve warrantied performance targets in the IPO prospectus further modifying the capital arrangements. While empirical research findings are mixed about the relationship between CEO shareholding and goal alignment, the manipulation of the share price by former CEO/founding group member Henry supports findings that share ownership may also lead to illegal activities (Connelly et al., 2010). Although laws can deter CEOs from wrongdoing, it may be difficult for shareholders to detect and/or prevent mismanagement because of information asymmetry as well as efforts to conceal actions. It suggests that regulators play a significant role in safeguarding the integrity of capital markets. It further supports our contention that multiple sets of governance systems cannot prevent bad/irresponsible acts. However, a responsibly led board of directors can act to prevent the prospect of wrongdoing and mitigate negative outcomes should they arise (Larcker & Tayan, 2016; see Chapter 4).

In this third point, we discuss how *different types of shareholders influence board responsibilities*. The argument that ownership structure plays a major role in shaping firm performance is hardly new or controversial, but the debate on how share ownership matters is far from being resolved. The implications of share ownership as a form of governance involves a diverse mix of shareholders and connects to a range of board objectives (Connelly et al., 2010). Among the types of shareholders, governments create special ownership structures that range from full ownership (state-owned enterprises) to mixed models of public and private ownership (hybrids) that may be self-regulated or adopt market-like mechanisms as in Solid Energy. Apart from commercial objectives, board responsibilities involve serving the principals' interests which may extend to other governance matters such as increasing market share or employment levels (Bruton et al., 2015). Despite variations in the types of ownership structures, the board's responsibility is to manage the long-term interests of the enterprise on behalf of the shareholder (government).

Among employees/founders as a type of shareholder, board responsibilities entail the alignment and engagement of interests such as motivation, commitment and performance (see Chapter 7 for social and psychological pathways) for the long-term interests of shareholders. Although the level of employee influence may vary informed in part by the nature of the share ownership programme and percentage of share ownership, boards need to ensure that employee participation in decision making is implemented throughout the company as in Diligent and Frequency.

Among listed companies, share ownership has shifted from individuals to large institutions with heterogenous interests (Fichtner et al., 2017). Board responsibilities in this context involve knowledge of the institutional investors (short or long term) which may have competing interests and to understand that long term or pressure resistant investors can exert a strong influence on a range of outcomes. Finally, directors as shareholders have the responsibility to act in the best interests of the company. They are, however, poorly positioned to act independently as monitors in closely held companies such as Diligent (Boivie et al., 2021; see Chapter 4).

Conclusion

The choice of a capital structure places demands on boards of directors to make decisions that will provide requisite financial resources as the company adapts to ever changing environmental conditions. Despite the importance of the capital structure for the survival and performance of the company, corporate governance and finance literature has tended to overlook the board's role in determining the arrangements and, relatedly, the ownership structure that may be affected by altering arrangements. For too long, the principal contributions have considered processes and structures that affect the company's optimal capital structure as *fait accompli*. In this approach, the board is a stand-in (or agent) for the shareholder/owner to protect their interests. If that was all that the board of directors do, then a set of rules for profit maximisation would void the need for boards on that matter.

In this chapter, we maintain that the corporate entity is composed of a legal person and a corporate fund, and the role of the board is to act in its best interests as the company operates in the world. The discretion given by law provides the board with the ability to consider the interests of employees, environment and local community. It also positions the board in a relationship with shareholders that is complex, organic and unlike any other that the board has with other corporate participants. It is a defining element of the corporation. Among the challenges faced by boards in a dynamic environment, there is a diversity of shareholders (identity) with a diversity of objectives (purpose) as well as different levels of ownership (concentrated or dispersed). These dimensions of share ownership are further complicated by differing time horizons among directors, shareholders, and managers.

We develop the argument that board led responsible leadership involves a 'political' negotiation or subjective judgement of shareholders' interests informed by imperfect information to act in good faith and in the best interests of the company. In this context, boards engage with shareholders to gain an understanding of interests and concerns formally through mechanisms such as the annual general meeting for accountability as well as informally. Collectively, these actions by boards help to build trust, tame shareholder activism, and acquire additional resources as aspects of its responsible leadership in governance role. However, these actions may not help to reconcile contrasting objectives about decisions taken in the best interests of the company where the government as shareholder (or another majority block shareholder) has a political objective tied to economic interests.

Notes

1 All data in the case study are based on public sources for the period 2007–2014. The material produced by the company included the company's IPO prospectus, annual reports, press releases and notices of annual general meetings, among others. It also featured material produced by third party sources which included court records, newspaper articles and reports, among others.
2 Weldon learned about Diligent through a personal connection. Alessandro Sodi and Mark Weldon were both competitive swimmers while in New York many years earlier.
3 The receiver confiscated a fleet of Mercedes-Benz and BMWs and a leased Lear jet. Gerald Henry declared bankruptcy owing 100 creditors nearly US$40 million including more than US$10 million to Bank of New Zealand and more than US$8 million to John Spencer, initial backer of Energycorp.
4 Judgement of Venning, J. The High Court of New Zealand Auckland Registry. CIV-2013-404-003144 [2014] NZHC 1853 paragraph 48.
5 FMA was established in 2011 under the Financial Markets Authority Act 2011. It replaced the Securities Commission.
6 Judgement of Venning, J. The High Court of New Zealand Auckland Registry. CIV-2013-404-003144 [2014] NZHC 1853 paragraph 41.
7 Judgement of Venning, J. The High Court of New Zealand Auckland Registry. CIV-2013-404-003144 [2014] NZHC 1853 paragraph 43.
8 Judgement of Venning, J. The High Court of New Zealand Auckland Registry. CIV-2013-404-003144 [2014] NZHC 1853 paragraph 32.
9 All data in the case study are based on field research and public sources. The research underpinning this case study included an in-depth interview with the former board chair and a director in the period 2007–2013. The material produced by the company included the company's annual reports and press releases, among others. It also featured material produced by shareholders (government) and third-party sources which included newspaper articles and reports, among others.

10 Palmer was recognised as 2009 *Deloitte/NZ Management* magazine Chairperson of the Year for Solid Energy and Air New Zealand.

11 Name changed to Crown Ownership Monitoring Unit in November 2009.

12 In the mixed ownership model companies are subject to the accountability provisions in the Companies Act 1993 and the Financial Markets Conduct Act 2013, rather than the provisions in the State-Owned Enterprises Act 1986. Regarding the shareholding, the Crown owns at least 51 per cent of the shares of the mixed ownership model companies and no one person owns more than 10 per cent of the shares (data from Controller and Auditor General, 2014).

13 This case study was written with the cooperation of the Frequency Project Management board. All data are based on field research and public sources. The research underpinning this case study included in-depth interviews with the board chair, founder/directors, directors and management appointed in the period 2012–2015. The material produced by the company included the company's website and promotional brochure. Material produced by third party sources included newspaper articles and reports, among others.

References

Aggarwal, R., & Goodell, J. W. (2010). Financial markets versus institutions in European countries: Influence of culture and other national characteristics. *International Business Review*, 19(5), 502–520.

Aggarwal, R., & Goodell, J. W. (2011). Institutional variations in expected equity premia: Role of financial architecture and governance. *Journal of Banking and Finance*, 35(11), 3090–3100.

Aggarwal, R., & Goodell, J. W. (2014a). Culture, institutions, and financing choices: How and why are they related? *Research in International Business and Finance*, 31, 101–111.

Aggarwal, R., & Goodell, J. W. (2014b). Cross-national differences in access to finance: Influence of culture and institutional environments. *Research in International Business and Finance*, 31, 193–211.

Aguilar, L. A. (2015). The important work of boards of directors. www.sec.gov/news/speech/important-work-of-boards-of directors.html.

Alves, P., Couto, E. B., & Francisco, P. M. (2015). Board of directors' composition and capital structure. *Research in International Business and Finance*, 35, 1–32.

Alves, P., & Francisco, P. M. (2015). The impact of institutional environment on the capital structure of firms during recent financial crises. *Quarterly Review of Economics and Finance*, 57, 129–146.

Antonczyk, R., & Salzmann, A. (2014). Overconfidence and optimism: The effect of national culture on capital structure. *Research in International Business and Finance*, 31(May), 132–151.

Antoniou, A., Guney, Y., & Paudyal, K. (2008). The determinants of capital structure: Capital market-oriented versus bank-oriented institutions. *Journal of Finance and Quantitative Analysis*, 43(1), 59–92.

Armour, J., Black, B., Cheffins, B., & Nolan, R. (2009). Private enforcement of corporate law: An empirical comparison of the United Kingdom and the United States. *Journal of Empirical Legal Studies*, 6(4), 687–722.

Arosa, C., Richie, N., & Schuhmann, P. (2014). The impact of culture on market timing in capital structure choices. *Research in International Business and Finance*, 31 (May), 178–192.

ASIC v Hellicar, 286 ALR 501 (2012).

Bebchuk, L. A. (2013). The myth that insulating boards serves long-term value. *Columbia Law Review*, 113(6), 1637–1694.

Bebchuk, L., & Kastiel, K. (2017). The untenable case for perpetual dual-class stock. *Virginia Law Review*, 103, 585–631.

Bebchuk, L., & Kastiel, K., (2019). The perils of small-minority controllers. *Georgetown Law Journal*, 107, 1453–1514.

Bertrand, M., & Schoar, A., (2003). Managing with style. *Quarterly Journal of Economics*, 118(4), 1169–1208.

Black, B. S., Cheffins, B. R., & Klausner, M. (2006). Outside director liability: A policy analysis. *Journal of Institutional and Theoretical Economics*, 162(1), 5–20.

Boivie, S., Withers, M. C., Graffin, S. D., & Corley, K. G. (2021). Corporate directors' implicit theories of the roles and duties of the boards. *Strategic Management Journal*, 42(9), 1662–1695.

Brailsforda, T., Oliver, B., & Pua, S. (2002). On the relation between ownership structure and capital structure. *Accounting and Finance*, 42(1), 1–26.

Bruton, G. E., Peng, M. W., Ahlstrom, D., Stan, C., & Xu, K. (2015). State-owned enterprises around the world as hybrid organizations. *Academy of Management Perspectives*, 29(1), 92–114.

Butler, S. (2016). BHS collapse: The key players and what the report says about them. *The Guardian*, 25 July.

Butler, S., & Ruddick, G., (2016). Sir Philip Green's reputation ripped apart in damning report on BHS demise. *The Guardian*, 25 July.

Céspedes, J., González, M., & Molina, C. (2010). Ownership and capital structure in Latin America. *Journal of Business Research*, 63(3), 248–254.

Connelly, B. L., Hoskisson, R. E., Tihanyi, L., & Certo, S. T. (2010). Ownership as a form of corporate governance. *Journal of Management Studies*, 47(8), 1561–1589.

Controller and Auditor General. (2014). State-owned enterprises: Results of the 2012/13 audits. https://oag.parliament.nz/2014/soe-audits/part5. Accessed 18 March 2022.

DeAngelo, H. (2021). Corporate financial policy: What really matters? *Journal of Corporate Finance*, 68, 101925.

DeAngelo, H. (2022). The capital structure puzzle: What are we missing? *Journal of Financial and Quantitative Analysis*, 57(2), 413–454.

Denis, D. J., & McKeon, S. B. (2021). Persistent negative cash flows, staged financing, and the stockpiling of cash balances. *Journal of Financial Economics*, 142 (1), 293–313.

Easterbrook, F. H., & Fischel, D. R. (1996). *The economic structure of corporate law*. Harvard University Press.

Executive Counsel to the Financial Reporting Council v Denison and PriceWaterhouseCoopers LLP, Particulars of Fact and Acts of Misconduct (2018 August 10).

Farre-Mensa, J., Michaely, R., & Schmalz, M. C. (2020). *Financing payouts*. Paper no. 1263, 27 December. Ross School of Business.

Fee, C., Hadlock, C., & Pierce, J. (2013). Managers with and without style: Evidence using exogeneous variation. *Review of Financial Studies*, 26(3), 567–601.

Fhr European Ventures Llp v Cedar Capital Partners LLC [2014] UKSC 45.

Fichtner, J., Heemskerk, E. M., & Garcia-Bernardo, J. (2017). Hidden power of the big three? Passive index funds, re-concentration of corporate ownership, and new financial risk. *Business and Politics*, 19(2), 298–302.

Fields, L. P., Fraser, D. R., & Subrahmanyam, A. (2012). Board quality and the cost of debt capital: The case of bank loans. *Journal of Banking Finance*, 36(5), 1536–1547.

Frank, M. Z., & Goyal, V. K. (2008). Trade-off and pecking order theories of debt. In B. Espen Eckbo (ed.), *Handbook of corporate finance: Empirical finance*, vol. 2(3), (pp. 135–202). Elsevier.

Frank, M. Z., & Goyal, V. K. (2009). Capital structure decisions: Which factors are reliably important? *Financial Management*, 38(1), 1–37.

Ghosh, C., Giambona, E., Harding, J. P., & Sirmans, C. F. (2011). How entrenchment, incentives and governance influence REIT capital structure. *Journal of Real Estate Finance and Economics*, 43, 39–72.

Graham, J., & Leary, M. (2011). A review of empirical capital structure research and directions for the future. *Annual Review of Financial Economics*, 3, 309–345.

Greenspon, J. (2019). How big a problem is it that a few shareholders own stock in so many competing companies? *Harvard Business Review*, 19 February. https://hbr.org/2019/02/how-big-a-problem-is-it-that-a-few-shareholders-own-stock-in-so-many-competing-companies.

Harford, J., Li, K., & Zhao, X. (2008). Corporate boards and the leverage and debt maturity choices. *International Journal of Corporate Governance*, 1(1), 3–27.

Hartevelt, J. (2012). English: Solid Energy not ready for sale. Stuff, 21 August. www.stuff.co.nz/dominion-post/business/7517479/English-Solid-Energy-not-ready-for-sale. Accessed 7 March 2022.

Howard Smith Ltd v Ampol Petroleum Ltd [1974] AC 821.

Hundal, S., & Eskola, A. (2020). Board of directors, capital structure, investment decisions and firm performance: An empirical study of Nordic firms. *Corporate Ownership & Control*, 17(4), 377–390.

Jensen, M. C. (1986). Agency cost of free cash flow, corporate finance and takeovers. *American Economic Review*, 76(2), 323–329.

Jensen, M. C., & Meckling, W. H. (1976). Theory of the firm: Managerial behaviour, agency costs and capital structure. *Journal of Financial Economics*, 3(4), 305–360.

Jiraporn, P., & Gleason, K. C. (2007). Capital structure, shareholder rights, and corporate governance. *Journal of Financial Research*, 30(1), 21–33.

Jiraporn, P., Kim, J. C., Kim, Y. S., & Kitsabunnarat, P. (2012). Capital structure and corporate governance quality: Evidence from The International Shareholder Services (ISS). *International Review of Economics and Finance*, 22(1), 208–221.

John, K., & Litov, L. (2010). Managerial entrenchment and capital structure: New evidence. *Journal of Empirical Legal Studies*, 7(4), 693–742.

Kay, J., & King, M. (2020). *Radical uncertainty*. W. W. Norton & Company.

King, M., & Santor, E. (2008). Family values: Ownership structure, performance and capital structure of Canadian firms. *Journal of Banking and Finance*, 32(11), 2423–2432.

Kirk, S. (2013). Partial privatisation better for Solid Energy—Key. Stuff, 29 October. www.stuff.co.nz/national/politics/9336610/Partial-privatisation-better-for-Solid-Energy-Key. Accessed 6 March 2022.

Knight, F. (1921). *Risk, Uncertainty, and Profit*. Hart, Schaffner & Marx.

La Porta, R., Lopez-de-Silanes, F., & Shleifer, A. (1999). Corporate ownership around the world. *Journal of Finance*, 54(2), 471–517.

Larcker, D., & Tayan, B. (2016). We studied 38 incidents of CEO bad behaviour and measured their consequences. *Harvard Business Review*, 9 June. https://hbr.

org/2016/06/we-studied-38-incidents-of-ceo-bad-behavior-and-measured-their-consequences.

Lemmon, M. L., & Zender, J. F. (2010). Debt capacity and tests of capital structure theories. *Journal of Financial and Quantitative Analysis*, 45(5), 1161–1187.

Lorca, C., Sáamchez-Ballesta, J. P., & García-Meca, E. (2011). Board effectiveness and cost of debt. *Journal of Business Ethics*, 100(4), 613–631.

Mayer, C. (2013). *Firm commitment*. Oxford University Press.

McNulty, T., & Nordberg, D. (2016). Ownership, activism and engagement: Institutional investors as active owners. *Corporate Governance: An International Review*, 24(3), 346–358.

Miller, M. H. (1977). Debt and taxes. *Journal of Finance*, 32(2), 261–275.

Modigliani, F., & Miller, M. H. (1958). The cost of capital, corporation finance and the theory of investment. *American Economic Review*, 48(3), 261–297.

Modigliani, F., & Miller, M. H. (1963). Corporate income taxes and the cost of capital. *American Economic Review*, 53(3), 433–443.

Moore, M. T. (2014). Private ordering and public policy: The paradoxical foundations of corporate contractarianism. *Oxford Journal of Legal Studies*, 34(4), 693–728.

Moreolo, C. S. (2021). Global asset managers record 4.9% net AUM increase in 2020. *IPE Magazine*, 3 June. www.ipe.com/global-asset-managers-record-49-net-aum-increase-in-2020/10053184.article.

Myers, S. C. (1984). The capital structure puzzle. *Journal of Finance*, 39(3), 575–592.

Myers, S. C., & Majluf, N. S. (1984). Corporate financing and investment decision when firms have information that investors do not have. *Journal of Financial Economics*, 13(2), 187–221.

New Zealand Exchange. (2014). Brian Henry admits market manipulation. Press release, 7 August. www.nzx.com/announcements/253603?msclkid=cb7828b0c63d11ec9a20fbac55f63021.

Ninness, G. (2009). Float with a sting like a bee. Stuff, 18 February. www.stuff.co.nz/sunday-star-times/business/169051/Float-with-a-sting-like-a-bee.

O'Boyle, E. H., Patel, P. C., & Gonzalez-Mule, E. (2016). Employee ownership and firm performance: A meta-analysis. *Human Resource Management Journal*, 24 (4), 425–448.

Palmer, J. (2012). *2012 strategic issues*. Treasury report: Solid Energy update. Se-2280181, T2012/348, 28 February, Annex A. Treasury.

Papadopoulos, K. (2019). Dual-class shares: Governance risks and company performance. Harvard Law School Forum on Corporate Governance, 28 May. https://corpgov.law.harvard.edu/2019/06/28/dual-class-shares-governance-risks-and-company-performance/.

Richard, H., Thaler, R. H., & Sunstein, C. R. (2008). *Nudge: Improving decisions about health, wealth, and happiness*. Yale University Press.

Setia-Atmaja, L., Tanewski, G. A., & Skully, M. (2009). The role of dividends, debt and board structure in the governance of family controlled firms. *Journal of Business Finance and Accounting*, 36(7–8), 863–898.

Small, V., & Rutherford, H. (2013). Elder deserves applause. Stuff, 14 March. www.stuff.co.nz/business/8424123/Palmer-Elder-deserves-applause. Accessed 6 March 2022.

Smellie, P. (2013). Miner's debt expansion all its own work say former leaders. *National Business Review*, 14 March. www.nbr.co.nz/article/solid-energy-debt-expansion-was-all-its-own-work-say-its-former-leaders-bd-137229. Accessed 7 March 2022.

Strine Jr, L. E. (2014). Can we do better by ordinary investors: A pragmatic reaction to the dueling ideological mythologists of corporate law. *Columbia Law Review*, 114(2), 449–502.

Stuff. (2009a). The rise and fall of Gerald Henry. Stuff, 8 February. www.stuff.co.nz./business/176014/The-rise-and-fall-of-Gerald-Henry.

Stuff. (2009b). Diligent chief gone in a boardroom minute. Stuff, 18 February. www.stuff.co.nz/business/176203/Diligent-chief-gone-in-a-boardroom-minute.

Summers, R. S. (1968). 'Good faith' in general contracting law and the sales provisions of the uniform commercial code. *Virginia Law Review*, 54(2), 195–267.

Treasury Report. (2011). *Solid Energy New Zealand scoping report.* Se-2192628, T2011/2373 item 46, 4 November. Treasury.

Treasury Report. (2012). *Solid Energy update.* Se-2280181, T2012/348 item 2, 1 March. Treasury.

UK House of Commons. (2016). BHS. July. https://publications.parliament.uk/pa/cm201617/cmselect/cmworpen/54/5402.htm.

van Ees, H., Gabrielsson, J., & Huse, M. (2009). Toward a behavioural theory of boards and corporate governance. *Corporate Governance: An International Review*, 17(3), 307–319.

Yan v Mainzeal Property and Construction Ltd (in liq) [2021] NZCA 99.

4 Uniting Leadership and Organisational Oversight

Introduction

Our primary focus in this chapter is on responsibilities of boards related to their oversight function. We argue that board of directors' *active* monitoring is essential in adding value to the company and its shareholders. Board oversight should provide reasonable assurance that the company's purpose, commitments, and objectives can be reliably achieved in a legal, ethical, and safe manner.

The board is distinctively positioned to carry out dynamic balancing of control, strategy and service tasks, and requirements of different internal and external governance actors (shareholders and investors, chief executive officer, among the directors, and across stakeholders). But responsibly led board oversight in the context of these relationships does not simply happen. It requires boards to provide leadership more expansively, considering its role is to act in the best interests of the company at any given time (Cikaliuk et al., 2020; Eraković & Jackson, 2012).

Decisions to act in the best interest of the company shape the way in which oversight is conducted. It also affects accountability for those decisions. We maintain that board accountability in an entity model of the corporation is more diverse and contextual than traditionally conceptualised in corporate governance and responsible leadership theory. Fiduciary duties are not the only legal duties directly placed on the board of directors or which fall within the board's purview in carrying out its leadership and governance functions. This chapter helps to develop a better understanding of board oversight and how it is mobilised in relation to formal and informal forms of accountability.

We begin this chapter by explaining major building blocks of directors' monitoring function. Here, we examine several characteristics that have been shown to be critical for boards in executing this role. The second section examines three aspects of board's responsible oversight: active and independent monitoring; formal and informal accountability; and engagement efforts. In the fourth section, we present two case studies of a finance company and an international software company. We conclude the chapter by discussing the most important learning points from the case studies.

DOI: 10.4324/9781003054191-4

The Board's Oversight Role

The board of directors is a governing body normally elected by and accountable to shareholders to direct and supervise the management of the company. The board establishes the strategic direction and objectives of the company and sets the policy framework within which the company operates.

Board roles are generally categorised into three groups: oversight, service and resource provision roles (Zahra & Pearce, 1989). The oversight role involves the directors' fiduciary duties of monitoring management on behalf of shareholders. Directors' responsibilities in this role include appointing and dismissing the chief executive officer (CEO) and other top executives, deciding executive remuneration, and monitoring managers to ensure that shareholders' interests are protected. The services role considers directors' advisory functions in formulating strategy and providing guidance to the CEO and top managers in other managerial and administrative issues. The resource role refers to directors' assistance in the acquisition of critical resources for the company.

According to the traditional view of the company (the shareholder perspective), shareholders are the owners of corporate assets, and managers and boards are their agents who are supposed to work in the interest of shareholders (principals). The main purpose of corporate governance is allocation and control of power and authority within a business. Within the agency theory framework, the corporate governance discussion is primarily concerned with the control of managers' self-interested behaviour and a board of directors' monitoring role (Fama & Jensen, 1983).

From a governance perspective on legal institutions, the oversight role is the primary purpose of the board of directors (Boivie et al., 2016). Directors owe fiduciary responsibility to the company and shareholders. Fiduciary duties include the duty of care and duty of loyalty. Essentially, fiduciary duties call on directors to make every attempt to be well informed before they make decisions, to act in good faith and the best interest of the shareholders, and to be independent in their decisions. From the perspective of finance theory, directors' source of power is derived from shareholders. Board members are selected by principals (shareholders) to monitor managerial behaviour (agents). By actively monitoring management actions and firm performance, the board can reduce agency costs and maximise shareholder value.

Active and Independent Monitoring

Corporate boards today operate differently from the boards in the second half of the last century. In the 1980s, they were mainly seen as having had a rubber-stamp function and provided advice and counsel to executive management when required (Tricker, 2020). Their monitoring role in a new era of corporate governance is more complex and demanding, involving independent judgement, diverse knowledge, and active engagement. It also requires adaptation in response to and in anticipation of change. Some changes are brought about by innovative forms of technology, different regulatory requirements and a new global environment. Other changes emerge from the natural environment and people. Regardless of the sources of change, corporate boards face increased pressure from shareholders and stakeholders to actively monitor choices made by management (Khanna et al., 2014).

There is a substantial body of literature that supports the importance of having experienced and competent members on the board of directors (see for example Carter & Lorsch, 2004; Kiel & Nicholson, 2003). However, competence as a director is not simply a function of professional and industry-based expertise. Boards require directors with additional relational skills to responsibly lead and effectively monitor. Skillsets, such as strategic thinking capabilities, team and leadership abilities and information-processing skills, cumulatively deliver value to the company in the form of board capital (Khanna et al., 2014; Mahoney & Kor, 2015).

Current corporate governance codes and regulations place strong emphasis on non-executive director independence. Regulators around the world share a view that director independence is central to effective board oversight and strong corporate governance. Although definitions vary, most studies and corporate governance codes broadly define an independent director as an outside director.

The constructive and collaborative behaviour of directors, particularly their information-processing capacity constrained by bounded rationality, is also important for effective monitoring. Among the individual, group, and firm level factors, Boivie et al. (2016) argue that dysfunctional board dynamics are a major information-processing barrier that impairs effective monitoring. Similarly, Veltrop et al. (2021) contend that board dynamics are crucial to directors' engagement in monitoring. A constructive information processing style, including open boardroom discussions, encourages directors' actions in seeking information from the CEO and improves their engagement in monitoring CEO decision-making. Thus, directors should be more proactive than reactive in their monitoring role and, as such, perform as a more effective check on management hegemony.

Findings from various streams of research suggest that board oversight goes well beyond traditional monitoring activities of formal incentives, control, and sanctions. Depending on the company, it may include a business model and strategy, its systems for making decisions, the selection and retention of employees, performance recognition (rewards) as well as its relationships with legitimate stakeholders (including shareholders) (Paine & Srinivasan, 2019). This suggests the need for an integrated approach to board oversight which includes formal and informal accountability.

Board's Formal and Informal Accountability

The board's legal and moral authority has traditionally been derived from its representation of shareholders or owners of the firm. This authority, legally translated into accountability for key strategic assets of the firm, guides their deployment toward the most productive, and shareholder-approved uses.

In this section, we examine board accountability from the perspective of corporate legal governance and the business judgement rule for collective and individual accountability. In addition, we integrate existing work on accountability and responsible leadership and examine the linkage between these constructs.

Formal/Legal Accountability

The board's accountability through its legal duty to act in the best interest of the company is, on one level, consonant with its role in providing leadership and strategic direction. The board can, and often is required, to look beyond the immediate interests of dominant shareholder groups to the longer-term position of the company as an entity, which may entail explicit consideration of the needs of diverse corporate stakeholders. The flexibility of this standard provides legal scope for board leadership.

Below the headline, the legal framework for accountability is more complex and specific. The core duty of the board to act in the best interests of the company is often supplemented by specific legal duties (e.g. reporting to shareholders and regulators), duties to individual shareholders (e.g. rights to dividends and voting, protections for minority shareholders), and to varying degrees duties that are effectively to creditors arising when the company is or close to insolvency. The different duties may be enforced by specific stakeholder groups through a variety of procedures. The shareholder is the central but not the sole beneficiary and actor. In some places, duties owed to individuals may be supported by public enforcement of either civil or criminal duties, especially where the conduct in question is tainted with fraud. Further expectations of the board may be created by securities regulation and stock market listing rules.

Securities regulations and listing rules impose duties on boards not only to protect actual or potential investors but also out of concern for market confidence and integrity. Many other laws, pursing a myriad of regulatory goals also impose duties directly on company boards and their management or otherwise hold directors and managers accountable for the actions they perform on behalf of the company. The law has developed difficult concepts by which the company may be held legally responsible for certain actions of directors and managers. These duties and more specific company law duties are often derisively labelled compliance. However, managing the risks associated with these duties is part of the leadership role of the board.

While duties of due diligence cohere with the notion that the board balances a range of considerations in making strategic decisions, other duties are strict and, in principle, prevail over considerations. Law enforcement is, however, never perfect and the probability that a law has been breached may be difficult to assess ex ante. Compliance itself may, therefore, in some companies be seen as a strategic decision.

The duties-complex that exists for board accountability reinforces the notion that the board is a nexus of leadership and governance within the company. The various duties mark the existence of the relationship that the board has or should have with management, shareholders, employees, creditors, and other stakeholders. These relationships are not symmetrical nor are they necessarily strictly reciprocal. Furthermore, boards typically make decisions by consensus. As a consequence, where a board is legally accountable for some decision or inaction, each individual director may face civil or criminal liability. Each member of a board has an incentive to ensure that the board is not dominated by one or a subset of directors, creating a propitious tension between the legal and practical imperatives for directorial independence and collaboration.

Informal Accountability

We consider informal board accountability as a complementary yet largely unrecognised approach in corporate governance. In a manner similar to codes of good governance, we maintain that a more expansive view of accountability co-exists and complements formal legal board accountability. In an empirical study that conceptualised the interactions with stakeholders as a critical aspect of responsible leadership, Pless et al. (2012) found that leaders (CEOs) with a low degree of accountability towards others aligned with the business objective of profit maximisation for shareholders. In contrast, leaders with a high degree of accountability perceive their accountability to extend beyond shareholders to stakeholders and a sense of legitimate business purpose that is morally relevant.

Although Pless et al. (2012) did not explicitly link the different responsible leadership orientations and stakeholders with psychological pathways, there are individual level routes (i.e. processes) in which leaders influence organisational processes and outcomes (Doh & Quigley, 2014; Stahl & Sully de Luque, 2014). At an individual level, leader inclusivity of stakeholders' perspectives involves trust, psychological ownership and commitment (see Chapter 7).

The psychological pathway also extends to the individual and their own inward sense of moral or internal accountability to their conscience. It involves a sense of 'felt accountability' (Hall et al., 2017). Morality broadly refers to what is the 'right' and 'wrong' way to behave or moral behaviour (Haidt & Kesebir, 2010; for a review see Ellemers et al., 2019). Morality is involved in the maintenance of social order. Moral guidelines for boards of directors, such as 'do no harm' or 'do good' can induce individuals to enact behaviour that has no direct value or instrumental use for them (e.g. fairness or empathy) (Ellemers et al., 2019; Stahl & Sully de Luque, 2014). 'Morality sometimes calls upon leaders to do things that are against their self-interest' (Ciulla, 2022, p. 29) in consideration of the greatest good in the performance of their duties. In this way, a good (responsible) leader is an ethical and effective leader (Ciulla, 2022).

Board's Engagement Efforts

Boards play a particularly critical responsible leadership role when it comes to account for how decisions are taken in the best interests of the company (Waldman & Galvin, 2008; Waldman et al., 2020). Consistent with the approach outlined in chapter one, we maintain that board responsibility is oriented toward 'the specific concerns of others, an obligation to act on those standards, and to be accountable for the consequences of one's actions' (Waldman & Galvin, 2008, p. 328).

The use of 'others' and 'act' in the definition of responsibility aligns with the increasing expectations of shareholders, management, and stakeholders about directors' involvement in the company's affairs. To perform their monitoring function boards should be knowledgeable about the operational and institutional environments of the company. Understanding needs of shareholders and other stakeholders presents not only a condition for an effective execution of their governance role but also a value adding activity through which directors protect corporate assets, provide access to resources, grow the company's business, and strengthen its reputation. Therefore, the development of relationships with internal and external stakeholder groups might be considered as one of the primary tasks of the board.

Some important aspects of relationships with shareholders have been discussed in the previous chapter. As stakeholders and shareholders demand greater accountability of boards and broaden their domain of corporate governance, boards need to anticipate and respond to diverse needs. We focus here on the boards' engagement with non-shareholder stakeholders.

Relationships with Non-shareholding Stakeholders

Responsibly led board oversight requires an investment in relationships with stakeholders who are aligned by shared values and corporate purpose. The focus on interaction with stakeholders indicates a much broader range of responsibilities for boards of directors than the more limited shareholder view. Theoretically, according to the stakeholder perspective, the directors act as trustees, balancing the interests of stakeholders, including shareholders, for mutual benefit and in so doing help to sustain assets rather than merely maximising their value. This pluralist approach to board roles and board decision-making places the board at the apex of an open system of relationships comprising internal actors (management, employees), external actors (shareholders and other financial capital providers, customers, suppliers), and board members. In practice, the 'Statement of the Purpose of a Corporation' released by the US Business Roundtable (2019) is a public pledge signed by 181 CEOs of major companies to adopt a stakeholder version of the corporation. Similar commitments have been made by large investment firms, including BlackRock, The Vanguard Group, and State Street (Chia & Suvanto, 2020). The first main principle of the UK Corporate Governance Code of 2018 recognises that stakeholders play a significant role in the success of companies (Financial Reporting Council, 2018).

Case Studies

The following two case studies, featuring a finance company and an international software company, help to illustrate how board oversight is conducted in relation to formal and informal forms of accountability and board engagement.

Case Study 4.1 Lombard Finance Demise[1]

Investors and other stakeholders could stop waiting to find out what happened to troubled finance company, Lombard Finance and Investments, and its mountain of debt. Board led leadership had not prevented its collapse. Sir Douglas Graham, chair of the company's high-profile board, and fellow directors faced an investigation about internal control and board oversight.

Lombard Finance and Investments Company History

In 2002, a group of five business colleagues came together to incorporate Lombard Finance and Investments as a privately owned and operated finance company. Some of them had worked together previously in the financial industry. Soon after incorporation, Michael Reeves, also known to them, joined the company as an executive director.

The new finance company filled a lending gap between conventional banks and property developers who needed more credit than banks were willing to approve. It also offered investors serious returns for their investments.

In 2005, the finance company announced its acquisition of an investment company listed on the New Zealand Exchange. The reverse takeover did not raise additional capital which simplified the listing process. The company avoided the full costs, regulatory requirements, and time constraints associated with an initial public offering. The newly listed entity became Lombard Group. It remained tightly held with around 85 per cent of shares owned by parties related to Lombard Finance and Investments. It was the only listed finance company specialised in property development. The parent company, Lombard Group, had its own business operations as well as subsidiaries that ran their own operations.

One of those wholly owned subsidiaries was Lombard Finance and Investments. It remained Lombard Group's principal profitable business. Lombard Finance and Investments had a track record of financial growth. Its total equity increased steadily from around US$220,000 in 2003 to nearly US$20 million (in rounded figures) in 2007.

Lombard Finance and Investments Operations and Management

Lombard Finance and Investments (hereafter referred to as Lombard Finance) was a financier. It acted as an intermediary or middleman, taking money from savers/investors and lending it to borrowers. The company periodically raised money from the public. Its investors were retail or 'mom and pop' investors: prudent but non-expert. It issued prospectuses and provided investment statements. These offer documents contained information about the investment policy, types of investment instruments (i.e. secured debenture stocks and others) as well as risks.

Its borrowers were predominantly property developers. The company's focus was residential rather than commercial real estate development (i.e. retail or office space). Most projects involved the construction of large subdivisions that transformed raw plots of land into neighbourhoods. Other projects involved apartments (including the presales) and a retirement village/multistage care facility. Depending on the scope, projects typically took years to be completed and needed substantial upfront development capital for infrastructure (e.g. roads, sewage, and power) before sales could happen.

Property loans were structured so that accrued interest was added to the loan balance and received on repayment of the loan rather than interest paid to the company on a monthly or quarterly basis. Often, further development funding was required to complete the project.

MANAGEMENT

Since 2002, Michael Reeves had been chief executive officer of the company. As CEO, Reeves had worked to expand the company's strategic vision and operational footprint through his leadership and management of its products, services and employees as well as all aspects of the company's fiduciary, financial and operating performance. He developed the company's organisational framework and culture to support its business strategy and established the controls for its financial management practices.

He brought more than 20 years of experience in commercial lending and merchant banking along with his experience gained as general manager of a wholly owned subsidiary of Brierley Investments to his role. Reeves was a non-independent director and majority shareholder of Lombard Group and a director of several private companies.

Board Leadership and Governance

At the time of the company's incorporation, three directors brought high-profile public-sector leadership experience to the board: Graham, Jeffries and Templeton. Although they were not celebrity directors in the conventional sense, they were highly visible former politicians (Cardow & Wilson, 2017). The first and most well-known was the Right Honourable Sir Douglas Graham. Having served as Ministers of Justice and the Serious Fraud Office as well as Attorney General, Graham was recognised for his role with treaty settlements informed by New Zealand's founding constitutional document, the Treaty of Waitangi, along with his reforms on financial reporting requirements for companies. He served as deputy chair of a crown entity investment fund. He brought a proven legal and policy track record as well as analytical skills to his role as board chair and independent director.

The second director was the Honourable William Jeffries. As a civil and commercial lawyer in private practice at the time he joined the board, Jeffries had formerly served as a Minister of Justice among other portfolios. He was a chief commissioner of a government entity that investigated aviation, marine, and rail incidents. He was known for creating cultural bridges as honorary Consul-General for Sweden since 1995. He brought a deep understanding and resolution of legal issues encountered in businesses and commercial transactions and strong communication skills to his role as an independent director.

The third director was the Honourable Hugh Templeton. As a former cabinet minister appointed to communications and economic portfolios as Minister of Revenue and Trade and Industry, he was involved in free trade agreements. He had also worked with the Prime Minister to promote domestic liquid energy exploration through infrastructure development. As an independent director, he brought to the board skills in the development, formulation and implementation of policies and strategies related to economic growth. Templeton served on the board until 31 March 2007.

Two other independent directors, Lawrence Bryant and Alan Beddie, brought a diversity of knowledge, skills and experience to the board in 2002. Lawrence Bryant, public affairs counsel, worked to align business interests and public policies. He brought his skills in lobbying and relationship building to the board. Previously, Bryant served as executive director of a national agricultural organisation and as a director of private companies.

Alan Beddie added financial markets experience gained through his 30-year career in banking and then insurance as an investment adviser before he began a financial consultancy firm. He was a director of private companies. Beddie served on the board until December 2006. He subsequently resigned from the board to act as chief financial officer until October 2007. Following that, he continued to provide those services which included guidance on financial reporting and accounting.

Board Leadership When it is Not Business as Usual

The board and management were mindful that the company's financial growth relied on high property prices. But early indicators pointed towards a downturn. In the finance industry, two major companies verged on collapse in early 2007 following several others over the past year. In March 2007, Reeves shared with the board that there was a general lack of confidence in the finance market. He proposed, and the board decided that its short-term strategy would focus on strengthening its liquidity, which included building a healthy cash reserve, until marketplace uncertainty passed.

Large Loan Subcommittee Established

In May 2007, the board created a separate large loans subcommittee, at the recommendation of its auditors. David Wallace, director of the parent company Lombard Group, was appointed chair. He was joined by Bryant, Jeffries (chair of the audit committee) and Reeves on the subcommittee to improve monitoring of large loan performance and how effectively risks were being managed. Despite his appointment, timing difficulties prevented Reeves from attending any meetings until November 2007.

Although Bryant and Wallace were 'strangers to the loan files', loan managers most familiar with the large loans in question had the directors' confidence. The loan managers were aware of a pattern where loans reached maturity dates which were then repeatedly extended, often when the loan was in default and past its due. Loan reviews generated substantial fees and short renewal periods were used. It pressured borrowers to repay, provide additional security, or take other measures to facilitate repayment. That operating practice had been repeatedly and uneventfully used with other loans over the past 5 years.

The loan managers provided forecasts for the timing of loan recoveries to the subcommittee. Major loan balances ranged from around US$6 million to more than US$20 million. Several had exceeded credit limits. The major loans from only five borrowers totalled US$60 million, which accounted for more than 50 per cent of the total loan book.

External Monitoring of the Company

At the July 2007 annual general meeting, Reeves reaffirmed to investors that the company's well established lending policies of local lending only and no related party lending were risk measures taken for investor safety.

In August 2007, the board responded to three inquiries about the company's financial health. Each entity was responsible for monitoring the company's compliance with its obligations. In the first request, the parent company, Lombard Group, confirmed with the New Zealand Exchange all relevant matters had been disclosed as part of its continuous disclosure requirement. Reeves used the request to issue a press release to explain the company's approach to cash management. It remained higher than the company's and industry's historical norms, which allowed the board to remain confident that its obligations to its investors could be met. Reeves commented, 'Going forward, the actual and opportunity costs of holding additional cash will mean that the environment is challenging and requires calmness and resolve'.

The second request came from the Securities Commission. It sought information about the company's profitability. The board concluded that the company's liquidity position was strong (it had nearly US$30 million in cash) and its security backing on the loan book had improved. The company reported that 'there had been no material adverse changes to Lombard's liquidity and asset quality analysis'.

The third request came from its trustee, Perpetual Trust. The trustee had also been receiving the reports from the large loan subcommittee. It was concerned about potentially unacceptable levels of risk for secure debenture stockholders. The trustee recommended an independent review. The board agreed.

Independent Report Findings

In mid-September, the directors had the report. It was a snapshot of loan recovery efforts and revenue in relation to investors' deposits. Among the report's findings, the assumptions about repayments, including the large loans, were not unreasonable. It also confirmed that variances in projections could be expected, and projections should be revised as circumstances changed. The report was concerned about a lack of diversified revenue. It pointed out, 'As reinvestments rates plummet from historical levels', the company would face increased pressure concerning its maturing investor deposits.

Investor confidence 'was serious and unlikely to be restored for some time', Reeves acknowledged. His concern followed on the heels of a prospectus issued a few weeks earlier inviting investor subscriptions. He suggested that the company explore revenue alternatives, including a line of credit from a bank. Reeves explained what would happen if the board decided to immediately wind down the company. He noted, 'it was estimated that, after recovery of all loans and repayments from all investors, there would be a surplus of around US$10 million'. With that, Reeves 'assured the board that the company would have no difficulty meeting the trustee's requirements'. Encouraged by the report's findings, the board's line of sight into the company's internal controls and processes remained unchanged.

Soon after the board meeting, Reeves sent a letter to be co-signed by Graham and him and distributed to investors. Graham disagreed with the tactic generally and specifically objected to content that referred to the company's independent review. He was clear that he did not want that type of letter distributed. Reeves disregarded Graham's decision. The letter was revised to remove the objectional content, signed only by Reeves and sent. Reeves and the marketing staff were prepared to overlook directors' wishes when it came to the use of promotional material.

Marketing and Investors

Marketing investment instruments required building investor trust and confidence. The parent company, Lombard Group, sponsored television programmes to position its brand with its investor demographic. The company produced its own promotional materials which included a prospectus, an investment statement and its own brochure, 'A Guide to Investing Wisely', along with its website. The directors also created a DVD edited at Reeves's direction. After viewing it, Bryant firmly advised against the use of it. The board understood that Reeves would let employees know it should not be distributed.

In September 2007, Graham and Reeves travelled throughout the country to conduct seminars with investors. It was an effective way to maintain investor relationships and attract interest in its recently issued prospectus. Although marketing personnel were in attendance, Reeves did not 'monitor the detail of all the information being made available or ensure that it was otherwise properly supervised' (Dobson, 2012 paragraph 316). Graham was not involved in monitoring material even though some chairs might have been more careful about what was on hand. Graham and the other non-executive directors were unaware of the DVD's use. Meanwhile, it continued to be distributed up to March 2008.

Monitoring Major Loans

In preparation for the board's meeting in early November, updated cash flow projections were ready. The directors discussed the effect of tight cash flow over the next six months, particularly if loan recoveries were late. Most finance companies were under stress. Receivers had been appointed to many companies in the industry, and the prospect of further collapse and its effect on investors' deposits was considered. They explored the idea of financial assistance from a bank and considered it would be highly unlikely.

Following that meeting, Graham and Reeves attended the large loans subcommittee meeting in mid-November 2007. The recent pattern of forecasts had improved; the gap between projections and recoveries had narrowed. But the projections, on average, only had about a 40 per cent accuracy rate since September. It meant, in short, that timely repayments from borrowers were not happening as expected.

Directors accepted management's explanations about repayment delays. Directors did not bring additional insight or information to test the reasonableness of assessments made by management. Importantly, directors did not probe management's assumptions about recoverability of the loans. Wallace, chair of the major loans committee, maintained that there had not been a lot of choice to extract repayment with some projects other than to provide continued support for their completion so that sales could be realised.

Management tried different tactics to bring about loan recoveries. In one effort, some first mortgages had been downgraded to second mortgages in exchange for cash which reduced borrowers' indebtedness to the company. Another effort saw employees and company affiliates purchase apartments at 60 per cent valuation, subject to a buy-back arrangement, to reduce that borrower's loans. That action, which should have immediately signalled that repayment was in doubt, did not until much later. In another project, an advance of nearly US$9 million was made to facilitate sales of a coastal subdivision.

In November, management arranged for the sale of a project in trouble to another developer. The loan, first issued in 2003, had been poorly monitored. It accounted for more than 20 per cent of the company's total loan book. It was also common knowledge that the project had been poorly managed by the borrower. An attempt to include two of the company's independent directors in the developer's entity was short lived. It lasted until June 2007. To terminate that borrower's association with the project, the company agreed to a US$14 million loan to a new developer. The project had a greater likelihood of completion with the new developer although it would take time.

Following that meeting, Graham emailed Reeves the same day to express his concerns about the company's liquidity. Graham had no doubt that everyone:

> is working hard to get the loans repaid or refinanced but the fact is that we are sailing very close to the wind now and the next two or three months will be critical. Some of our exposures are difficult and dependent on a number of positive events occurring. If they do not, or there are delays, we run the risk of running out of cash. I know that consideration is being given to obtain a line of credit from the bank but we both know how obstinate the banks can be and I do not think we can rely on that. A private placement of prefs may relieve the pressure but I have doubts it will succeed in the present climate with the exposures we have. I would not want to be a party to any capital raising which misrepresents the true position.
>
> (*Jeffries v R* [2013] NZCA 188 paragraph 49)

At the next board meeting in late November, the board reviewed the latest projections for loan recoveries and the company's cash position. A worst case scenario, discussed by the board, recognised the company's vulnerable position if loan payments were not received. Meanwhile, funding options explored by Reeves had not moved beyond preliminary discussions. The board deferred any decision until its next meeting.

In the lead up to the December 2007 board meeting, Reeves confirmed that the company's cash position had decreased from its high of nearly US $30 million in August to less than US$8 million. The board's current situation was in contrast with the independent report which had projected that the company would have more than US$20 million in cash at the end of December. That report had contained an important provision: a healthy cash reserve depended on the timely repayment of major loans.

The board's strategy to reduce the loan book in an orderly manner and increase its liquidity had led to a concentration of large loans among a few borrowers. But recoverability issues meant the company could not collect on the loans. The company ran the risk of being out of cash in less than a few months.

Board Decision to Seek More Investors

The board wanted to retain its current investors and attract new ones. Maturing investor deposits would need to be paid from the company's cash reserve. As it had often previously done, and consistent with the practice of finance companies, the board decided to issue an amended prospectus. An amended prospectus would test investors' calmness and resolve for the prospect of strong returns amid an increasingly uncertain property market. More importantly, it would provide a needed revenue stream.

The amended prospectus had to be filed before the 9-month window since the company's last audited financial statements closed. In anticipation that the board would approve an extension, the original September prospectus had been reviewed in October by the same legal firm that prepared it. In consideration of the company's changing financial situation, an extra step was taken. The draft was reviewed by another legal firm. Neither expressed any concern with the contents. The amended prospectus stated that the material position of the company had not materially and adversely changed since the audited financial statements issued on 31 March 2007. The board approved and signed the amended prospectus in late December 2007. Over the next 3 months, nearly US$8 million was generated from new investors and those who reinvested.

The Wind Down

In February 2008, Reeves's report for the board meeting stated, 'It is clear that a managed well-orchestrated wind down of Lombard Finance is an inevitable reality'. In February, Reeves and Beddie pursued the sale of a large development project, the retirement village/multistage care facility. Although the sale reduced the borrower's indebtedness to the company, Graham and the other directors learned about the extent of the shortfall on the sale after the transaction was completed. In early March, another major development project, the coastal subdivision, was sold but the company was left with a substantial outstanding balance.

Reeves arranged for an independent reviewer to provide a fresh report on the status of its loans. The balance for the total loan book had been reduced by around 15 per cent. However, large loan balances had increased for three of the five borrowers. They totalled around US$80 million in April 2008, up from US$60 million a year earlier.

Meanwhile, the parent company, Lombard Group, converted its US$1.5 million unsecured investment in the company to secured debenture stock. Shortly thereafter, in early April, the board announced to its 4,400 investors that it would be seeking a moratorium which immediately halted repayment obligations to its investors.

The board's proposal for a moratorium was rejected by the company's trustee, Perpetual Trust. Instead, the trustee appointed receivers. The company was placed into receivership on 10 April 2008. Convictions were obtained against Graham, Jeffries, Bryant, and Reeves for breaches of the Securities Act 1978. They were confirmed on appeal. Along with community work and home detention, reparations of US$150,000 were also required to be paid with those monies distributed to investors. Investors sustained substantial losses. In 2019, the receivers concluded the disposal of receivership property. Over the period of the receivership, it had only been able to realise 20 per cent or US$20 million of the property loan book.

Case Study 4.2 Diligent Board at the Crossroads[2]

David Liptak, non-executive director and chair of Diligent Board Member Services considered the software company's latest application developed for iPads. Its strong sales increased annual revenue as costs of the board led remediation of the company's oversight role neared US$10 million. Liptak and the other directors now faced scrutiny from stakeholders whether these control improvements would provide enough flexibility for future compliance with evolving business policies and practices as well as laws and regulations of the New York-based, New Zealand-listed company.

Diligent's Company History

In 2003, a small team of consultants founded Diligent Board Member Services (hereafter referred to as Diligent), a software firm that developed a governance software application called Diligent Boardbooks, in New York. The company pioneered a secure web-based portal for board members, management, and administrative staff to speed and simplify how board materials are produced, delivered, reviewed and voted on.

Within five years, the company became the first United States-based firm listed on New Zealand's stock exchange. Diligent's initial projections for growth were ambitious, fuelled by its vision as 'a global company able to meet the needs of every significant board in the world in the near future'. In 2007, the initial public offering fell short of its intended mark and Brian Henry, CEO, resigned immediately. Investor disappointment with the lack of transparency and the absence of full disclosure about Henry's controversial background persisted. With the global financial crisis, Diligent's future seemed uncertain. For two full years, 2008 and 2009, Diligent was a loss-making company. In 2010, the company rebounded.

Diligent Company Operations and Management

Besides its key clients in the financial industry, Diligent expanded into other industries ranging from transportation to health to mining. Its clients included Air New Zealand, Bombardier, Heineken, New Zealand Rugby Union, Gwinnett Medical Centre, and Rio Tinto. In 2012, the number of employees in the United States, New Zealand, the United Kingdom, Australia, Singapore, Canada and Hong Kong had grown to 138. The company began to enjoy some success in its international operations. Revenue from the regions (excluding the United States) had grown to 18 per cent. The Asian-Pacific market contributed nearly 4 per cent and Europe provided 14 per cent to total revenues. The North American market remained the company's largest market with 25 per cent of Fortune 1000 companies using Diligent's Boardbooks.

In 2012, Diligent was added to New Zealand's Top 50 Index of the 50 largest and most liquid companies listed. For the second year in a row, Diligent received acknowledgement as one of the Fastest Growing Technology Companies in North America, a prestigious recognition given by Deloitte. High customer confidence in and satisfaction with the product led to a 97 per cent client retention rate which was among the best-in-class for software as a service company.

MANAGEMENT

Since 2007, Alessandro Sodi had been president and chief executive officer of the company and served on the board as an executive director. Sodi, with his business development and client relationship experience, was well versed with governance application development, having worked with Henry and other founding members in New York from 1998 to the company's listing in 2007. Sodi set strategy and direction for the company, developed the company's culture and values, and led the executive team from its US-based company headquarters. He collaborated with the other board directors to oversee the company's activities including an infusion of capital in 2009 from two US-based private investment companies.

Board Leadership and Governance

NEW BOARD CHAIR

In 2009, John Liptak joined the board as a non-executive director. His appointment came with the block ownership of Series A preferred shares which provided much needed capital for the company. He was elected as board chair in 2010 by other holders of the preferred shares. As founder and managing member of a New York-based investment partnership for innovative companies since 1995, Liptak brought strategic and analytic skills as well as extensive experience in the financial industry. He also provided continuity in board membership. Liptak was not eligible for election at the annual general meeting given the special provisions for his type of share ownership.

He joined Rick Bettle, former chief executive of a New Zealand-based commercial law firm and an experienced board chair in business, health and transportation, serving most recently as Diligent's board chair. As one of the independent directors for the company's IPO, Bettle added financial and legal skills to the board. Another director that brought continuity to the board with the company's IPO was Peter Huljich. As managing director of a New Zealand-based wealth management company founded by his family in 2007, he brought his 10 years of investment experience to the board as an independent director.

Mark Russell, senior commercial partner for a New Zealand-based law firm, added his experience in corporate finance and restructuring, compliance and initial public offerings as an independent director appointed initially for the company's IPO. Sharon Daniels, executive director and chief marketing officer, and one of the founding members of the company, brought creative and analytic capabilities to the board gained in her 20 years' experience of branding and strategic business development.

DIRECTORS RESIGN

In little more than a year following Liptak's appointment to the board, Daniels stepped down from the board and her role as chief marketing officer to launch a new US-based consulting firm. In 2011, Huljich resigned from the board which included his membership in the Audit and Compliance Committee. Later that year, Huljich pled guilty to misleading investors from his wealth management company for investments in Diligent.

In the absence of a board succession plan the director vacancies went unfilled. For nearly a year, the Audit and Compliance Committee operated with only Russell and Bettle rather than the requisite three independent directors. The New Zealand Exchange raised the issue with the company. Diligent's subsequent application for a temporary waiver was denied. The rule was important to the integrity of the market 'as it ensures that issuers maintain an appropriately comprised audit committee and thereby maintain a robust audit process'. Russell disagreed. He explained, 'Diligent understands the need to comply with the listing rules but we do not see this as a major issue'. Meanwhile, the board searched for a director who would also serve on the Audit and Compliance Committee.

CHANGES TO BOARD STRUCTURE AND DIRECTORS AMID GROWTH

The company continued its growth strategy by investing in sales and marketing to further expand internationally and across new industries. It increased spending on research and development to improve Boardbooks's operating system and products. The company 'was growing like a house on fire', Liptak explained to shareholders at the 2012 annual general meeting, 'so we are taking advantage of that as much as possible'. In an intensely competitive market, Sodi pointed out, 'it is hard to divert resources to something else when you are growing'.

In the midst of growth, the board began to take steps to revise its own structure and composition. The board adopted staggered term limits of one to three years for board membership continuity and flexibility. Board size was adjusted to allow for no fewer than four and no more than seven directors.

Two new directors joined the board. In 2012, Joseph Carrabino Jr, an independent director based in the US, brought his deep knowledge of the financial services industry, experience with corporate restructuring and reorganisation, and senior leadership experience as a partner in a global private investment firm to the board. Mark Weldon, recent former CEO of the New Zealand Exchange, joined the board as an independent director. Weldon had recruited Diligent to list on the New Zealand Exchange. The directors hoped Weldon would contribute his knowledge, skills and experience in strategy development, corporate finance, governance, entrepreneurship and operations.

Shortcomings Laid Bare

The board's initial steps to improve its visibility into the company's internal controls and processes had not gone far enough. Diligent had a material weakness in its internal controls over financial reporting, Liptak acknowledged. Its control and compliance systems and processes needed to be reviewed and revised, stakeholders' interests needed to be better protected, and the company's culture needed to be improved.

In December 2012, at the eleventh board meeting of the calendar year, the board unanimously authorised and empowered an *ad hoc* Special

Committee to launch an investigation into the internal control environment of the company. The board appointed its newest and independent directors, Weldon and Carrabino, to conduct the investigation along with United States and New Zealand law firms to serve as legal counsel throughout the review.

Initially focused on the amount and type of compensation awarded to Sodi and other executives, the board delegated broad powers to the Special Committee to take all necessary action. The Special Committee first investigated share option issuances. It found three instances in which Sodi and another executive were awarded shares in excess of the caps set out in compensation packages.

The Special Committee then turned its attention to Diligent's compliance with regulations since its listing on the New Zealand Exchange in 2007. The review and analysis included both United States and New Zealand regulatory obligations and the New Zealand Exchange listing rules. They identified numerous instances in which Diligent was not in compliance. Based on its review, the Special Committee made two important determinations: one, that the instances were 'inadvertent and attributable in part to the constrained resources of the company in a period of financial difficulty in the years following its listing'. Two, the complex regulatory and compliance obligations across multiple jurisdictions with differing regulations and requirements were contributory factors to the company's current problems.

Regardless, it was clear to the Special Committee that Diligent's internal control environment put the company at risk. It found that senior management charged with compliance were not well-versed in the complexities of the legal and regulatory regimes applicable to the company. As a general matter, it also found that the advice of outside advisers was not sought. Finally, it found that 'the company did not maintain robust compliance procedures or review regulatory effectiveness or compliance practices, and that the role of senior management in compliance was not clearly defined or regularly evaluated'.

In 2013, the Special Committee presented its findings to the board. With the recommendations in hand, it would be up to the board to decide which changes would be made. Following the completion of its investigation, the Special Committee disbanded.

Disclosure and Sanctions

Diligent advised the New Zealand Exchange of its findings. Both agreed that Diligent had breached six listing rules over an extended period. The seriousness of rule violations ranged from minor to major. The violation of four minor listing rules involved 37 notification failures about Diligent's activities, mostly concerning stock option conversions. The two more serious violations had to do with the employees' stock option plan and directors' remuneration.

In the first major instance of listing rule violation, the board had repeatedly given too many shares to Sodi and another employee for their executive compensation contracts between 2007 and 2011. For Sodi, a total of 4.1 million shares exceeded the limit. A further 250,000 shares were in excess for a senior manager. The Special Committee pointed out, 'These awards were determined to be reasonable compensation at the time and were an important incentive component of the employees' compensation packages'.

The second major violation involved directors' remuneration. Compensation for directors' service had never been authorised by a shareholders' resolution. The Tribunal found that 'Diligent's internal controls and procedures were insufficient to ensure compliance with the Listing Rules'. For its six violations, Diligent was publicly censured and incurred a small penalty of US$13,000.

New Disclosure and Additional Sanctions

In less than six months since its initial notification of violations, Diligent once again alerted the New Zealand Exchange of a problem. There was an error with the timing of the company's revenue recognition practice. Revenue from new customer contracts was incorrectly recognised from the beginning of the month rather than from the actual start date. The company's financial statements for 2010, 2011 and 2012 needed to be restated. Sodi explained, 'We are fully committed to ensuring the prompt and thorough resolution of these matters and providing our shareholders with the most accurate disclosure possible'.

It turned out to be a time-consuming process that forced the postponement of the company's 2013 annual report and annual general meeting along with other financial reports. Over that six-month period, investors traded in Diligent without the benefit of relevant, reliable financial information. The Tribunal found that investors were exposed to 'an information balance where those "inside" the company are in possession of information not available to the market'.

In determining the settlement agreement, the Tribunal pointed out:

> as a large and prominent company, there is a market expectation that Diligent would have in place the appropriate governance, internal controls and resources to ensure compliance with its reporting obligations under the Rules. Diligent's failure to do so impacts on the integrity of the market.

The Tribunal also considered aggravating factors. The company had already been the subject of disciplinary action. Once again, the company received a public censure along with US$82,000 in fines and costs.

Remediation

The board began to modify the company's governance structures and processes including the flow of information, policies, and management to improve its system of internal control.

BOARD STRUCTURE AND COMPOSITION

In 2013, the board announced that it would 'reinforce as a "tone at the top" that an effective control environment is a core value of Diligent'. To help realise its commitment, the board restructured its standing committees from four to three. The Audit and Compliance Committee, the Compensation Committee, and Nomination Committee were refocused with revised charters. The Stock Issuance Committee, which consisted of Liptak and Sodi as members to oversee the issuance of shares to employees and directors, was eliminated.

The board developed a new compensation plan for its directors. The changes in the plan reflected 'the board's belief that this new remuneration package is consistent with governance best practices in aligning board remuneration with shareholder value by including a substantial equity component'. It was approved by shareholders at the 2013 annual general meeting.

There were also some changes among the directors. In early June 2013, Bettle, who was standing for re-election, resigned with immediate effect. His nomination, which had been disputed by the New Zealand Shareholders Association, was withdrawn. Bettle subsequently pleaded guilty to five Securities Act charges for signing offer documents that contained untrue statements in relation to failed finance companies.

The directors also participated in the first individual and board performance assessment. Three new United States-based directors joined the board between 2013 to 2014. Collectively, they added their software and technology industry experience, strategy, and corporate finance skills to the board. Having completed the company's restatement process, Carrabino resigned from the board in May 2014. He commented, 'I am proud of the work we have done and believe the Board's efforts during the past two years have put Diligent on a path to a stronger future'. Three months after Carrabino's departure, Weldon announced his resignation. He had a new position as a CEO for a media company.

BOARD–MANAGEMENT RELATIONSHIP

In consideration of its goal to improve its internal system of control, the board and Sodi made changes to its management. The Special Committee had found that the company had operated without sufficient levels of qualified personnel in its executive, accounting, finance and tax functions.

New senior executives were appointed including a chief financial officer and general counsel along with additional employees. The company implemented training on its new contract and revenue recognition procedures for its accounting, sales and legal personnel. It also trained its expanded cadre of 264 employees in the United States, New Zealand and its international sales offices, which included United Kingdom, the Netherlands, Germany, France, Australia, Hong Kong, Singapore, Brazil and Canada, on the company's new policies and procedures.

Following a 2013 meeting with Liptak and Sodi, the New Zealand Shareholders Association pointed out that 'significant resources are now being deployed to avoid recurrences of the kind of governance failures' experienced to-date. The Shareholders Association announced its support for the appointment of the 'new executives with far more international experience. This positive action is a good sign and should lead to far better standards going forward'.

The board hoped to retain Sodi and had entered into a three-year employment agreement in 2011. The findings of the internal Special Committee had the potential to jeopardise that relationship. Having cancelled 4.1 million excessive shares previously awarded, the board proposed that Sodi receive a cash award of $4.2 million, 2.25 million shares, and future consideration for performance-based shares. Sodi agreed. The New Zealand Shareholders Association reviewed and recommended in favour of the proposed solution. In 2013, the plan was approved at the annual general meeting.

The reporting systems, policies, and activities to maintain and monitor compliance were overhauled. To ensure the integrity of the financial statements complied with the financial acts and listing rules in New Zealand, a new audit firm was appointed. To improve the quality of the information that the board and management used to make decisions, new financial reporting and accounting software was implemented.

STAKEHOLDERS

The board adopted new policies to communicate the relationship between the company's vision and values and its day-to-day operations. In a new ten-page code of conduct for employees and directors, a set of expectations about which actions were required, acceptable or prohibited was specified in detail to deter wrongdoing and to promote conduct with integrity:

> Diligent expects all its employees and directors to maintain the highest ethical standards as set out in our Code of Conduct. The directors support the principles set out in the 'Codes of Practice for Directors' issued by the Institute of Directors in New Zealand. Whilst recognizing that the Code expresses principles and does not purport to determine the detailed course of conduct by directors on any particular

matter, the directors are committed to the highest standards of behaviour and accountability.

For directors, a conflict of interest or even the appearance of a conflict of interest, prevented them from performing company duties and responsibilities honestly, objectively, and effectively. Other prohibited actions involved family members, undue influence, and competitors of the company.

A fraud policy was adopted to prohibit dishonest or fraudulent activities and established procedures for reporting activities. A trading policy to prevent insider trading by employees and directors and their family members or other related parties was adopted. To avoid even the appearance of an improper transaction, directors and employees were required to sign an acknowledgement and certification that they agreed to be governed by that policy in relation to the purchase and sale of shares.

Diligent also adopted a whistle-blower policy and hotline for employees to report misconduct. The company launched an anonymous and confidential reporting website and a hotline—both of which were operated by an independent third party.

The Road Ahead

Liptak and the directors were mindful that the remediation process, which had put a strain on time and resources, also served to restore stakeholder confidence. With implementation efforts well underway, the board looked to further minimise the risk of noncompliance as a company incorporated in the United States and listed in New Zealand. As part of its oversight role, the board established an *ad hoc* New Capital working group to analyse options ranging from a move to a new exchange to privatisation to the company's acquisition. For Liptak, all options merited consideration.

Discussion

With these two case studies, we aimed to draw attention to board responsible leadership (or lack of it) in performing their oversight role. Although the case studies illustrate different monitoring issues, both emphasise problems of accountability in executing directors' duties and managing relationships with external stakeholders (shareholders and investors). Our discussion points are developed around these topics.

Among *the models of accountability and their 'to whom for what' focus*, there are several dimensions that have implications for organisational behaviour and board behaviour specifically (Dubnick, 2011; Hall et al., 2017). One, there is an expectation that an actor will take responsibility for its conduct or decision (responsibility). Two, the actor will make its actions transparent (transparency). Three, the actor will agree to be judged in relation to a set of standards (answerability). Four, the third party has the right to sanction the actor if the actor does not inform or explain its decisions (consequence).

These four dimensions of accountability are clearly exemplified in the case of Diligent. First, the new chair of the board took responsibility to develop new and robust governance practices, the lack of which led to the 2009 debacle (see the case study in Chapter 3). Second, the chair clearly communicated the board's intentions and actions with the company's shareholders. Third, the proposed changes (reduced board size, board membership continuity, board composition, director appointment process) were in accord with agreed company's and institutionally accepted good corporate governance standards. Finally, the New Zealand Exchange (the third party) used its right to review and validate Diligent's internal control and procedures.

The board has a formal relationship for accountability that is established under the law and in its charter. It is a configuration that involves checks and balances of the board's performance through mechanisms (e.g. annual general meeting and annual general reports) and processes for enacting sanctions. But stakeholders are not empowered the same way as shareholders. Although the model of board accountability cannot be transferred directly to other relationships, alternative forms of accountability to match the relationships can be developed. We concur with other researchers (Bower & Paine, 2017; Mayer, 2021; Stroehle et al., 2019; Waldman et al., 2020), that a broader perspective of accountability is needed for corporate boards that includes not only what is good for the company but also what is beneficial for stakeholders.

Together with shareholder passivity and relative lack of power, especially among dispersed small shareholders, many boards have preserved arrogance in their attitude towards shareholder and stakeholder interests (Ingley et al., 2011). However, as we have previously noted, greater accountability by boards and a broadening of their oversight role sit at the centre of calls for *active and responsible boards* and, in protection of their reputation, assets and legitimacy, companies also can no longer expect to ignore shareholder and stakeholder interests (Doh & Guay, 2006).

The second point relates to *directors' duties and duty orientation.* Directors owe fiduciary duties to the shareholders and the company they serve. However, as the Lombard Finance case study illustrates, these duties are obscured when the owners and managers sit on the board. In the case of closely held companies, the importance of truly independent directors and independent judgement is even more pronounced. One of the most important director's duties, as we emphasised at the beginning of this chapter, is to (proactively) monitor management and give strategic directions. If directors in their executive decision-making capacity rely on uncontested information supplied by management, as in the case of Lombard Finance, the purpose of the board is unclear. Boards usually work in strategic partnership with management (Boivie et al., 2021), but as monitors they need to act independently.

One approach that better accommodates the moral domain of informal accountability is a duty orientation. It invokes personal/individual accountability (Waldman et al., 2020). Duty orientation concerns 'what individuals believe they owe to their groups in terms of loyal service and fidelity to the group's members, its missions and tasks, and its moral codes' (Hannah et al., 2014, p. 222). It emphasises an individual's perceived responsibility to take actions that serve the good of the organisation and its stakeholders rather than their own self-interest (Haidt & Kesebir, 2010; Hannah et al., 2014). Accordingly, the duty orientation aligns with the responsible integrator leadership orientation identified by Pless et al. (2012) (Waldman & Balven, 2014; Waldman et al., 2020). In the case of Diligent, individual directors accepted accountability for the obligations of team membership. The directors put the interests of the company ahead of their own as a personal and moral decision in support of the investigation led by fellow directors to identify their own mistakes (e.g. excessive share allocations, overlooked shareholders' resolution). They went beyond the minimum required for a conscientious performance with the adoption of ethics codes and trading policies accompanied by a third-party operator. Finally, they identified new directors informed by a board performance assessment.

Our two case studies portray monitoring issues and initiatives in closely held companies where the board members are also investors and major decision makers. The main question is then related to the relationship between the boards and company investors/shareholders. Thus, our third point focuses on the question: *who monitors the monitors*?

In the situation of multiple agency problem where different principals have divergent interests (such as in our two cases), the board of directors' role to represent the common interests of the principals is consistent with the requirement for the board to act in the best interests of the company on behalf of shareholders/owners. Because the common interest is complex and not well defined, it may also be part of the board of directors' role as the ultimate decision-maker to determine what the common interests are, based on the board's understanding of the company and its constituents.

In the case of Lombard Finance, there was a clear conflict of interests between directors and outside investors. Directors were interested in the survival of the business which involved high-risk behaviour and immediate returns without communicating their intentions with other shareholders. The outside individual investors, on the other hand, placed their deposits at risk hoping for long-term high returns. In their actions, the board did not represent the common interest. Outside investors did not have knowledge, access to information, established procedures nor power to impose pressure on directors and managers to act on their behalf at critical moments.

Our case studies complement other research which has shown that inside ownership, especially in the financial sector, can increase risk-taking behaviour of main decision-makers (Dinç, 2006) and that the 'wealth effect' (directors' equity ownership), generally, may have a negative influence on directors' effective monitoring (Kumar & Sivaramakrishnan, 2008). Thus, the boards (even well composed) do not necessarily act in the interest of shareholders and increase shareholder value.

So, what about shareholder monitoring? While shareholder passivity is presented by contractarians as a virtue, empirical evidence demonstrates that shareholders are not always passive (Appel et al., 2016; Tonnello & Gatti, 2019). Activism by some had led to a greater priority of their interests, such as policies that affect dividends, CEO compensation as well as research and development. A consolidation of shareholding in institutional investors, the organising power of social media (e.g. January 2021 GameStop short-selling saga; Chohan, 2021), and changing social expectations are driving further change.

A number of authors and institutional shareholders view investor activism as a positive force for change in governance practices (see Benton & You, 2019; Florou & Pope, 2008). However, this activism may be an inequitable answer to the need for corporate board reform, as certain shareholders may in effect seize board functions, without authorisation from other shareholders to do so (Ingley et al., 2011). Hence, shareholder activism is a partial solution to the deeper problem of the underperformance of corporate boards. We acknowledge that shareholders may be justified in taking action to draw attention to poor governance and firm performance.

While we support the idea of responsibly led boards implementing governance reforms, government also has the capacity and responsibility to initiate such reforms. In the case of Lombard Finance and other New Zealand finance companies at the time, the regulatory regime was weak (Cardow & Wilson, 2017). Government regulation could certainly be a viable solution, or at least a partial solution. Or, as one of the commentators of the Lombard Finance fiasco pointed out, 'in the same way that companies require knowledgeable directors, a thriving market economy requires competent and active government, including regulators, working in partnership with business' (Mayhew, 2012).

Conclusion

In this chapter, we have argued that the monitoring role of boards needs to include a combination of internal and external governance systems that extend beyond formal regulations and legal requirements. Effective monitoring involves active engagement by the board with shareholders and non-shareholder stakeholders. It requires more than 'good' board composition with knowledgeable, skilled, experienced, and independent directors. It is also more than monitoring the financial performance of the company. We maintain that it includes formal and informal elements that affect the quality of the board's relationships among the directors, within the company and across non-shareholder stakeholders and shareholders as the board makes decisions.

The dynamic quality of the board's relationships plays a central role in affecting the quality of board oversight. As research suggests and the case studies illustrate, board oversight may improve with the adoption of different practices that lead to high quality stakeholder relationships. Conversely, it may deteriorate with changes in practice that diminish the quality of stakeholder relationships. The changing nature of relationships for effective board oversight requires that boards develop the ability to manage the interplay between internal governance factors (such as board members' individual commitments and duty orientation) and external governance factors (such as such as laws, securities regulations and listing rules as well as institutional requirements).

Some of the measures to improve the board's capacity for effective oversight involve active and independent monitoring, formal and informal accountability along with engagement efforts. In this way, we may better understand how responsible board leadership shapes a combination of governance practices that may be in the company's best interests. We also gain insight into the constraints of effective board oversight as the nature of the tasks, obstacles to the adoption of effective practices, and leadership enacted varies with specific board decision-making contexts.

Notes

1 All data in the case study are based on public sources for the period 2002–2019. The material produced by the company included the company's annual reports, press releases and notices of annual general meetings, among others. It also featured material produced by third party sources which included court records, newspaper articles and reports, among others.

2 All data in the case study are based on public sources for the period 2007–2014. The material produced by the company included the company's IPO prospectus, annual reports, press releases and notices of annual general meetings, among others. It also featured material produced by third party sources which included newspaper articles and reports, among others.

References

Appel, I. A., Gormley, T. A., & Keim, D. B. (2016). Passive investors, not passive owners. *Journal of Financial Economics*, 121(1), 111–141.

Benton, R. A., & You, J. (2019). Governance monitors or market rebels? Heterogeneity in shareholder activism. *Strategic Organization*, 17(3), 281–310.

Boivie, S., Bednar, M. K., Aguilera, R. V., & Andrus, J. L. (2016). Are boards designed to fail? The implausibility of effective board monitoring. *Academy of Management Annals*, 10(1), 319–407.

Boivie, S., Withers, M. C., Graffin, S. D., & Corley, K. I. (2021). Corporate directors' implicit theories of the roles and duties of boards. *Strategic Management Journal*, 42(9), 1662–1695.

Bower, J. J., & Paine, L. S. (2017). The error at the heart of corporate leadership. *Harvard Business Review*, 95(3), 50–60.

Cardow, A., & Wilson, W. (2017). Independent celebrity directors in closely held financial institutions. *Asia Pacific Management Review*, 22(2), 61–69.

Carter, C. B., & Lorsch, J. W. (2004). *Back to the drawing board: Designing corporate boards for a complex world*. Harvard Business Press.

Chia, D., & Suvanto, L. (2020). Boards beware: Accountability is rising. https://corpgov.law.harvard.edu/2020/12/05/boards-beware-accountability-is-rising/ Accessed 1 March 2022.

Chohan, U. W. (2021). Counter hegemonic finance: The Gamestop short squeeze. https://papers.ssrn.com/sol3/papers.cfm?abstract_id=3775127.

Cikaliuk, M., Eraković, L., Jackson, B., Noonan, C., & Watson, S. (2020). *Corporate governance and leadership: The board as the nexus of leadership-in-governance*. Elements in Corporate Governance Series. Cambridge University Press.

Ciulla, J. (2022). Why ethics is at the heart of leadership. In N. Pless & T. Maak (eds), *Responsible leadership* (2nd edition; pp. 21–38). Routledge.

Dinç, I. S. (2006). Monitoring the monitors: The corporate governance in Japanese banks and their real estate lending in the 1980s. *The Journal of Business*, 79(6), 3057–3081.

Dobson, J. (2012). The Queen v Douglas Arthur Montrose Graham, Michael Howard Reeves, William Patrick Jeffries, Lawrence Roland Valpy Bryant. In High Court of New Zealand (Ed.), *Reasons for verdicts of Dobson J. in R v GRAHAM HC CRI-2010-085-2538*. Wellington, New Zealand.

Doh, J. P., & Guay, T. R. (2006). Corporate social responsibility, public policy, and NGO activism in Europe and the United States: An institutional-stakeholder perspective. *Journal of Management Studies*, 43(1), 47–73.

Doh, J. P., & Quigley, N. R. (2014). Responsible leadership and stakeholder management: Influence pathways and organizational outcomes. *Academy of Management Perspectives*, 28(3), 255–274.

Doh, J. P., & Stumpf, S. A. (2005). Towards a framework of responsible leadership and governance. In J. P. Doh & S. A. Stumpf (eds), *Handbook on responsible leadership and governance* (pp. 3–18). Edward Elgar.

Dubnick, M. J. (2011). Move over Daniel: We need some 'accountability space'. *Administration & Society*, 43(6), 704–716.

Ellemers, N., van der Toorn, J., Paunov, Y., & van Leeuwen, T. (2019). The psychology of morality: A review and analysis of empirical studies published from 1940 through 2017. *Personality and Social Psychology Review*, 23(4), 332–366.

Eraković, L., & Jackson, B. (2012). Promoting leadership in governance and governance in leadership: Towards a supportive research agenda. In A. Davila, M. M. Elvira, J. Ramirez & L. Zapata-Cantu (eds), *Understanding organizations in complex, emergent and uncertain environments* (pp. 68–83). Palgrave Macmillan.

Financial Reporting Council. (2018). The UK corporate governance code. www.frc.org.uk/getattachment/88bd8c45-50ea-4841-95b0-d2f4f48069a2/2018-UK-Corporate-Governance-Code-FINAL.PDF. Accessed 14 February 2021.

Florou, A., & Pope, P. (2008). Are boards and institutional investors active monitors? Evidence from CEO dismissal. *Managerial Auditing Journal*, 23(9), 862–872.

Fama, E., & Jensen, M. C. (1983). Separation of ownership and control. *Journal of Law and Economics*, 26(2), 301–326.

Haidt, J., & Kesebir, S. (2010). Morality. In S. T. Fiske, D. T. Gilbert & G. Lindzey (eds), *Handbook of social psychology*, vol. 1 (pp. 797–832). John Wiley & Sons.

Hall, A. T., Frink, D. D., & Buckley, M. R. (2017). An accountability account: A review and synthesis of the theoretical and empirical research on felt accountability. *Journal of Organizational Behaviour*, 38(2), 204–224.

Hannah, S. T., Jennings, P. L., Bluhm, D., Peng, A. C., & Schaubroeck, J. M. (2014). Duty orientation: Theoretical development and preliminary construct testing. *Organizational Behaviour and Human Decision Processes*, 123(2), 220–238.

Ingley, C., Rennie, M., Mueller, J., Cocks, G., Warrick, D., & Eraković, L. (2011). Reformed and engaged boards—not activist shareholders. *World Review of Entrepreneurship Management and Sustainable Development*, 7(3), 302–329.

Jeffries v R [2013] NZCA 188.

Kumar, P., & Sivaramakrishnan, S. (2008). Who monitors the monitor? The effect of board independence on executive compensation and firm value. *The Review of Financial Studies*, 21(3), 1371–1401.

Khanna, P., Jones, C. D., & Boivie, S. (2014). Director human capital, information processing demands, and board effectiveness. *Journal of Management*, 40(2), 557–585.

Kiel, G. C., & Nicholson, G. J. (2003). Board composition and corporate performance: How the Australian experience informs contrasting theories of corporate governance. *Corporate Governance: An International Review*, 11(3), 189–205.

Mahoney, J. T., & Kor, Y. Y. (2015). Advancing the human capital perspective on value creation by joining capabilities and governance approaches. *Academy of Management Perspectives*, 29(3), 296–308.

Mayer, C. (2021). The future of the corporation and the economics of purpose. *Journal of Management Studies*, 58(3), 887–901.

Mayhew, D. (2012). Lessons to be learnt from Lombard's mistakes. *New Zealand Herald*, 22 May. www.nzherald.co.nz/business/david-mayhew-lessons-to-be-learnt-from-lombards-mistakes/S3SR5LJN4SBQW4PYUSHUXZB6EU/.

McNulty, T., & Nordberg, D. (2016). Ownership, activism and engagement: Institutional investors as active owners. *Corporate Governance: An International Review*, 23(3), 346–358.

Paine, L., & Srinivasan, S. (2019). A guide to the big ideas and debates in corporate governance. *Harvard Business Review*, 14 October. https://hbr.org/2019/10/a-guide-to-the-big-ideas-and-debates-in-corporate-governance.

Pless, N. M., Maak, T., & Waldman, D. A. (2012). Different approaches toward doing the right thing: Mapping the responsibility orientation of leaders. *Academy of Management Perspectives*, 26(4), 5–65.

R v Graham [2012] NZHC 265.

Stahl, G., & Sully de Luque, M. (2014). Antecedents of responsible leadership behaviour: A research synthesis, conceptual framework, and agenda for future research. *Academy of Management Perspectives*, 28(3), 235–254.

Stroehle, J. C., Soonawalla, K., & Metzner, M. (2019). *How to measure performance in a purposeful company? Analysing the status quo*. Future of the Corporation Series. British Academy. https://papers.ssrn.com/sol3/papers.cfm?abstract_id=3504530.

Tonnello, M., & Gatti, M. (2019). Board-shareholder engagement practices: Findings from a survey of SEC-registered companies. *Directors Notes*, December, 1–44.

Tricker, B. (2020). *The evolution of corporate governance*. Elements in Corporate Governance Series. Cambridge University Press.

US Business Roundtable. (2019). *Statement of the purpose of a corporation*. Business Roundtable. https://opportunity.businessroundtable.org/wp-content/uploads/2019/08/BRT-Statement-on-the-Purpose-of-a-Corporation-with-Signatures.pdf.

Veltrop, D. B., Bezemer, P.-J., Nicholson, G., & Pugliese, A. (2021). Too unsafe to monitor? How board–CEO cognitive conflict and chair leadership shape outside director monitoring. *Academy of Management Journal*, 64(1), 207–234.

Voegtlin, C., Patzer, M., & Scherer, A. G. (2012). Responsible leadership in global business: A new approach to leadership and its multilevel outcomes. *Journal of Business Ethics*, 105(1), 1–16.

Waldman, D. A., & Balven, R. (2014). Responsible leadership: Theoretical issues and research directions. *Academy of Management Perspectives*, 28(3), 224–234.

Waldman, D. A., & Galvin, B. M. (2008). Alternative perspectives of responsible leadership. *Organizational Dynamics*, 37(4), 327–341.

Waldman, D. A., Siegel, D. S., & Stahl, G. K. (2020). Defining the socially responsible leader: Revisiting issues in responsible leadership. *Journal of Leadership & Organizational Studies*, 27(1), 5–20.

Zahra, S., & Pearce, J. (1989). Boards of directors and corporate financial performance: A review and integrative model. *Journal of Management*, 15(2), 291–334.

5 Value Creation

Introduction

Value creation by companies has long been associated with economic relationships between management and shareholders. Most accounts focus on a specific conception of the corporation strongly associated with shareholder value creation which fosters an impoverished view of board leadership in corporate governance. In this chapter, we draw on an entity conception of the corporation to propose a framework that integrates a finer grain understanding of board led responsible leadership in governance and establishes a link between these constructs and value creation. We use the framework to facilitate an understanding of how instrumental and integrative orientations of responsibly led boards of directors and stakeholder and purpose driven corporate governance affect value creation across stakeholders, including shareholders. The framework allows us to compare insights from four cases of large, listed companies and distil theoretical and practical implications for boards of directors and those who support and interact with them.

During the last decade or so, responsible leadership—a relational, values-centred approach aimed at influencing value creation, including processes for governance—has emerged as an influential perspective for boards of directors of large, listed companies. Numerous corporate boards of directors around the world have experimented with aspects of responsible leadership through initiatives which further the interests of customers, employees, communities, and societies. At the same time, the topic continues to draw the attention of management and legal scholars given contested models and theories of the corporation and its purpose along with the conceptual and practical challenges associated with value creation and board led responsible leadership in governance.

Board led responsible leadership in governance is concerned with value creation, which connects it to strategy alongside issues of process, choice, and change. This is particularly important because it allows us to integrate a major theme in the strategic management literature into the responsible leadership in governance approach for an entity conception of the corporation. It is also of great importance to boards of directors focused on

DOI: 10.4324/9781003054191-5

responsibly leading and governing the performance of large, listed companies and those that support and interact with them.

Our interest here is the actual behaviours of boards of directors to create value. Stated differently, rather than assume boards of directors will enact leadership in ways that enhance the firms' performance, we treat board leadership as critical to further the integration of responsible leadership and governance. The clear implication of this approach is that without considering how responsibly led boards of directors purposefully create value across stakeholders, discussion of value creation remains in the abstract, removed from the actual practice of governing large, listed companies.

What will differentiate this effort from other related work is our conception of the modern company as an entity and its link with board led responsible leadership in governance. This position informs a proposed framework between these constructs and value creation. Accordingly, the question we address in this chapter is, how do responsibly led boards of directors create value? Central to this undertaking, we pay close attention to the strategies and actions of boards of directors of large, listed companies to generate value in relation to stakeholders.

The remainder of this chapter is structured as follows. Following this introduction, we define what we mean by value and value creation. The third section examines a contractarian view of the corporation and the limits of its approach for board leadership and value creation. The fourth section focuses on the entity conception of the corporation and the relationship of instrumental and integrative responsible leadership orientations and value creation in stakeholder and purpose driven governance. The fifth section, featuring four cases, illustrates different approaches of responsible leadership enacted by boards of directors in strategically creating value for stakeholders, including shareholders, over time. The final section of the chapter presents conclusions.

Value and Value Creation Definitions

In this chapter, we maintain that value itself is not fixed or tangible. Value is defined in relation to customers, investors, employees, suppliers and other stakeholders through engagement with stakeholders (International Federation of Accountants, 2020). Companies create value in the context of six capitals. Two of the most well-known forms are financial and manufactured capital (material goods/fixed assets). Four additional capitals provide a fuller range of the resources and relationships companies use to create value: intellectual capital (ideas), human capital (people), social and relationship capital (society), and natural capital (environment). Together they represent stores of value that are the basis of a company's value creation (International Integrated Reporting Council, 2013). The capitals are dynamic, that is, they can be built up, run down and depleted over time. However, they need to be maintained to generate benefits in the future.

Conceptions of the Corporation and Value Creation: Contractarian and Entity

We enter the long-standing debate about the role of the corporation with simplified common understandings despite the variations in theories and models that scholars from different traditions have contributed concerning its nature and purpose (for a review see Watson, 2015, 2019). In this chapter, we refer to a contractarian view of the corporation and an entity conception of the corporation.

Contractarian View and Value Creation

For a long time, the study of the corporate form and its purpose seemed rather out-dated. Certainly, the energy created by the Berle–Dodd debate of the early 1930s had long since dissipated. Concerns about the type of value created and for whom value was created seemed to recede. Broadly speaking, the corporation was widely viewed as an entity separate from its shareholders, and that entity had an expansive role in shaping aspects of society (Paine & Srinivasan, 2019; Watson, 2015).

In the 1970s, a new theory of the firm (agency theory) and a vastly different view of value creation emerged to gain prominence and influence performance. The corporation was recast as a 'nexus of contracts' existing explicitly and implicitly among agents (actors) including the board of directors, shareholders, employees, creditors and customers (Easterbrook & Fischel, 1996; Jensen & Meckling, 1976). As a legal fiction, rather than as a separate and real entity, the corporation has no responsibilities to society (Bower & Paine, 2017; Watson, 2015). In this view, value creation is narrowly defined and focused on the shareholder. This approach is often captured by Friedman's (1970) argument that the proper role of business is to focus on wealth creation for shareholders. Maximising shareholder value as a goal aligns with the belief that stakeholders' interests are more appropriately served by government, other social institutions, and non-profit organisations.

Agency theory, which dominates as a conceptual framework (Åberg et al., 2019; Daily et al., 2003; van Ees et al., 2009), addresses issues related to the delegation of decision rights (Fama & Jensen, 1983; Jensen & Meckling, 1976), size and characteristics of boards (Dalton et al., 1998; Finkelstein & Mooney, 2003), and ownership structure of firms (La Porta et al., 1999) to name a few. Strategy scholars investigate the demographics (attributes) of top management teams and firm outcomes (Finkelstein et al., 2009; Hambrick & Mason, 1984) and the nature of decision making, risk, and uncertainty (for a review see Eisenhardt, 1989).

From a legal perspective, directors' responsibilities towards company stakeholders are widely contested in the Western world (see Clarke, 2014; Plessis, 2016). More recently, corporate law has demonstrated that company law systems do not insist that boards focus exclusively on returns to shareholders (Sjåfjell, 2016). The complex relationships between the board and corporate stakeholders cannot be understood in terms of principal–agent relationships and residual rights of control. Accordingly, accounts of board leadership and governance have had to turn to different approaches (e.g. behavioural, contingency) and models and theories of the corporation to advance progress on both the conceptual and empirical fronts (Eraković & Jackson, 2012; Huse 2007, 2018; Mayer, 2018; Paine & Srinivasan, 2019; Wilson et al., 2017).

Entity Conception and Value Creation

A conception of the modern company as an entity, that is, as a non-person legal person, aids in positioning the value creating activities of the board beyond the singular focus of shareholder interests (Bower & Paine, 2017; Watson, 2019). The modern company as an entity holds a capital fund that consists of many types of value or capital which acquires and generates other forms of value or capital as it operates in the world. The board's role is not to act exclusively as the agent of shareholders in bringing about shareholder value through the maximisation of the capital fund. To the contrary, its role is to act in the best interests of the company which involves providing leadership more expansively (Cikaliuk et al., 2020). The board, when enacting responsible leadership in governance, must ensure that value creation extends from the entity itself to shareholders and other stakeholder groups.

Responsibly led boards consider and assume responsibility for the effect of its decisions that shape and guide companies' different activities across stakeholders for performance outcomes which extend beyond financial returns and relate to manufactured, human, social and natural capital along with financial capital. Instead of accepting that boards will act in ways that enhance the company's capabilities and advance its strategy, we treat the board's leadership role in value creation as worthy of study (Åberg et al., 2019; Eraković & Jackson, 2012; Huse, 2018). Boards play a particularly critical role when it comes to the creation and adjustment of company strategies that affect the company's resource base and the prospect of value creation (Hendry et al., 2010; Pugliese et al., 2009; Stiles & Taylor, 2001). Boards which make investments in opportunities that best fit the companies' capabilities also need to consider changes in the wider environment including different stakeholders' expectations because they may not necessarily align.

The role of the board is not to mediate between interest groups that may be in conflict—we do not consider the board to be a mediating hierarch (Blair & Stout, 1999). Instead, the role of the board is to act in the interests of the entity itself at any time. Viewed from the board's perspective, responsible leadership in governance takes the interests of stakeholders for value creation—including those internal and external to the company—and assesses and balances all relevant interests. In this way, the board's determination of the best interests of the company are a political exercise to keep stakeholder interests in harmony for the company's long-term value creation strategies. Responsibly led boards of directors go beyond regulatory and statutory requirements to comply with the law and pursue business practices that create value for consumers, employees, suppliers, shareholders, communities, and the environment. Accordingly, boards of directors enact more nuanced responsible leadership orientations for value creation than the 'do no harm' and 'do good' conventions suggest (Stahl & Sully de Luque, 2014).

Governance and Responsible Leadership Integrative Framework

In this section, we integrate existing work on responsible leadership and governance and examine the connection between these constructs and value creation. We consider stakeholder and purpose governance, two distinct approaches of corporate governance, and the responsible leadership orientations that influence how value is created: instrumental and integrative responsible leadership. The goal is to integrate and synthesise these constructs to present a framework which builds on the work of Maak et al. (2016) and Pless et al. (2012) that is meaningful for scholars and practitioners.

Stakeholder Governance and Instrumental Responsible Leadership

There is an increasing body of work concerning value creation by companies that adopt a more expansive view of value and the pursuit of a broader social objective (the stakeholder view) than shareholder profit maximisation. Accordingly, our focus is sharpened to how an instrumental responsible leadership orientation of boards of directors affects value creation in stakeholder governance.

In this approach, stakeholders are explicitly considered in the value creation decisions by boards of directors. The idea of promoting stakeholders' interests, that is, stakeholder governance, is considered good business practice which creates financial value for shareholders and benefits for stakeholders (Jones et al., 2018; Porter & Kramer, 2006). The boards of directors of companies with stakeholder governance make decisions that may be characterised as enlightened self-interest or enlightened shareholder value (Freeman, 1984; Mayer, 2020; US Business Roundtable, 2019). Board decisions for value creation point to a legal recognition to take into consideration stakeholder concerns (see legal corporative governance literature that discusses these models Gunasekara, 2013; Plessis, 2016, 2017; Sjåfjell, 2016; Vasudev, 2012) and the resolution of conflicts of interest which reside with the judgement of the board (Bainbridge, 2003, 2020).

In practice, the approach is reflected in the UK Companies Act 2006, which Clarke (2014) labelled as a 'discretionary pluralism model' (p. 276) as well as in Australia and New Zealand (Plessis, 2017), as described in Chapter 2. The US Business Roundtable (2019) released a 'Statement of the Purpose of a Corporation' signed by numerous CEOs of major companies as a public pledge to shift from shareholder primacy to a stakeholder version of the corporation.

As scholars have persuasively argued and professional bodies have recognised, it is socially divisive if companies are only oriented towards the pursuit of profit maximisation. We view the board's role in value creation to be a demonstration of responsible leadership. Its position at the intersection of relationships between the CEO, among directors, and with other stakeholder groups lends an importance to its value creating activities. It is particularly useful at this point in this discussion to introduce the instrumental responsible leadership orientation (Maak et al., 2016; Pless et al., 2012). The focus of this orientation of responsible leadership is on performance and achievement of company objectives, such as realising growth or competitive advantage by understanding and addressing key stakeholders' interests (Siegel, 2009; Waldman, 2011; Waldman & Siegel, 2008). Instrumental responsible leadership involves knowing what key stakeholders' value (i.e. needs, interests, and concerns) and articulating a vision that 'rings true' in the promotion of shared interests.

Stakeholder Relations

Stakeholder interaction is critical for value creation and comprises an integral element of responsible leadership, especially for governance processes (Doh & Stumpf, 2005; Pless & Maak, 2011). The relational strategies assume a shared future with selective stakeholders finding common ground to create long-term economic value for shareholders and other value for stakeholders if it is also beneficial for shareholders (Doh & Quigley, 2014; Freeman et al., 2010; Pless et al., 2012; Waldman & Galvin, 2008). A recognised contribution of the board (especially non-executive directors) is their boundary-spanning activity (see Barratt & Korac-Kakabadse, 2002; Filatotchev & Nakajima, 2014; Pugliese et al., 2009). Prior empirical research has found that companies with close stakeholder relationships, developed through an ethical approach, that is, treating them well and managing for their interests, helps to create firm value, which tends to be measured in terms of financial performance (for a review see Villalonga, 2018).

Leadership

The leadership behaviours associated with an instrumental responsible leadership orientation focus on performance, including establishing goals and making tangible commitments or incentives towards achieving defined goals with a well-defined, limited set of stakeholders (Maak et al., 2016; Siegel, 2009; Waldman & Galvin, 2008). Accordingly, investments in employee training are a means to gain competitive advantage, adopting prosocial policies prevents legal actions and save costs, and implementing ethical guidelines complies with external rules and regulations. In this orientation, investments are made in stakeholder groups as a reciprocal exchange to create value in the context of various capitals including intellectual, social, human and relationship, and natural (International Integrated Reporting Council, 2013). Non-monetary contributions, as part of the exchange, include factors such as commitment/loyalty, trust, and obligation among others (Doh & Quigley, 2014).

The kind of instrumental responsible leadership discussed here is not motivated exclusively by personal or corporate reputational aggrandisement (Bartlett & Ghoshal, 1994; Pless & Maak, 2011). Stakeholder groups can discern between companies which appear moral but are motivated by shareholder wealth maximisation and those that are authentic. This discernment can translate into value-adding or -destroying behaviour (Gartenburg & Serafeim, 2019; Jones et al., 2018). Motivation, in this sense, seems to matter as much as action (Christensen et al., 2014; Maak & Pless, 2019; Pless et al., 2021; Waldman, 2011).

Strategic Emphasis

To create a competitive edge relative to competitors, strategic emphasis is directed towards economic performance and key stakeholders to generate tangible and intangible benefits. In terms of decision making, leaders are perceived as being rational and apply business case logic to justify choices (Pless et al., 2012; Siegel, 2009). The directors acting collectively engage in a political bargaining process with consideration of costs and benefits (financial and non-financial) of key stakeholder groups given the jointness of their interests. To be able to perform these analyses and make decisions, some investments in stakeholder groups are made without an expectation of profit and ultimately become embedded as structures, policies, and guidelines which inform strategic decisions (Waldman & Galvin, 2008; Waldman & Siegel, 2008).

Purpose Governance and Integrative Leadership

In our framework, we retain the conception of the modern company as an entity and bring together purpose driven governance with integrative responsible leadership to better understand value creation where boards' actions focus on the common good. In some companies, a purpose is incorporated into its articles of association or charter and refers to legally defined types of for-profit corporations with an explicit social or environmental purpose, other than profit maximisation. In others, corporate purpose is realised through strategic rather than financial controls in governance (Filatotchev & Nakajima, 2014; Thomsen, 2020).

Our focus expressly addresses the broader contribution of a company's value creation effort beyond profit measures alone by incorporating a social objective. 'Purpose is the statement of a company's moral response to its broadly defined responsibilities, not an amoral plan for exploiting commercial opportunity' (Bartlett & Ghoshal, 1994, p. 88). As Mayer (2021, p. 2) states, 'Purpose is therefore about finding ways of solving problems profitably where profits are defined net of the costs of avoiding and remedying problems'. This definition of purpose and profits recognises that a purpose company can generate profits, which does not contradict the aim of creating other types of value.

Purpose, then, is a means to recognise a company's larger social role, a means to motivate employees and other stakeholders (such as customers) that identify with the company, and a means to provide a foundation for strategy (Freeman & McVea, 2001; Gartenburg & Serafeim, 2019). Corporate purpose is determined by the board of directors, ideally but not necessarily with block shareholders as some may have different interests, and preferably revisited at the annual general meeting to affirm its continued relevance (Mayer, 2021; Thomsen, 2020).

We are at a good point in this discussion where it is useful to introduce integrative responsible leadership to further an understanding of its relationship with value creation and boards of directors of companies with corporate purpose. An integrative responsible leadership orientation draws attention to the activities leaders undertake across different domains of business and society to create value with a broad and balanced approach (Maak et al., 2016; Pless et al., 2012).

Stakeholder Relations

This orientation recognises that relational strategies are inclusive of all legitimate stakeholders as an integral element (Maak et al., 2016; Pless & Maak, 2011). The legal and formal basis of these relationships with stakeholders does not necessarily determine the influence that the stakeholders may exercise. It is the role of the board of directors to scan widely, identify and invest in relationships with formal/legal and informal/non-legal or less favoured stakeholder groups which may be essential not only for the company's survival but also its sustainability. The onus is placed on directors of the board in which alternate viewpoints held by stakeholder groups are brought together and reconciled or actively integrated based on a set of shared core values (Doh & Quigley, 2014; Freeman & McVea, 2001; Maak & Pless, 2006).

The extent to which proactive stakeholder relations are fostered varies from company to company, and depends in part, on the corporate purpose which is made credible through the actions of boards of directors.

Accordingly, board led responsible leadership, which is both hierarchical and shared, can work in tandem to build and maintain stakeholder relationships for desirable outcomes (Pearce & Conger, 2003; Pearce et al., 2014).

The collective responsibility of the board for the long-term success of the company is the first of the main principles in the revised UK Corporate Governance Code (Financial Reporting Council, 2018) and, importantly, recognises that stakeholders play a significant role in the success of companies. Its second main principle sets out that boards establish a company's purpose, values and strategy. While the board is accountable formally at the annual general meeting to shareholders, in the context of integrative responsible leadership and corporate purpose, the boards' accountability includes not only what is good for the company but also what is beneficial for society (for a review see Hesketh, 2019; Stroehle et al., 2019).

Leadership

The leadership behaviours associated with the integrative responsible leadership orientation raise stakeholder aspirations and invoke higher order values among stakeholders (Maak et al., 2016). Such leadership can inspire stakeholders and influence behaviours related to value creation for socially responsible outcomes not only for internal and external stakeholders but society at large (Christensen et al., 2014; Pless et al., 2021; Stahl & Sully de Luque, 2014). In this way, board leadership is realised through individual and collective efforts, regardless of formal role (van Ees et al., 2009; Huse, 2018). Recent work on corporate boards has underscored the importance of the board itself acting as a team and sharing leadership (Conger & Lawler, 2009; Vanderwaerde et al., 2011).

Effective responsible leadership entails a compelling and credible purpose that engages stakeholders. It involves a consistency of actions over an extended period (Walman & Galvin, 2008). At the individual actor level, such purpose is promoted through sense giving and the moral labour of responsible leadership (Maak & Pless, 2019). The role of emotional and meaning related aspect of leadership as purpose fosters a sense of togetherness and connects stakeholders' contributions to a higher purpose or goals greater than the organisation (Kempster et al., 2011).

Strategic Emphasis

From a strategic perspective, boards of directors facilitate an inclusive decision-making process with a range of stakeholders perceived to be legitimate to enable long-term value creation. Because the identity, motivation, and roles of stakeholders are dynamic (Doh & Quigley, 2014; Pless & Maak, 2011), boards shape and adapt their interactions over time. Decisions by boards of directors involve judgements which concern benefits and harms between different groups of stakeholders (Bainbridge, 2020; Freeman & McVea, 2001; Mayer, 2020). Although cost-benefit analyses are taken into consideration, there is a perceived moral obligation consistent with the company's purpose to develop strategies to ensure the long-term support of all stakeholder groups. Stated differently, profits are a necessary product or outcome to be able to continue rather than the rationale for the board's decisions that fulfil the company's purpose.

To recap, instrumental responsible leadership in stakeholder governance and integrative responsible leadership in purpose governance add different perspectives on the board's role in value creation in an entity conception of the modern company. A question arising from this discussion is as follows. Are there some specific factors that distinguish how responsibly led boards of directors are successful in value creation, and if so, what are they? We address this question in the next section.

Case Studies

In this section, we use the framework to consider value creation in the context of how boards of directors enact responsible leadership in large, listed companies. In each of the four cases, we describe the instrumental and integrative leadership orientation of boards of directors and the stakeholder and purpose governance models, highlighting value creation strategies as they play out over time with stakeholders. Following each case, we link the board of directors' behaviours to precepts of responsible leadership in governance to illustrate the board's role for value creation across stakeholders for the viability and sustainability of the company and the social wellbeing of the wider community.

Case Study 5.1 Lansdowne Group Strategic Adaptation[1]

Robin Sweeney, chair of the Lansdowne Group, and John Taggart, managing director and deputy chair, surveyed the architect's rendition of the company's latest fulfilment centre to support its e-retail growth strategy. The pace of online sales growth now passed sales growth for the retail chain's large network of physical stores. Board led responsible leadership in governance would be needed to create value for stakeholders, including Taggart with his majority ownership interest, in the transformation of this iconic company once again.

Setting a New Tone: The Initial Public Offering

John Taggart began his involvement with the Lansdowne Group when its parent company streamlined global operations, divesting its less profitable companies. In preparing the company for new ownership, Taggart decided to buy the struggling retailer. All of Taggert's retail management sensibilities were put to the test as he transformed the troubled retail chain. He revamped the product lines. He closed stores, invested in the business, and built the brand.

A decade later, the turnaround, diversification and expansion plans had succeeded with a chain of stores throughout the country. Taggart recognised that future value creation opportunities resided in taking the company public. As a practical matter, the initial public offering (IPO) would raise capital relatively inexpensively, which could be used to accelerate growth and profitability with new stores.

Listing the company required a board of directors. Consistent with his lean management approach, Taggart preferred an efficient board that would facilitate access to capital and ensure the checks and balances were in place for good governance. The first independent non-executive director appointed was Richard Holmes. As a merchant investment banker and former principal in a wealth management company, Holmes had helped to create the largest reseller of telecommunications company and, as chair, had recently taken it public. Holmes had acted as an informal consultant and occasional tennis partner over the past decade to Taggart.

Two additional appointments were made. Edward Kirkland was appointed as a non-independent executive director. With his 30 years of experience in legal, accounting and financial roles within the company, he and Taggart had a strong working relationship. As a non-executive director, international retail billionaire Robert Goodman, who rarely joined the boards of companies other than his own, accepted Taggart's invitation. Goodman had invested personally in the Lansdowne Group as well as through his own company.

With the directors appointed and the company valuation in hand, the role of board chair needed to be filled. Robin Sweeney's reputation brought her to the attention of Taggart and Holmes. Intrigued, she met with Taggart. Sweeney's diverse leadership and governance experience as a director and chair in large, listed companies, private companies, and state-owned enterprises landed her the role. As chair, Sweeney would be responsible for the board and governance; Taggart, as managing director, would focus on running the company. Sweeney, who thrived on challenges, agreed and the IPO unfolded with Taggart retaining majority share ownership as planned.

Strengthening the Management and Governance in a New Corporate Ambiance

The board and management recognised that steps needed to be taken to transition from a private to a publicly listed company. There were governance systems and processes to be developed, disclosure of financial and non-financial information reports to be prepared, and minority shareholder rights to be protected. A system of internal control, which would allow effective oversight, guide employees' action, and provide transparency as a listed company was essential.

Considering these goals, Taggart made two changes the Lansdowne Group's management to strengthen financial and operational areas. He created and appointed to the role of chief financial officer (CFO) an internationally experienced retail financial manager. He subsequently appointed a chief operating officer (COO) who had held senior roles across the company.

There were also some changes at the governance level. Three years after the IPO, Goodman retired from the board. Stephan Mason, who had participated in most of the board meetings as Goodman's alternate since the IPO, joined the board as a non-executive director. Mason brought additional financial skills, extensive contacts, and retailing experience to the board.

BUILDING GOVERNANCE SYSTEMS AND PROCESSES

The board worked closely with management to create and approve policies and procedures for implementation. One of the major changes related to the protection and limitation of access to business assets by Taggart, the majority owner. No longer able to purchase property at will, all decisions involving more than $1 million required the board's approval.

The board adopted a corporate Code of Conduct that defined ethical business practice expected within the company ranging from conflicts of interest to payments, gifts, and entertainment. The board established a policy on share trading by directors and senior managers. The board also formalised related party transactions policies. In disclosing commercial transactions conducted in the normal course of company business in its annual report, the board sought transparency for minority shareholders and potential investors.

The board established two committees, Human Resources and Audit, chaired by Sweeney and Holmes. A separate Nominations and Governance Committee was not established. The board determined that those issues were best served as a shared board-level responsibility.

In shaping the company's philanthropic activities, the board selected a national charity that the company rallied around to help improve the quality of life for children. In a long-term commitment to the charity, Kirkland was appointed to its board.

BOARD MEETINGS

From the outset, the CFO and COO, along with members of senior management, regularly participated in the full 3–4-hour monthly board meetings. At the board meetings, Sweeney aimed to integrate operationally oriented questions with queries about strategic plans and governance processes to engage management and directors. Sweeney commented: 'There is a need to grow and develop management … and the board also. This need arises when you have not worked as a team before'.

Board's Willingness to Support Radical Organisational Changes

In 2008, Sweeney and Taggart decided it was time to revisit whether the company could be better positioned to create value with a different business model. The emergence of the global financial crisis (GFC) dropped the pace of profitability below expectations. Faced with time and financial pressures, Taggart was keenly aware that they needed to think of something quite different.

The board met to explore what they might do. The board resisted the temptation of sweeping employee layoffs and marketing cutbacks which could come back to haunt the company. Goodman, well versed in the retail franchise model, offered Taggart and his executive team a site visit of his industry-leading company for inspiration. They gained insights for adapting their own company's practices, including its organisational structure, decision-making practices, and employment practices. In evaluating strategic fit for the proposed radical organisational changes, the board decided that a profit-centre structure would position the company for sustainable, stable profitable growth for the long term. Taggart explained the restructure:

> We had to introduce two or three things at the same time. We did the restructure, put in the new incentive profit share plans, and it just worked like a dream. It was bold. It was different. There was no one in this country that has run a similar scheme, but it has worked great for us.

NEW STRUCTURE AND OPERATIONS

The goal, Taggart pointed out, was to develop an operations structure that would 'empower and incentivise store managers to create more profit from every store'. A new role, retail business manager, was created and the regional management layer was eliminated. New operating procedures, such as the sales and service programme, were launched to 'create resilient business managers who could stand on their own feet and operate'.

ALIGNMENT OF REWARD AND REMUNERATION FOR PERFORMANCE RESULTS

For business managers to succeed, the shift involved adopting an ownership sensibility with commensurate accountability. It meant running the profit centre as if it was their business within the framework of rules, such as health and safety, while sharing a passion for customer service. A new performance-related compensation system allowed managers to earn an incentive bonus and employees were eligible for a discretionary bonus.

NEW MANAGEMENT INFORMATION SYSTEM

The company needed a new inventory management and financial reporting system to bring about the improvements. Not all directors were convinced that the company could implement a new integrated system of accounting, sales and payroll without taking twice as long and costing twice as much as budgeted. The board made the bold decision to go ahead. Taggart explained:

> The global financial crisis was not going to last forever from where we sat. And when it did finish, I was going to have the best management and merchandise and financial system you could buy in the world in what was a very trying and difficult time. But we still chose to make that significant investment.

The company was one of the first retailers to anticipate, adjust, and meet its goal as a top specialist category performer emerging from the GFC. It held its market share and implemented its new management information system on time and under budget. Based on the company's performance, the board was well positioned to investigate growth opportunities.

Finding New Avenues for Growth (2011–2015)

BOARD LEADERSHIP: ONLINE FOR ORGANIC GROWTH

In the period between 2011 and 2012, when the company's growth strategy, long dominated by expansion efforts through building and acquiring brands and properties for its consumer electronics and apparel categories, began to evolve with another option—online retailing. Online retail demanded a complex distribution system, a reliable, scalable and secure online platform, and innovative marketing. It also required the knowledge, skills and experience of the board, management, and staff to lead this transformation. The company would be a late entrant, at least a decade behind other competitors in gaining a foothold in the market.

Over a year, the board deliberated about the financial commitment, technology requirements, and organisational capacity to make this strategic shift for growth. Taggart was not very enthusiastic about the resource commitment, and he could not see how entering digital retail fit with customer service. The board pored over reports about trends in the domestic marketplace, digital retail transformation trends, and domestic and international competition. While some directors were leaning toward an entry into online retail, it was not a foregone conclusion.

In 2011, the board decided to start small with a soft launch of the website to grow their share of the market while also keeping an eye on competitors' response. Dissatisfied with the initial costly marketing strategy by an external agency, Holmes used his digital expertise and worked with management to wind down that campaign. In its place, they developed a cost-effective organic approach to immediately improve visibility.

One of the executives explained the company's timing and speed for entering online retail:

> You can't not be there; it is just a matter of when you are there. While the board would have liked us to have been there earlier, I think that we got it right. Part of our values is being innovative, and to me, innovative means working smart.

REDEFINING RETAIL BASICS

In 2012, the company posted record profit. Having seen the potential of e-retail with strong earnings growth, Taggart explained how the company's primary focus would remain, as always, on the retail basics—merchandise, marketing, and interesting stores—which involved:

- improving the quality and value of its product ranges;
- creating impactful, relevant promotions delivered to its customers via a medium of their choice and channel of their choice;
- continuing to improve inventory management and analysis skills to drive profit through improved product availability;
- keeping costs firmly under control; and
- improving the service offered to customers.

MARKETING STRATEGY

The company's commitment to retail basics extended to its marketing strategy. Tried-and-true promotional campaigns on television and in print media were favoured. Taggart pointed out that 'the proposition of really good quality famous brand name products at real good prices is just irresistible'.

This marketing approach was adapted to each of the company's key segments. The apparel line featured the same spokesperson over 25 years in a discount-powered campaign targeting the key customer demographic, women in age range of 30–50 years old. The other key segment of the company's activities, consumer electronics, featured campaigns that targeted younger customers with no particular skew to male or female. Now that consumers could shop anytime and anywhere, the company aimed to position its brands on social media sites as it looked to expand its influence as a trusted brand.

The company made quick progress in growing its online sales as new customers migrated to its digital retail space. Concerns were no longer lurking and the board 'saw massive potential in further developing online capabilities'. Catherine Parsons, a newly appointed independent director with domestic and international experience for online retail of consumer products, explained:

> The whole customer dynamic is about personalisation and understanding your customer behaviour. We all know that data is everything now. We must be able to capture and effectively use that data, which would be a big step for the Lansdowne Group.

Stepping Up

Between 2013 and 2015, the Lansdowne Group continued to produce record bottom line profit. Dividends to shareholders, which had increased every year for the past 5 years, were on track for another strong performance. The company had enjoyed many successes, built up a loyal customer base, and developed an industry leadership position. Online sales, once a concern among directors and management, were anticipated to outpace the rate of growth of in-store sales. The board looked to embark on the next phase of growth, scanning internationally and domestically.

The board was willing to expand its presence to more than one country through its e-retail strategy. As one director explained, the company 'faced increasing competition for business arising from a global marketplace that is very much online'. The board decided to adopt a deliberate low cost, low risk approach by only building fulfilment centres in other countries on its growth path.

Evolving Board Leadership in Governance Relationships

CHAIR–MAJORITY OWNER (MANAGING DIRECTOR) RELATIONSHIP

Sweeney's board chair leadership and governance knowledge, skills and experience had helped transform the company's capability to create value. Recognised nationally for service to the country in business management, she had 'a way of bringing Taggart along' as one director explained. The original understanding struck between Sweeney and Taggart did not waiver over 14 years. As chair, Sweeney was accountable for board governance and Taggart was the entrepreneurial retailer interested in developing an innovative and profitable business.

Sweeney pointed out that she had not modified her board leadership style to accommodate an organisation's ownership structure:

> Different models [ownership structures] should not take you away from the principles of good governance or responsibility. They might be shareholders, they might be stakeholders, but the board must preserve its independence. The standards do not or should not change.

As majority shareholder, Taggart remained unconvinced that he 'held any greater voting power than board and other strategic management'. Despite his considerable influence over the policies and management of the company, a director commented on the successful relationship: 'What John Taggart and Robin Sweeney have achieved with the Lansdowne Group is an openness and willingness to contribute at times beyond a pure governance mandate'.

BOARD–MANAGEMENT RELATIONSHIP

The success of the relationship extended to Sweeney's view of the board as a team. Sweeney explained:

> It does not need to be a large board to have a diversity of views, but you need these complementary skills, and there needs to be an acknowledgement of people and their skills. It is important that you allow people to demonstrate leadership. And that management see that there is this recognition and pride in different roles.

One of the executives explained how the directors provided valuable perspectives, innovative opinions and creative approaches for constructively challenging management:

> In the board meetings, we gain a whole different set of views because they are operating in different spheres. It creates a healthy tension. The demands of the board are always slightly more than we can achieve. The expectation that they set does add value because there is a stretch goal. Without the structure that Robin Sweeney and Richard Holmes have brought over the years, the business would not be the same.

INDEPENDENT DIRECTORS–EXECUTIVE DIRECTORS RELATIONSHIP

The board adapted conventional governance practices which would have limited their tenure. The continuity of the directors' tenure had allowed them to gain deep insight into the company, and its capabilities as well as each other's. Sweeney commented:

> We have reached a stage that we have a successful model. We still challenge and stimulate one another around the board and challenge and stimulate management, and they challenge us. But nothing can last forever—and this length of service is unusual by my standards, and by traditional standards. It surprises me. I do critically look at how I think I am performing. I have no hesitation if I don't think I am able to contribute or I am not performing, that I would walk. But we do need to continue to have fresh thinking; and that applies for both board and management.

In 2015, Sweeney initiated a director succession discussion, only the third time in the 14 years of her role as board chair. The first time arose with the retirement of Goodman, a non-executive director. His alternate, Mason, joined the board. The second time had followed the resignation of Mason for a potential conflict of interest in the highly competitive retail industry. After a two-year gap, Catherine Parsons, an independent non-executive director, had joined the board in 2013. Now Sweeney faced the retirement of two long-serving directors—Holmes, an independent director and Kirkland, an executive director. Both had been directors on the board since the IPO. It would be an opportunity to bring 'freshness, experience, and different ways of looking at things' that would be relevant for the future needs of the Lansdowne Group.

Discussion

In the case study we wanted to highlight the ways in which the board can provide instrumental responsible leadership in stakeholder governance for value creation and to link these activities that the board performs when developing and adapting its strategies for sustained performance. The case study, featuring a majority shareholder/managing director of the Lansdowne Group, demonstrates that the board engaged in balancing key stakeholders' interests with value creation in an industry undergoing change. We have identified four steps taken by the board to reconcile stakeholders' interests that were significant for improving the company's competitive positioning, profitability, and growth prospects.

The board of directors *engaged in targeted active management of its relationships* with stakeholders. A range of tactics, which extended from an exchange of information to adoption of a management approach, was used to influence its key stakeholders. Tactics for customers included marketing research, advertising, and market development to influence consumer purchase decisions. Tactics for affecting its ability to attract and retail talent and improve public relations (i.e. loyalty to the company) involved a variety of training programmes for employees and incentive schemes as well as donations to charities. To engage with management, the board used an informal dialogue for the board meetings. Shareholders connected with the board of directors at the annual general meeting. The board's actions are consistent with a relational role of the board as a boundary spanner to manage key stakeholders for instrumental reasons (Freeman & McVea, 2001; Jones et al., 2018; Maak & Pless, 2006; Siegel, 2009).

The board *sought 'win–win' solutions* with key stakeholders to improve the company's competitive advantage. The board led the development and directed the adaptation of its business model with the support of its key stakeholders as the environment shifted. The directors of the board had detected an external threat (GFC) to the viability of the company itself, which is consistent with the directors of the board acting as networkers to pre-empt issues that arise from too narrow of a board structure/board composition (Doh & Stumpf, 2005; Maak & Pless, 2006). The board's systematic analysis and collaboration aligned the interests of key stakeholders and brought ethical considerations into effective decision making under situational and time constraints, which demonstrated the board's service role in strategy for long-term value creation (Åberg et al., 2019; Pugliese et al., 2009).

The board *brought values to bear on decisions*. The board chair, along with an independent non-executive director, served in their roles for an extended period which brought a sense of constancy and commitment to broader social values to the board's leadership role. Broadly based values guided how the directors of the board collectively approached key stakeholder interests as it developed and adapted its corporate strategies and advised management. As Waldman and Galvin (2008, p. 334) explain, 'executives who place too much emphasis on rational, quantifiable profit maximization may find that their values or desires go unrequited'. The board balanced a reward system and corporate culture that stressed profits and efficiency with a consideration of social values and non-financial stakeholders' interests.

Consistent with the *achievement of the company's objectives*, the board evinced clear-sighted decisions for profitability and growth, and creating value for customers who wanted high quality products at low prices. The board declared their intention to shift to online retail only when the risk of failure (e.g. technology problem, consumer apprehension) was lower and the majority shareholder/managing director was convinced of the scalability within currently served markets and internationally for growth. The application of digital technologies, including mobile, social media, analytics, and platforms, involved a transformation of the business to enable enhanced customer experience, streamlined operations, and greater profitability and growth. It is not a surprise that the majority shareholder/managing director would want to exercise his monitoring role for shaping the company's strategies and to implement his preferences in the transformation of the company's business model, given that he had the ability and incentive (Villalonga, 2018).

Case Study 5.2 Auckland International Airport Growth 1998–2005[2]

In late 2005, Wayne Boyd, board chair of Auckland International Airport (AIA), and the board of directors surveyed the latest expansion of the international terminal. A new wall of windows provided a commanding view of the flat, former agricultural land to the north, which appeared ideal for the board's plan to build a second runway, a hotel, and an expanded commercial park within the next four years.

As Boyd toured the site with four fellow directors, he reflected on the board's exercise of responsible leadership in governance that had promoted the transformation of the former state-owned enterprise into one of the world's most cost-efficient and best-performing airports in less than 10 years. Boyd contemplated, 'How can we continue to create value for our stakeholders without losing our key focus on long-term, stable growth?'

Early History (1950s–1970s)

In 1955, a recreational landing strip on a dairy farm became the site selected for Auckland's international airport. In 1966, the government officially opened New Zealand's gateway to world with a three-day grand air pageant and ceremony. AIA introduced airlines, passengers, and cargo as part of an economic growth strategy for New Zealand. In its first year of operation, the airport handled approximately 750,000 passengers, 22,000 aircraft movements, and 8,300 tonnes of freight. A decade later, AIA opened a new international terminal to meet customer demand, improve quality of service for passengers, and enhance revenue streams through retail.

Corporatisation of AIA (1980s–1995)

In 1988, AIA was incorporated as part of New Zealand's economic reform. Its ownership was split between the Crown (central government) with 51.6 per cent shareholding and 29 local councils (local governments). Four months later, trading, which was restricted to government entities, led to share ownership concentrated among five local councils. The Crown's share remained unchanged.

By 1994, AIA's performance exceeded the board's goal of 10 per cent return on shareholder funds. The government relaxed the original ownership restrictions, allowing 1 per cent of AIA equity to be purchased by a New Zealand based private investment firm, Infratil Investments, in 1995.

From State-Owned Enterprise to Publicly Listed Company (1996–1998)

The central government decided it would no longer retain an ownership stake in AIA. The board began preparations for an IPO. In 1996, the directors welcomed Wayne Boyd's appointment to the board. Boyd brought his experience as a lawyer and investment banker along with his experience as chair of freight, energy, and steel manufacturing companies to the role of AIA board chair. With Boyd's strength in strategy, regulatory issues and financial performance skills, the directors that would lead AIA through an IPO included Sir Laurence Stevens, Sir Wilson Whineray and Anthony Frankham.

Sir Laurence Stevens was appointed to the AIA board in 1988. He served as board chair for eight years, before stepping aside with Boyd's appointment as his successor; Stevens continued as a director for two more years. Stevens, former president of the New Zealand Manufacturers' Federation (the forerunner of Business New Zealand), was credited for his role in promoting closer economic relations between Australia and New Zealand through free trade.

Sir Wilson Whineray was appointed to the AIA board in 1992 and chaired the board's remuneration committee. He served as the managing director of one of New Zealand's largest companies, Carter Holt Harvey, from 1987 to 1993 and then became that company's board chair from 1993 to 2006.

Anthony Frankham joined the AIA board in 1994. As a chartered accountant, Frankham gained expertise in financial and accounting practices as a partner of Deloitte. Frankham's appointment to the board had initially been recommended by the largest local government shareholder, Auckland City Council.

In 1997, Joan Withers joined the board. Withers had experience as chief executive officer for the Radio Network of New Zealand. Withers brought a proven track record of driving growth through transformational change, coupled with a strong client/customer orientation and a wide network of contacts, to the board.

In 1998, two appointments to the board were made. Michael Smith was welcomed to the board. With his nearly 30 years of corporate experience, Smith brought additional financial skills and strategic acumen, which included acquisition and diversification strategies. John Goulter, chief executive officer of AIA for the past decade, was appointed as managing director. As CEO, Goulter brought business experience and a reputation for developing organisations and leadership talent.

In 1998, AIA was the first airline company in the Southern hemisphere to be listed. With the exit of its majority shareholder, the company gained access to additional capital for three strategies: (1) rebuilding and extending the runway, (2) expanding retail activities, and (3) developing commercial property. The IPO unfolded as planned leading to 67,787 new shareholders.

Post-IPO Performance

In 1999, the board listed AIA on the Australia Stock Exchange (ASX) as a perquisite for Australian institutional investors, having exceeded its surplus after tax result by 21.3 per cent in the first year as outlined in the Prospectus/Investment Statement. Two of the five regional councils sold their shares.

In 1999, for the first time in AIA's history, retail revenue surpassed landing charges. Goulter explained that, although 'the runway is key to our business', the company pursued further expansion of retail business and commercial property development. Goulter explained:

> Being listed in both New Zealand and Australia has placed us under increased shareholder attention and it was extremely important that the

Company begin its tenure as a listed entity on a credible basis by achieving what it said it would.

POST-IPO AWARDS AND HONOURS (1999–2000)

Following its IPO, AIA's achievements were recognised by domestic and international business communities. Goulter won recognition, most notably being named the *New Zealand Herald* Business Leader of the Year in 1999. AIA's 2000 Annual General Report placed first in a communications competition by the Airports Council International Pacific.

In 2000, AIA won the Retail and Restaurants Award from New Zealand Tourism for the World of Shopping retail complex in the International Terminal. New Zealand Tourism also awarded AIA with the Tourism Innovator Award for the human resource development and training programme for the 150 Bluecoat Volunteer Hospitality Ambassadors. That same year, AIA was named runner up for the best retail website for the Netguide Award. It was also named runner up in the Top 200 Business Ethics Award by *New Zealand Management* magazine. In 2000, AIA featured prominently in *International Business Traveller* magazine, ranking fifth in a list of the Top 20 International Airports. It earned recognition in the category for best airport shopping and ranked sixth for world's most efficient airports.

POST-IPO VISION AND CORE VALUES

As AIA continued to build its reputation for sound financial performance as a top 10 New Zealand Exchange (NZX) listed company, the board and senior management aligned strategy and organisational development to instil a service orientation. In 2000, with Goulter's leadership, a 'Future Focus' session was conducted with AIA's 282 employees. They reflected on AIA's past and shared their ideas on the future of AIA. Following the session, AIA adopted a vision 'to be a world-leading airport enterprise where people come first'. In striving to achieve this vision, AIA's values focused on people, environment, safety and returns (economics), as well as a commitment to being proactive, responsible, and ethical.

Recalibrating Aeronautical Revenue (2000–2001)

In 2000–2001, the board identified that revenue generated for airfield activities paid by airlines, including landing, aircraft parking, refuelling and common area terminal service charges could be increased. The board, aware that AIA operated in a market where competition for airfield activities was limited, needed to take steps so that it did not abuse its market power in setting prices that could be deemed excessive. The board dedicated four of its twelve meetings to address pricing issues.

The outcome of the consultative process led to a dispute. AIA's largest customer, Air New Zealand, initially sought to contest the new fees in New Zealand's High Court before a negotiated deal that saw a backdated reduction was reached. In its decision for the fee increase, the board emphasised it had tried to balance the interests of shareholders, its customers (in the form of airlines), visitors to New Zealand, the travelling public, and the region.

Appointment of a New CEO (2002–2003)

The board announced Goulter's retirement in July of 2002 (effective September 2003). Goulter had been the inaugural CEO and managing director since AIA's incorporation in 1988. Goulter's leadership was recognised by many, culminating in his being named the *Deloitte/Management Magazine* Executive of the Year. He also won recognition as the *National Business Review* New Zealander of the Year and was inducted into both the Enterprise New Zealand Trust and the Manukau City Business Halls of Fame.

Goulter established strong relationships with AIA's local community, which extended to the local Māori people, the Tangatawhenua (Tainui), secondary schools like Aorere College, and the Life Education Trust, a health-based programme for children. He secured a memorandum of understanding for the construction of a Marae as a major component of AIA's commitment to the community. A Marae served as a religious and social meeting place for Māori communities. He described the significance of the Marae for AIA's relationship with Māori communities as 'in essence, an illustration of an extension to our triple bottom-line management responsibilities, a cultural responsibility to go with our social, economic and environmental performance responsibilities'. The opening of the world's first airport Marae was scheduled for November 2005 to coincide with AIA's 40th anniversary.

In July 2003, following an international search process, the board selected Don Huse as the new CEO to succeed Goulter. The board decided that a separation between the role of chief executive officer and managing director would be implemented. Thus, Huse was not appointed to the board as a managing director. As one director explained, 'That doesn't minimise the role of the chief executive and the role of management. There is a relationship that must work between management and the board'. Huse, a chartered accountant, was previously chief financial officer of Sydney Airport Corporation, chief executive of Wellington International Airport, and a director of TransAlta New Zealand. His responsibilities included the development and implementation of strategies, recognition of wider stakeholder interests, and growing sustainable shareholder value.

The Board's Continued Evolution (2004–2005)

The board set its sights on the expansion of AIA's business in a 'responsive, sustainable and secure manner'. Boyd expected his fellow directors to fully understand their commitments and responsibilities:

> I am about moving the board and company forward. As chair I engage with my board members. I draw them out to ensure we get the decision-making and the diversity of thought that one would expect from that sort of group.

In 2004, Boyd was recognised by his fellow directors with a second nomination as QBE Insurance Chairman of the Year in the *Deloitte/Management* magazine Top 200 awards. A colleague described Boyd's exercise of board chair leadership:

> He does seek consensus, but he is very much a chair who is in charge of the meeting, but he is not aggressive or autocratic. He is very much a consensus builder. He is good with management. He is disciplined and demanding but he is a good manager of people. He recognises strengths and weaknesses of managers, and he drives them to give good outcomes.

In 2004, the board reviewed its practices, following the release of the ASX Principles and NZX Code for principles of good corporate governance and best practice recommendations. The board moved quickly to fine tune its practices. The audit committee expanded its focus to include risk management and the external auditor requirement to appoint a new partner after a five-year rotation. A nominations committee for the selection and induction of new directors was established to develop a succession plan and implement an annual performance review for board members.

In April 2004, the board announced Dr Keith Turner as the first new independent non-executive director since AIA had been listed. Turner had been appointed as chief executive officer in 1999 of Meridian Energy, the largest electricity generator in New Zealand. His vision and commitment to effecting major industry reform as a government liaison brought skills, contacts, and experience in planning and development for commercial success to the board. In 2005, Whineray stepped down from the board following 14 years of service.

A Platform for Growth (2004–2005)

At the time of Huse's appointment, the aviation industry was showing signs of recovery in international traffic volumes following the terrorist attack in Bali, the war in Iraq, and the outbreak of Severe Acute Respiratory Syndrome (SARS). In 2004, passenger movements, a key performance indicator, well exceeded 10 million for the first time. It was a milestone for AIA and a significant international benchmark which moved AIA into the top 100 airports worldwide in terms of passenger movements.

In 2004, the board launched a two-year comprehensive master planning initiative. As an asset-intensive infrastructure business, the board was looking forward 5–25 years, projecting how AIA would meet both current and anticipated growth. The directors set out to identify and understand what was important to their stakeholders in aeronautical and non-aeronautical facilities and services which encompassed airfields, terminals, freight, retail, car parks, roads, property development, and land use.

In parallel with generating the masterplan, the board continued to annually review and refine the long-term corporate strategy. The corporate strategy focused on five key initiatives to provide a platform for growth: Delivering capacity enhancement; active capital management; maximising yield, enhancing strategic relationships; and delivery capability.

DELIVERING CAPACITY ENHANCEMENT

In 2004, Huse embarked on the largest and most complex infrastructure development programme since commercial operations started, nearly 40 years earlier. The projects aimed to add value by growing AIA's four core businesses—aviation, retail, car parking, and property. Activities included an upgraded runway and security, expanded retail business and car parking facilities, and new property investment projects with commercial tenants to meet the needs of the more than 10,000 people who worked in the vicinity of the airport.

ACTIVE CAPITAL MANAGEMENT

In 2005, the board implemented changes to its capital structure which included enhanced distributions to shareholders through a special dividend, a share buy-back, and an ordinary dividend increase. To keep the share price attractive for its 20 per cent retail investor base and to entice new investors, the board decided on a stock split. The number of shareholders reached 53,005 up from 50,859.

MAXIMISING YIELD (RETURNS ACROSS AERONAUTICAL AND NON-AERONAUTICAL ACTIVITIES)

AIA embarked on a renewed consultative process for the 2007 scheduled reset of aeronautical charges following the landing fee dispute in 2000–2001.

ENHANCING STRATEGIC RELATIONSHIPS

In 2005, tourism's role as New Zealand's largest export industry earner continued to gain recognition as a competitive advantage. In strengthening its relationships with tourism internationally, Huse accepted an appointment for the Pacific Regional Council of the Airports Council International, an association of the world's airports with 569 members operating over 1,640 airports in 177 countries and territories. In 2004, a member of the senior management team accepted an appointment on the board of Tourism Auckland, furthering AIA's commitment to working with the industry to achieve tourism growth.

DELIVERING CAPABILITY

This element of the corporate strategy encompassed AIA's commitment to improve human resources management, operations, technology, corporate decision-making, and risk management. The board recognised that the expanding scope and scale of AIA's operational and development initiatives required additional resources to deliver on the growth strategy. The board supported an investment in building organisational capability through the recruitment of senior management talent. Other initiatives included workforce planning and organisational development across the company. The development of a workplace culture promoting productivity and performance was encouraged through learning and development, performance management as well as an incentive scheme with rewards and recognition.

The Board's Next Moves

In February 2006, Prime Minister Helen Clark was joined by Boyd, the directors and senior management, along with a host of dignitaries in a double celebration for the 40th anniversary of AIA and the official opening of the expanded International Terminal, completed on time and on budget.

In less than a decade, the board had created a legacy of a world-class gateway for New Zealand from the former state-owned enterprise, retaining its initial ranking as a top 10 listed company on the NZX. AIA's vision for the future—the board's masterplan for airport development over the next 25 years—neared completion. Board led responsible leadership in governance was needed to continue the collaboration among the directors, senior management and stakeholders in pursuit of AIA's transformation journey.

Discussion

We wanted to feature the measures that can be taken by the board to provide integrative responsible leadership in purpose governance for value creation and to connect these activities that the board performs with its strategies for long-term sustainable growth. The case study demonstrates that the board developed and adapted its strategy as the company evolved from its pre-IPO origins as a state-owned enterprise to a top performing publicly listed company. We have identified four ways in which the board sought to fulfil its obligations through responsible leadership in governance and improve its long-term sustainability.

Positioned at the centre of a network of stakeholder relations, *the board adopted an outward-looking approach* associated with creating value. The board engaged in building relationships which helped impart financial and non-financial information needs for decision making, such as its investors with the stock split to keep the stock price attractive for retail investors. It also promoted relationships with the tourism industry domestically and internationally. The board interacted with a broad range of legitimate stakeholders which facilitated communication, collaboration, and alignment (Maak et al., 2016).

The board *promoted alignment between its corporate purpose and social objectives*. The board engaged in diversified, coordinated strategies to demonstrate congruency between corporate purpose and social objectives. Some of the initiatives undertaken included an allocation of funds for community projects related to health and education and Māori support for the construction of a Marae. The board took steps to improve the quality of work life for its employees through training and development programmes and new employee recruitment to senior management positions. Among its initiatives employee involvement in setting a new vision and values for the company helped to ensure that the vision was truly shared—and not developed by senior leadership—and guided the development of shared responsible leadership throughout the company for value creation (Bartlett & Ghoshal, 1994; Pearce et al., 2014).

The board *demonstrated a commitment to people, planet and profit (the triple bottom line)*. The board sought to demonstrate and widely communicate the company's activities in fulfilling its purpose and how it had done. In providing transparency, it used non-financial data for its report to focus on the environmental and social impacts of the company's activities. Companies with significant market power or a near monopoly, such as a national commercial and cargo service airport, have an intrinsic social objective (see Mayer, 2018). Evidence from empirical studies, including meta-analyses, that investigate whether there is a relationship between a company's social and financial performance find the overall effect is positive but small with a range of results given mediating factors. Results are clear about the negative effects for misdeeds on financial performance (for a review of the large body of empirical work on the link between environmental/social performance and financial performance see Villalonga, 2018).

The board *adapted its strategy over time for corporate performance* congruent with its corporate purpose. Given the asset intensive nature of the company, the board made decisions over a long-time horizon as it transitioned the company from a state-owned enterprise to a recognised top performing company. The board also demonstrated that it did not always get it right in the eyes of its customers (airlines) with the reset of the aircraft landing charges. A concern for harm to its reputation saw a negotiated settlement. The company had developed a reputation for ethics, having been runner up for a business ethics award, and an award-winning board chair and CEO and the risk for reputational damage among its stakeholders was not congruent with its values. Consistent with Waldman & Galvin (2008), it illustrates that board led responsible leadership can only be undertaken over the long haul and in different situations, and there may be challenges along the way.

Case Study 5.3 Auckland International Airport Strategic Transformation 2008–2015[3]

Sir Henry van der Heyden thought back over the past three years since he had been appointed as chair for the AIA board. Board led responsible leadership had led to newfound success: The transformation of an airport into a leading global tourism infrastructure company. It was one of the best performing publicly listed companies in New Zealand, and proportionally, the busiest airport in Australasia for international traffic.

Its corporate purpose in tandem with responsible leadership has sustained the company's transformation momentum through changes in executives and directors. The reinvention of New Zealand's premiere gateway to the world had followed an accelerated change in the company's business model and the board's engagement in strategy. From the outset, first as a director appointed following a failed takeover bid, and then as board chair, van der Hayden recast the relationship between the board and management, among directors, and with stakeholders. On the threshold of his final term as chair, he recognised the board would soon be at a crossroads in setting AIA's strategic direction for the next five years affecting economic and social value across its stakeholders.

Auckland International Airport (1955–2007): Brief History

From its beginning in 1955 on rural dairy farmland, AIA had grown into an international company, operating as a gateway for travel, tourism and trade for airlines, passengers, and cargo. The company evolved through two ownership phases. In 1988, during its first phase, the airport became a state-owned corporatised organisation, operating commercial activities. Share ownership was split between the Crown (government) as majority owner, and local councils. In 1998, its second phase, AIA became the first airport company in the Southern hemisphere listed on a stock exchange at the Crown's request. Local councils retained their block share ownership while the Crown's divested shares were acquired by institutional and retail investors.

In 2007, the board faced foreign ownership bids. The bids divided the board and damaged relationships with shareholders. Following the resignation of the board chair, Anthony Frankham accepted the appointment of board chair. The takeover activity was a catalyst for the election of three shareholder nominated directors to the board. In 2008, the government declared AIA as a strategic asset, quashing any foreign ownership bids.

Board Engagement in Strategy Formation: 'Flight Path for Growth'

In 2008, the board appointed a new CEO, Simon Moutter, to undertake a strategic reset. The board committed to a new vision to 'be the recognised market leader in creating value from business centred on hubs for large-scale movement of people and goods'. The company captured the purpose behind its vision: 'We believe our primary business role is to play our part in growing travel, trade and tourism for the markets we serve'. The board believed their efforts would achieve benefits for passengers, customers and shareholders: 'Passengers will have a better travel experience, our customers and business partners will enjoy a more mutually beneficial partnership, and our shareholders will realise greater value from their investment'.

In 2009, the board unveiled its new strategy, 'Flight Path for Growth' that aimed to create a healthier commercial environment, increase cost efficiency and capital productivity and pursue growth in revenue. The purpose and business model had evolved from operating New Zealand's largest gateway to driving growth in travel, tourism, and trade.

APPOINTMENT OF NEW DIRECTORS (2009)

In 2009, at the annual general meeting (AGM) two new independent non-executive directors were elected: Sir Henry van der Heyden and James Miller. As an experienced chair of the world's largest exporter of dairy products, among other companies, van der Heyden brought strategic expertise, commercial acumen and a global outlook to the board. Miller brought additional regulatory, risk management and financial skills, and experience.

PARTIAL ACQUISITIONS

In 2010, the board was presented with an opportunity for influencing flight routes as part of its growth strategy—an ownership stake in an overseas airport company. Moutter learned of the privatisation of two airports in Australia and believed its advantages, which included flexibility for the company to respond entrepreneurially and rapidly, would lend AIA a competitive advantage. The prospect of expanding into Australia through the North Queensland Airports involved a difficult discussion among directors. The decision, once made, would affect the options for future growth as one director explained:

> There was a big debate about should we just be a one site business and really concentrate the value we get out of one site, or should we become a multi-site business. Was there any synergy for route development of having several destinations? Was there any synergy in the cross-fertilisation of one airport's experience to another?

Ultimately, the prospect of AIA gaining access to rapidly growing Asian markets because of the desirable destinations served by the Australian airports, and the capacity of the company to influence the flight routes of airlines, informed the board's decision to invest.

Several months later, in a move to strengthen its domestic growth strategy, Moutter presented the board with an option to purchase shares in New Zealand's fastest growing airport, Queenstown. Its market potential and its popularity among tourists for the four-season resort town and surrounding region imparted strategic importance. Building on the momentum of the overseas share purchase, the board acted quickly. Moutter's successor recalled, 'Taking a position in other airport companies made a lot of sense. We knew about airports. We had a model around how to stimulate growth in markets'.

APPOINTMENT OF A NEW CHAIR AND A DIRECTOR (2010)

Following the completion of the Queenstown share purchase, Frankham decided to retire and championed Joan Withers as the incoming chair. She accepted the appointment. In October 2010, Brett Godfrey joined the board. Having retired as chief executive officer after founding Australia's second largest airline, Virgin Blue, he brought his deep understanding of international aviation and tourism to the role.

New Airline Customers

The company developed its core capability to attract new customers (airlines) which extended to China Southern, the third largest airline in the world. The strategy paid off. The Prime Minister of New Zealand, John Key, who was also serving as the tourism minister, met the inaugural flight from Guangzhou to welcome the chief executive and president of China Southern Airlines.

Beyond Business as Usual

The vision of creating value from the movement of people and goods extended to how directors and management approached non-aeronautical business strategies for retail, property, and car parking. In 2011, AIA earned 49 per cent of its total income from these sources. As one director noted, 'the board started thinking more holistically about the whole business'. Another director explained:

> Growing businesses means you look at crazy ideas at times. You need people who have been in those situations and know how to manage risk and judge the amount of risk you are prepared to take for the reward that might be available to you. You need to reflect on your shareholder and understand inherently where the average shareholder might be in that risk continuum.

The board approved the redevelopment of the international terminal. The objective was to improve customer experience and increase passenger spend rates while still growing passenger volume.

AIA earned rental income from space leased in facilities, which included terminals and cargo buildings, and stand-alone investment properties. AIA had a 'property bank' for the airport's long-term growth, including a deferred second runway. In a joint venture between Tainui Group Holdings (a Māori-owned investment group), Accor Hospitality and AIA, the first airport hotel was built. In May 2011, Māori King Tuheitia Paki and New Zealand Prime Minister John Key officially opened the Novotel, designed by local architects.

The car park business did not escape transformation. A flexible price management model, along with an online reservation system, was introduced based on customer demand. As one director summarised, 'It is part of the overall package we are offering, whether it is car parking, hotels or retail and duty free; that is all part of a broad offering to the consumer'.

Creating a New Strategic Plan for 2012 Onwards

In 2012, board chair Withers commented:

> We firmly believe that Auckland Airport needs to help set the tourism and trade growth agenda, challenge the collective industry to be ambitious about its growth targets, and to be relentless about how those ambitions can and will be realised.

She elaborated, 'Leadership will be a key factor in both our own organisational performance and in the success of New Zealand travel, tourism and trade'.

To achieve these aims, Withers ensured that the board took steps on both the selection of a new CEO and directors, including the appointment of a new chair. Her tenure on the board had reached the maximum term limit.

APPOINTMENT OF A NEW CEO (2012)

In 2012, the board prepared once again for one of the most important strategic decisions it needed to make—selection of a new CEO. The search process included directors' input on the skills, attributes and industry knowledge that they considered important for the role. Adrian Littlewood, general manager of retail and commercial, had been with AIA since 2009. He had led the growth and development of that division (excluding commercial property) which accounted for 40 per cent of AIA's non-aeronautical income.

APPOINTMENT OF A NEW CHAIR AND DIRECTORS (2012–2013)

The directors turned their attention to further aligning the knowledge, skills and experience of the board members with the strategic direction of AIA. Two new female directors, 'unusual suspects', joined the board: Justine Smyth and Michelle Guthrie. During their careers, they gained significant international governance and executive experiences: Smyth as a group financial director for Lion Nathan, one of Australia's largest food and beverage groups, and a partner of Deloitte; and Guthrie as managing director of the Australian Broadcasting Corporation and an executive at Google Asia International Pacific based in Singapore. Their appointment, which reflected diversity of thinking, experience and skills, attested to the board's grasp of and insight into the evolving needs of the board and company.

Six months prior to the imminent retirement of Withers, the board announced van der Heyden as the incoming board chair. His personal professional goal was to lead and support the growth of strong, internationally competitive and sustainable businesses like AIA that contributed to New Zealand's economy and the well-being of its people. This commitment was supported by AIA's inclusion in the Dow Jones Sustainability Asia Pacific Index since 2012 and the FTSE4Good, an ethical stock market series of indices since 2008.

Revitalised Strategy: 'Faster, Higher, Stronger'

In 2013, the board unveiled its new five-year strategic plan Faster, Higher, Stronger which aimed to 'grow faster, aim higher and become stronger'. The objective was to build on the momentum of the past years yet respond to changes in aviation markets, customer expectations, and the commercial property market. The four themes for the next phase of growth were to: Grow travel markets; strengthen consumer business; be fast, efficient, and effective; and invest for future growth.

The company continued its pursuit of growth through innovation and technology. In April 2013, AIA became the first airport company in the world and the first business in Australasia to partner with Sina Weibo, one of China's largest social media sites. It was part of the digital marketing strategy to grow New Zealand's share from high growth markets, with China being one of the fastest growing tourism markets in New Zealand.

By 2014, a shared commitment to the strategic transformation paid off. Revenue increased by 6 per cent from the previous year. In addition to growing travel markets, AIA focused on investing in retail, property, and long-term infrastructure to keep lifting performance.

The Board's Working Relationships

ALIGNMENT OF BOARD-MANAGEMENT DYNAMICS

Van der Heyden adopted two approaches for directors and management engagement: one, scheduled board meetings; two, flexible, direct communication with notification to van der Heyden about the activity. It encouraged transparency. The trust generated was palpable, as one director explained:

> I never get a sense that I am missing something, as if there is a huge topic that has not been raised or they are hiding something or something is not being discussed. I think that really is tremendous credit to Adrian Littlewood, but I also think it is Henry van der Heyden really feeling like we should put everything on the table. The point of the board is to really have a true understanding of the business; the good, the bad, and the ugly.

In keeping directors engaged in an ongoing dialogue about strategy, van der Heyden promoted diversity encapsulated by both gender and thinking around the board table. The board's gender diversity was among the vanguard for the country. In late 2014, three of the eight directors were women with the appointment of Christine Spring. She brought international aviation infrastructure development and strategic planning expertise.

While gender and age diversity found expression in the composition of the board, the diversity of thinking gave the board its edge. Van der Heyden pointed out, 'I'm looking for different views, because different views, different experiences, different knowledge—that is when you get the best out of a board'. Rather than leading a position, van der Heyden encouraged openness of board discussions and thinking about options that informed an intrinsic part of AIA's growth strategy.

ALIGNMENT OF BOARD CHAIR–CEO RELATIONSHIP

In his role as chair, van der Heyden used the same rule with Littlewood as he had with other CEOs. He pointed out, 'I will never tell a chief executive what to do', otherwise accountability shifts. He explained:

> My role as chair is to give the chief executive space. I can mentor, I can coach, I can coerce, I can tell him what I think but I always say,

'Ultimately this is what I think, but it [must] be your decision'. So, I force recommendations.

Van der Heyden summarised the significance of the relationship between Littlewood and himself: 'The relationship between the chair and the chief executive is such a big value driver within the business. If you get that relationship right, it is actually one of the biggest value drivers'.

The benefit of the relationship between them was tangible, as one director pointed out: 'I think that there is no sense that Adrian Littlewood and Henry van der Heyden are not in lock step around what they are trying to get done'.

ALIGNMENT OF BOARD RELATIONSHIPS WITH STAKEHOLDERS

The continual challenge for the board and management involved aligning strategy and relationships with stakeholders, including shareholders, for value creation. The company positioned itself as a responsible business which supported people, the community and the environment to make a long-term contribution to its employees, investors, the people of Auckland and New Zealand and the global community. Its position as a responsible business helped to attract and retain employees, reduce its operating costs, and manage its impact on the environment.

With its commitment to purpose embedded in company practices, policies and procedures, the board implemented three changes. Van der Heyden brought about a new relationship between the board and management for its strategy planning cycle. The fundamental role of the board, he explained, 'is to set direction and feel comfortable with the strategy'. He revamped the strategy setting process, including ownership of the agenda for its annual strategy session by the directors rather than van der Heyden or Littlewood.

A second thrust involved an overhaul of board papers, re-oriented towards strategy from an operational focus. Van der Heyden explained: 'The monthly board meeting agenda is strategic rather than operational. It is all about looking forward—otherwise boards become compliant-focused rather than value adding'.

A third thrust involved a refreshed commitment to its stakeholder relationships. The board recognised the continued need to be transparent and accountable to both internal and external stakeholders, as well as local and international communities and the environment. The company's identified stakeholders included travellers and visitors, its business partners (airlines and border control agencies), tenants, businesses working at and around the airport, members of the South Auckland and Auckland communities, New Zealanders, its employees and investors.

As one director pointed out, the relationships reflected 'a zipper approach'. 'Some of those relationships are at Henry van der Heyden's level, chair to chair. Some of them are board to board. Some of them are Adrian Littlewood to his CEO colleagues'. In a global perspective, the director expanded on the significance of relationships:

> If you look out wider beyond New Zealand, we play a role in the global economy and from our network perspective in terms of how we sit in facilitating activity between Asia and South America, Australia and North America. We play a role in that global transportation of people and freight, but it is also in terms of how we integrate with Customs, Immigration and Security … Some parts we affect and influence; other parts we are a party to an influence.

The relationships with management and the board were key to value creation. Van der Heyden explained:

> So, you get alignment of strategy between the chair and the CEO, and alignment of strategy between the board and management. Those [two sets of] relationships are the biggest economic value drivers within a business. If you get all those things right, you are going to create a lot of value.

Financial Outcomes of the Growth Strategy

In 2015, continuing with its strategic plan for growth, AIA delivered on its financial commitment with total revenue up by 6.9 per cent. AIA achieved revenue growth through a combination of strong aeronautical and non-aeronautical performance. The exception was the North Queensland Airports which reflected, in part, a softening of the Australian economy. The changes implemented meant that AIA 'did not have a lazy balance sheet structure' as one director stated. Investors surveyed reported that AIA's capital structure now with the debt equity mix was right.

The board's continued commitment to corporate purpose and responsible leadership in governance reflected in AIA's ranking at the top of the New Zealand Exchange for its first time. In a bold move the board provided a bonus payment for all employees not involved in the company's incentive scheme as a financial reward for their efforts.

The Board's Next Steps

Van der Heyden considered the projected growth in passenger numbers over the next three-to-five years. AIA was positioned as a mid-point between Asia and South America, and 'travel always follows trade'. This presented opportunities for AIA as a gateway for destination tourism and as a transit hub. In two years, the board would be launching into a new five-year strategy setting cycle. Van der Heyden contemplated the board's next move.

Discussion

In the case study we wanted to highlight the ways in which the board can provide integrative responsible leadership in purpose driven governance for value creation and to connect these activities that the board performs when improving the company's long-term growth and survival prospects. The case study demonstrates that the board sustained a strategy for the strategic renewal of the company to create value for its stakeholders regardless of the transitions in executive and board leadership. We have identified four ways by which the board exercised integrative responsible leadership that were significant for reshaping the purpose driven company and creating value for economic and social wellbeing.

The board *invested in an information-rich position in a network* of stakeholder relationships. The board made investments in relationships across all legitimate stakeholder groups in recognition that some are more durable and time sensitive. The relationships were intrinsic to the board's approach to its business model transformation and extended widely to public and private businesses, industry associations, and government which supports the board's role as a boundary spanner (Filatotchev & Nakajima, 2014; Maak et al., 2016). The investments were not evaluated as to whether they would create profit in the short term or even in the long term. Research suggests that placing a financial value on the relationship is difficult (see Hesketh, 2019; Stroehle et al., 2019, for a detailed explanation of why such assessments are difficult). More importantly, the investments in the relationships built an understanding of stakeholders' interests, needs and concerns to provide a basic sense of compatibility or alignment as each learned more about the nature of the other's critical expertise and increased the quality of the relationships.

The board *combined and connected the interests of stakeholders* with its corporate purpose. The board was able to create value by purposefully focusing on building new relationships while sustaining extant ones as the board dynamically aligned interests with its corporate purpose. Over the span of three board chairs and two CEOs, the board mostly demonstrated efforts to engage in relationships linked to a higher social purpose benefitting the company and country rather than an exclusive instrumental goal of improving the returns to shareholders (Pless & Maak, 2011). The exception, of course, was the takeover quandary (see Chapter 6). The integrative responsible leadership orientation of the board allowed for better informed strategic decisions, in part, because the board was knowledgeable about the potential consequences of its choices for creating value with and for stakeholders (Maak et al., 2016).

The board clearly *articulated values that were adopted consistently* in tandem with its corporate purpose. Besides the factors that addressed stakeholder relations, values related to the board's enactment of integrative responsible leadership were critical for facilitating strategic and organisational change. In recent work, there has been progress on the importance of the board's role in promoting and modelling ethical behaviour within the board and by the board in its interactions with others, including the CEO (Conger & Lawler, 2009; Stiles & Taylor 2001; Waldman & Galvin, 2008). In the context of purpose driven governance, values were respected and embedded throughout the company and aligned with strategy, structure and organisational processes to implement strategic change and sustainable business practice.

Informed by its purpose driven governance, the board *adopted a longer term, broader strategic view of sustainable corporate performance.* Having confronted the need to reconfigure existing strategy, the board was actively involved in strategy formulation, strategic decision making, and strategic restructuring for renewal. Recent evidence suggests that board involvement in strategic activities leads to higher firm performance (for a review of these studies see Pugliese et al., 2009). In developing an interconnected approach with stakeholder groups, the board outlined its strategies and sought insights in shaping future directions (e.g. engagement with the hotel project generally and with Tainui Group Holdings (a Māori-owned investment group) specifically). The decision making exercised by the board of directors reflected consideration of both the short- and long-term time horizon in setting strategy as part of purpose driven governance (Mayer, 2018; Paine & Srinivasan, 2019). The board demonstrated that it actively balanced stakeholder interests to create value that delivered on economic and social objectives.

Case Study 5.4 Aldridge Energy Strategic Renewal[4]

Stephanie Bennett, chair of Aldridge Energy, surveyed the oil and gas onshore processing plant, a strategic investment for the company. The board had initiated a strategic renewal to strengthen the company's long-term competitive position and further integrate its social equity and environmental commitments into its business model. Board led responsible leadership in governance of the renewal efforts faced scrutiny from shareholders and other stakeholders.

Aldridge Energy Company History

Aldridge Energy, formed in 1999 by government, was involved in generation, trade and retail of electricity and gas. A decade later, it was a diversified generator from a fuel point of view with gas, hydro, wind and coal. In 2014, the company was partially privatised. The Crown (government) reduced its shareholding from 100 to 51 per cent through an IPO. Aldridge Energy was now among the country's largest listed electricity and gas retail businesses.

Aldridge Energy Company Operations and Management

The company handled three major components for its business: generation, trade and retail. Electricity generation depended on water, wind or steam from heat produced by burning fossil fuels (coal and gas). Trade involved selling or purchasing electricity through the national wholesale market to other power producers and companies. Retail included residential, industrial, and commercial consumers purchasing electricity, natural gas and liquified petroleum gas (LPG).

GENERATION ASSETS

Aldridge Energy operated its generation assets under several resource consents, easements, and mitigation and relationship agreements.

THERMAL ENERGY

The company owned and operated Cordova Power Station, a large capacity electricity generation facility, capable of providing over 20 per cent of the country's electricity needs. The facility was made up of two modern gas-fired and two coal/gas-fired generating units.

RENEWABLE ENERGY

The company had three hydro schemes. Water from these schemes flowed through eight power stations. The company also operated a commercial wind farm.

OIL AND GAS

The company had 31 per cent shareholder interest in an oil and gas joint venture. Along with light oil, the off-shore field produced natural gas and LPG.

MANAGEMENT

Since 2008, Owen Hillman had been at the helm of the company with nearly 1,000 employees. As CEO, Hillman had worked to diversify and strengthen the company's foothold throughout the country with strategic, operating and capital plans. Hillman worked closely with the board and management to bring about changes in the 'must run' generation activities and culture, including a commitment to employee health, safety and well-being. Finally, he was accountable for the company's financial position and performance as well as other social and environmental indicators.

Board Leadership and Governance for Mixed Ownership Performance

In 2014, Stephanie Bennett, as chair, led the board of eight independent, non-executive Crown-appointed directors through an IPO with institutional and retail investors acquiring 49 per cent share ownership as planned. In 2009, Bennett had accepted an appointment as board chair. She brought deep knowledge of the country's energy industry, a proven crisis management track record, and public service leadership experience. She understood the government's ambition to transform the company from a state-owned enterprise to mixed model ownership.

NEW AND INCUMBENT DIRECTORS ELECTED (2014)

In 2014, as the company's first annual general meeting (AGM) as a publicly listed company approached, the board considered whether as a team, it had the requisite skill, knowledge, experience and diversity. At the AGM, two new directors were elected: Colin Mason and Murray Walker. They brought wide-ranging experience with listed companies and regulated industries as director, chair and CEO. Colin Mason added financial markets experience through his international investment banking career. Murray Walker brought deep knowledge of monetary policy issues, a proven marketing track record and extensive international senior leadership experience. Harold Newcombe, with his business development and strategy expertise across a range of sectors, was re-elected to the board.

DIRECTORS RE-ELECTED (2015)

In 2015, the board conducted its annual performance review. The board confirmed among its directors a diversity of skills and experience to meet both the governance requirements and steer the strategic goals of the company in the short and medium term. In 2015, all three directors were re-elected at the AGM. Philippa Mills, the board's longest serving director, brought extensive experience in finance and accounting practices to her role as deputy chair. Neil Andrews added his experience as a consulting engineer along with expertise in asset management. Stephanie Bennett brought strategic acumen, relationship building skills and insight to her Crown approved reappointment as board chair.

They re-joined Marama Bachmann and Robert Fowler for continuity in board leadership. Marama Bachmann's background in law supported her deep understanding of regulatory issues that affected the energy industry and the communities in which the company operated. Robert Fowler brough additional expertise in executive finance and strategic management.

Board Leadership for New Approaches to Shareholders and Stakeholders

The board and management were mindful that the company's capability to make a sustainable financial return for its shareholders was integrated with their management and protection of the very resources enabling value creation. The company had direct and indirect social, economic and environmental impact throughout the country.

The board, knowing the importance of enduring relationships for the company's long-term stability, adopted a range of policies and practices for its stakeholders. The company's identified stakeholders included the communities in and the land on which it operated its generation assets and business activities, its employees and customers, as well as its shareholders, its suppliers and creditors and the local and central government regulatory bodies and non-governmental organisations with which it interacted.

The board recognised the need to adapt some relationships given its new mixed ownership model. Bennett explained her approach as board chair:

> In the chairmanship role, it is not chairing meetings, it is not understanding the governance frameworks—you must be able to do all of that—you also have to have both foresight and insight which is usually about people. While the dollar interests of the company are what they are, if you get the relationships right, it serves the company very well indeed.

BOARD LEADERSHIP FOR ENGAGEMENT WITH SHAREHOLDER GROUPS

The board approved new communications protocol for institutional investors, retail investors, and the Crown to keep the visibility of the company front and centre. Bennett and other directors initiated meetings and functions so that relationships could be developed, and communications regularised. Formal reporting requirements for Treasury, the Statistics agency and the Office of the Auditor General continued as required.

BOARD LEADERSHIP FOR ENGAGEMENT WITH EXTERNAL AND INTERNAL STAKEHOLDER GROUPS

Board led responsible leadership, collectively and individually enacted, developed and sustained stakeholder relationships within and outside of the company. The board recognised the role of Aldridge Energy to integrate social equity, environmental management and economic growth to create sustainable value. As one director pointed out, 'The shareholder is important and is critical, but actually how we interact with the environment and other stakeholders is equally important'.

IWI (INDIGENOUS PEOPLE OF NEW ZEALAND)

The board and management had developed many types of relationships, from being a tenant on Māori-owned land to agreements on how the two parties would work together to address the effects of company activities on iwi and initiatives that support land/community development.

Over time some of the relationships had soured. In 2009, after her appointment as chair, Bennett had taken steps to rebuild relationships by resolving a 10-year multimillion dollar legal battle over water rights. Bennett took steps to institute different ways the board would engage with iwi including hosting formal meetings and attending community events.

ENVIRONMENT

The company implemented an environmental management system, used independent audits and reported publicly on its environmental performance. The company collaborated with organisations protecting and enhancing biodiversity and promoting social well-being in the areas in which it operated its generation activities, including outdoor programmes for youth. Annual consultative meetings brought together stakeholders, such as the Department of Conservation, iwi as well as regional fish and game councils. The engagement was, as one director explained, 'about being really present as a board, showing leadership, showing that we believe that is it the right thing. It was also about giving confidence that we were going to continue to deliver the quality service that they had been used to'.

EMPLOYEES

Along with policies and practices to support employee learning and development and to promote health and safety, the board promoted workplace diversity principles. In 2014, the board adopted a holistic diversity policy anchored in diversity of thought, including differences resulting from employee experiences and capabilities, and family and cultural heritage.

The board approved a three-year road map which stemmed from its diversity strategy. The company implemented a series of programmes and tools to promote diversity. It established partnerships for programmes for women and indigenous employees, launched initiatives to change recruitment and retention practices, and tracked progress with a descriptive diversity dashboard report for the board's quarterly review.

Post-IPO Financial Performance

In 2015, the company delivered results that exceeded the prospective financial information in its listing prospectus. The board declared a dividend in line with the share offer prospectus. Increased visibility as a listed company brought greater awareness of the company's financial performance in relation to others. A director pointed out:

> We are actively compared by the analysts and, therefore, by the investors. The value of the shares reflects both their influence and view on it. It brings in the competitive aspect and the immediate market valuation on how good you are, which does not happen with a SOE.

With its mixed ownership status, the company faced restrictions. It could not issue any shares (the Crown had to hold its 51 per cent majority). It had to maintain its credit standing and to produce regular dividends. A director commented:

> It puts a discipline on us, because we must be clever to come up with a solution. But it is not the freedom that a genuine public company should have. If we want to reinvest, we must sell something or reposition the company. It is a constraint, but you can still do it. That is the way the Crown wants it.

Board Leadership for a Strategy Reset

In 2014, with the IPO in the board's rear-view mirror, there was a collective sense that strategy needed to regain prominence in the board's discussions. Between late 2014 and early 2015, the board conducted two strategy workshops. In the first session, directors and management assessed scenarios. A director described the strategy setting process:

> We have had a free and open dialogue on what the options might be and what the risks might be of any of these scenarios as a board and as a management team in the same room together. It has been vigorous, challenging, and confronting at times. We are, as an industry, facing a lot of uncertainty and change. The board or management alone will not develop the best answers. It is imperative that we work well together, and we have done so on the strategic review thus far.

Over the next several board meetings, the board and management collaborated to refine the strategic focus. The board engaged in 'deep dives' into the main areas of the business exploring issues, strategy and progress made. The company's purpose called for Aldridge Energy to be the provider of energy solutions and services for the country's people.

> In terms of the industry, we see potentially there may be a paradigm shift, in terms of what we have seen in telecommunications and other industries, where there are significant shifts in consumer control and consumer influence. The focus of the company right now is getting the company prepared for a potential change in the environment that may enable and require us to go down a slightly different path to the legacy-type utility businesses. We are taking some exploratory steps in

various directions while we wait for greater certainty over what that environment is and what the appropriate strategy may be.

Board Leadership and Governance for Long-Term Prosperity

In 2015, the company faced capacity oversupply, a more efficient transmission network and a relatively flat demand for electricity. Strategic renewal efforts would need to be 'bold and agile where necessary and where new opportunities existed', Bennett pointed out. She elaborated: 'We have no intention of meandering into the new energy future. We intend to move the company forward with pace'.

The board focused its strategic direction effort into developing new revenue streams, generating greater value from its operating practices, and continuing service improvements for its customers. The strategic direction effort was aligned with the company's core values of respect, drive, imagine, and support.

CUSTOMERS (RETAIL)

As a large electricity retailer, the company was a target for niche retailers and other mainstream competitors looking to grow their own market share. Over the past year, the company had stabilised the erosion through cost-effective service, innovative fixed-term contracts and steady prices.

The company also saw a decline in natural gas customers. Like the electricity market, the gas market remained competitive, with new entrants and existing competitors vying for residential and commercial customers. The company responded with innovative natural gas packages and pricing models.

In contrast to the retail performance in the natural gas market, the company was making significant gains in the LPG retail market. As the sole buyer from the joint venture oil and gas facility, the company had a potentially strong area of growth.

The board recognised that an industry leadership position required a clear commitment and communication of strategic intent. The acquisition and retention of customers was a key aspect of strategic renewal efforts. 'We are trying to shift the company to be more of a customer-focused company rather than a resource-based energy company'.

WHOLESALE MARKET (TRADE)

System-wide upgrades to the transmission network and newly constructed renewable generators by competitors sharply reduced the risk that the lights would not be kept on. These changes, along with improved water management and lower consumer demand led a new situation for the company.

At the peak of winter, the coal units at Cordova sat idle; it was simply more economical to buy from other generators than to operate Cordova.

In 2015, wholesale prices had dropped lower than 2008 price levels. The new normal threatened the trade/wholesale business; an oversupply by lower cost generators would have immediate and lasting effects on the company's financial performance.

THERMAL AND RENEWABLE GENERATION

The board decided to reduce its thermal generation capacity at Cordova. In early August 2015, the board announced that it would close the two remaining units by the end of 2018, unless market conditions changed dramatically. The decision cut to the heart of the country's energy security. A director explained the significance of the board's decision to end coal-fired electricity generation: 'It is not our job to provide energy security for the country now that we are a commercial operation. We have to serve the needs of all shareholders and make the best commercial decisions that we can'.

Bennett 'took soundings' with government and gained insight into how it might react politically. As one director explained, those indicators were taken into consideration. It did not change the board's decision; it affected how they thought about implementing and communicating it.

The Crown's exclusively preferred view no longer applied. Bennett pointed out:

> We will still, from time to time, give the shareholding ministers a heads up on things that are not market related, but are strategic. For example, when I was announcing that we would shut down the coal fired units, that has a much broader public policy implication. So, I picked the phone up. In the last three days, I have made a certain number of calls: Owen Hillman has been called; and Cordova; and dealing with stakeholders and our iwi partners and people. We have a process of making sure that the economic interests of the company are not compromised by really putting significant strength on relationships. But the balance of commercial against political has certainly shifted.

In mid-August 2015, Hawthorne Resources, the company's supplier of coal for the thermal generators, entered receivership, triggering Aldridge Energy's ability to cancel its contract without financial penalty. At the board's next meeting, the board decided to exit that contract, strengthening its commitment to change the company's energy portfolio.

The oil and gas field, a joint venture that produced crude oil, natural gas and LPG, had been in operation since 2010. In 2014, international crude oil prices had plummeted and stayed low, but current higher production levels of natural gas, oil and LPG resulted in higher sales volumes and revenue contributions. The board, with its joint venture partners, needed to consider its options to extend the life of the off-shore field or to vary production levels. Recently commissioned studies would provide a re-assessment of the reserves. Decisions around field development and future capital expenditure would not likely occur in the short term.

As part of its plans to further explore renewable energy, the board endorsed a new ventures group with a focus on solar initiatives aimed at adjusting its generation portfolio.

New CEO Search

In 2015, the directors embarked on one of the most important roles for any board, the selection of a new CEO. From a strategic renewal perspective, they sought a CEO who would want to go on a journey with the board in determining which options to pursue for long-term sustainability.

The Board's Next Moves

Bennett and the directors completed their inspection of the oil and gas processing plant and prepared for their meeting with local iwi before returning to the corporate office. With the first 18 months as a publicly listed company behind them, Bennett, and the directors were mindful that stakeholders including shareholders would want evidence of financial performance along with social and environmental considerations for the company's long-term sustainability.

The board's efforts to align and adapt the company through strategic renewal had brought many successes with the company leading its peers in many rankings. Bennett contemplated the issues and potential actions for the board to create value across the spectrum of stakeholders as thoughts turned to selecting a new CEO.

Discussion

In the case study we wanted to feature the measures that can be taken by the board to provide integrative responsible leadership in purpose governance for value creation and to connect these activities that the board performs with its strategies for sustainability. The case study, which involves the government as the majority shareholder of Aldridge Energy, demonstrates that the board continuously integrated and balanced the interests of new and extant stakeholders for value creation in the 18 months after the IPO. We have identified four ways by which the board was able to align stakeholders' interests that were significant for increasing its market share, growth prospects, and profitability over the long term.

The board *developed and invested in a network of stakeholder relations* to create options and strategies. The directors of the board generally, and the board chair specifically, acted as coordinators and cultivators of relationships with stakeholders that extended beyond the company (Maak & Pless, 2006). Effective engagement by the board of directors created value with stakeholders through three pathways: (a) communication which enabled the exchange of information between the board and stakeholder groups, such as shareholders; (b) knowledge sharing/learning which helped to produce and diffuse changes needed to improve organisational outcomes; and (c) intrinsic motivation (psychological) which fostered trust, commitment, and an emotional connection (Doh & Quigley, 2014). Engagement by the board of directors promoted relationships that extended beyond a box ticking exercise or a one-off activity which generated an understanding of the needs, interests, and concerns of stakeholders.

The board *integrated the interests of stakeholders* in its strategic decisions. The board's decision to end coal-fired energy generation benefited its stakeholders in two ways: (a) increased shareholder value achieved by cost-cutting with the elimination of an inefficient line of business; and (b) improved community wellbeing and environmental effects with the end of coal-fired generation activities. The board's decision was informed, in part, by an analysis which concluded that the risk of harm to customers was negligible. On the one hand, the board's actions fit a 'win–win' scenario (Porter & Kramer, 2006; Siegel, 2009). On the other hand, the company's purpose guided the board's decision. The board's actions aligned with the rationale of why the utility company was created and its purpose. The directors of the board exercised their decision-making role in what they believed to be congruent with the values, purpose and pursuit of a viable path for the company's future.

The board *reframed its relationship with shareholders consistent with its corporate purpose.* As a board of directors of a publicly listed utility company, it was particularly critical that the shareholders were aligned with the company's purpose and performance. Consistent with good governance, the board generally and the board chair specifically reframed the relationship with its majority shareholder (the government). The shareholder was offered no special or valuable information about the closure of the coal-fired generators and the change in the role of the company as the country's 'energy backstop'. The board operated with independence from the effects of its majority shareholder for its decision, which is consistent with the belief that boards should be insulated from shareholder influence and intervention for decisions within its ambit (Bainbridge, 2003; Blair & Stout, 1999).

Informed by its purpose driven governance, the directors of the board *brought values to bear* on its decisions. The board recognised that historical experiences would not necessarily be value creating in the context of new institutional and retail investors that might be less patient with dividend claims, despite the company's stated value of restrained profit maximisation. The board set the behaviours, ethical norms, and values with its actions and expectations throughout the company and with its stakeholders, including its shareholders. From a purpose driven perspective, the values set by the board underpinned the board's approval of investments into employee training, revised selection and hiring practices, and progressive policies which enabled employees to connect their personal values and the company's purpose (Jones et al., 2018; Pless & Maak, 2011). In this way, the actions of the directors of the board connected both shareholder and stakeholder expectations to the company's values and purpose.

Conclusion

More than 50 years ago, Milton Friedman (1970) argued for a clear separation between the interests of companies, individuals, and government. He set out a framework in which publicly listed companies, as a legal fiction, best serve consumers, employees and shareholders when maximising shareholder value. Other responsibilities—and stakeholders—are best left to individuals and governments. Among its deficiencies, a contractarian view of the corporation fosters a reactive, financial control role for the board of directors with little room for enacting responsible leadership.

We argue that corporate governance and responsible leadership are better served by a conception of the modern company as an entity. The modern company, as an entity, holds a fund consisting of many types of value that it converts to capital as a going concern. However, the creation of many types of value is nontrivial. From our point of view, the integration of responsible leadership and governance calls into relief how boards of directors proactively engage in value creation. We propose the present framework as an instrument to facilitate an understanding of responsibly led boards of directors that differently engage with stakeholders to create value for the company and generate social benefits for the common good. We develop the argument that boards of directors successfully create value to the extent that they able to articulate and share a responsible leadership orientation among directors, between the board and CEO, and with stakeholders (including shareholders) to align practices, behaviours and policies in governing stakeholder and purpose driven companies.

The extension of instrumental and integrative responsible leadership orientations to boards of directors introduces a refinement for stakeholder and purpose governance for value creation. By highlighting different board led responsible leadership orientations in the four cases, we identified issues of performance and opportunity for value creation across stakeholders. Our analysis suggests that boards with an instrumental responsible leadership orientation and stakeholder governance selectively create value with stakeholders, including shareholders, consistent with the corporate goals of the company for growth, profit and market share.

Our analysis also suggests that boards with an integrative responsible leadership orientation and purpose driven governance concertedly shape efforts to bring about social, environmental, and financial objectives. A commitment to corporate purpose enables boards to integrate social objectives into the business model and to balance broader stakeholder interests over the short- and long-term across a range of performance measures including, but not limited to, profit. Our analysis further reveals that long-term, stable block and majority share ownership by government (local and national levels) allow boards to widely and proactively engage with stakeholders to create value. This expands our awareness of the board's leadership role in realising corporate purpose by examining the activities undertaken to transform and align the company for successful evolution.

This expansive approach to value creation, we think, speaks to the enabling potential of responsible leadership integrated with governance to contribute to a better understanding of effective governance practices and leadership processes of boards of directors. Concerning future research, we think that a deeper understanding of board led responsible leadership, which is crucial to strategy, can help us to better understand value creation across stakeholders over time. We also realise the importance of more in-depth investigation of responsibly led boards of directors with different conceptions of what comprises value and for whom (including value creation and appropriation). Finally, an examination of value creation by responsibly led boards of directors in different institutional contexts could help us better understand the implications for those that support and interact with them at the individual, team, organisational and societal levels.

Notes

1 This case study was written with the cooperation of the Lansdowne Group board. All data are based on field research and public sources. The research underpinning this case study included in-depth interviews with the chair, managing director/CEO, directors and executive management appointed in the period 2001–2015. The material produced by the company included the company's annual reports, press releases and notices of annual general meetings, among others. It also featured material produced by third party sources which included newspaper articles and reports, among others.

2 This case study was written with the cooperation of the Auckland International Airport board. All data are based on field research and public sources. The research underpinning this case study included in-depth interviews with directors appointed in the period 1998–2005. The material produced by the company included the company's annual reports, press releases and notices of annual general meetings, among others. It also featured material produced by third party sources which included newspaper articles and reports, among others.

3 This case study was written with the cooperation of the Auckland International Airport board. All data are based on field research and public sources. The research underpinning this case study included in-depth interviews with the chair, former chairs, directors and CEO appointed in the period 2008–2015. The material produced by the company included the company's annual reports, press releases and notices of annual general meetings among others. It also

featured material produced by third party sources which included newspaper articles and reports, among others.

4 This case study was written with the cooperation of the Aldridge Energy board. All data are based on field research and public sources. The research underpinning this case study included in-depth interviews with the chair, directors, CEO and executive management appointed in the period 2009–2015. The material produced by the company included the company's IPO prospectus, annual reports, press releases and notices of annual general meetings, among others. It also featured material produced by third party sources which included newspaper articles and reports, among others.

References

Åberg, C., Bankewitz, M., & Knockaert, M. (2019). Service tasks of boards of directors: A literature review and research agenda in a new era of governance practices. *European Management Journal*, 37(5), 648–663.

Bainbridge, S. M. (2003). Director primacy: The means and ends of corporate governance. *Northwestern University Law Review*, 97(2), 547–606.

Bainbridge, S. (2020). *Corporate law: Concepts and insights* (4th ed.). Foundation Press.

Barratt, R., & Korac-Kakabadse, N. (2002). Developing reflexive corporate leadership: The role of the nonexecutive director. *Corporate Governance: The International Journal of Business in Society*, 2(3), 32–36.

Bartlett, C. A., & Ghoshal, S. (1994). Changing the role of top management: Beyond strategy to purpose. *Harvard Business Review*, 72(6), 79–88.

Blair, M. M., & Stout, L. A. (1999). A team production theory of corporate law. *Virginia Law Review*, 85(2), 247–328.

Bower, J. J., & Paine, L. S. (2017). The error at the heart of corporate leadership. *Harvard Business Review*, 95(3), 50–60.

Christensen, L. J., Mackey A., & Whetton, D. (2014). Taking responsibility for corporate social responsibility: The role of leaders in creating, implementing, sustaining, or avoiding socially responsible firm behaviours. *Academy of Management Perspectives*, 28(2), 164–178.

Cikaliuk, M., Eraković, L., Jackson, B., Noonan, C., & Watson, S. (2020). *Corporate governance and leadership: The board as the nexus of leadership-in-governance.* Elements in Corporate Governance Series. Cambridge University Press.

Clarke, T. (2014). Dangerous frontiers in corporate governance. *Journal of Management & Organization*, 20(3), 268–286.

Conger, J. A., & Lawler, E. E. (2009). Sharing leadership on corporate boards: A critical requirement for teamwork at the top. *Organizational Dynamics*, 38(3), 183–191.

Daily, C., Dalton, D., & Cannella, A. (2003). Corporate governance: Decades of dialogue and data. *Academy of Management Review*, 28(3), 371–382.

Dalton, D. R., Daily, C. M., Ellstrand, A. E., & Johnson, J. L. (1998). Meta-analytic reviews of board composition, leadership structure, and financial performance. *Strategic Management Journal*, 19(3), 269–290.

Doh, J. P., & Quigley, N. R. (2014). Responsible leadership and stakeholder management: Influence pathways and organizational outcomes. *Academy of Management Perspectives*, 28(3), 255–274.

Doh, J. P., & Stumpf, S. A. (2005). Towards a framework of responsible leadership and governance. In J. P. Doh & S. A. Stumpf (eds), *Handbook on responsible leadership and governance* (pp. 3–18). Edward Elgar.

Easterbrook, F. H., & Fischel, D. R. (1996). *The economic structure of corporate law.* Harvard University Press.

Eisenhardt, K. M. (1989). Agency theory: An assessment and review. *Academy of Management Review*, 14(1), 57–74.

Eraković, L., & Jackson, B. (2012). Promoting leadership in governance and governance in leadership: Towards a supportive research agenda. In A. Davila, M. M. Elvira, J. Ramirez & L. Zapata-Cantu (eds), *Understanding organizations in complex, emergent and uncertain environments* (pp. 68–83). Palgrave Macmillan.

Fama, E., & Jensen, M. (1983). Separation of ownership and control. *Journal of Law and Economics*, 26(2), 301–325.

Filatotchev, I., & Nakajima, C. (2014). Corporate governance, responsible managerial behavior, and corporate social responsibility: Organizational efficiency versus organizational legitimacy? *Academy of Management Perspectives*, 28(3), 289–306.

Financial Reporting Council. (2018). The UK corporate governance code. www.frc.org.uk/getattachment/88bd8c45-50ea-4841-95b0-d2f4f48069a2/2018-UK-Corporate-Governance-Code-FINAL.PDF. Accessed 14 February 2021.

Finkelstein, S., Hambrick, D. C., & Cannella, A. A. (2009). *Strategic leadership: Theory and research on executives, top management teams, and boards.* Oxford University Press.

Finkelstein, S., & Mooney, A. C. (2003). Not the usual suspects: How to use board process to make boards better. *Academy of Management Perspectives*, 17(2), 101–113.

Freeman, R. E. (1984). *Strategic management: A stakeholder approach.* Pittman Books.

Freeman, R. E., & McVea, J. (2001). A stakeholder approach to strategic management. In M. Hitt, R. E. Freeman & J. S. Harrison (eds), *The Blackwell handbook of strategic management* (pp. 189–207). Blackwell.

Freeman, R. E., Harrison, J. S., Wicks, A. C., Parmar, B. L., & de Colle, S. (2010). *Stakeholder theory: The state of the art.* Cambridge University Press.

Friedman, M. (1970). The social responsibility of business is to increase its profits. *New York Times Magazine*, 13 September. www.nytimes.com/1970/13/archives/a-friedman-doctrine-the-social-responsibilty-of-business-is-to.html.

Gartenburg, C., & Serafeim, G. (2019). Corporate purpose in public and private firms. https://papers.ssrn.com/sol3/papers.cfm?abstract_id=3440281.

Gunasekara, G. (2013). Privacy as a stakeholder interest in New Zealand: Transparency in corporate governance practices. *New Zealand Business Law Quarterly*, 19(4), 271–294.

Hambrick, D. C., & Mason, P. A. (1984). Upper echelons: The organization as a reflection of its top managers. *Academy of Management Review*, 9(2), 193–206.

Hendry, K. P., Kiel, G. C., & Nicholson, G. (2010). How boards strategise: A strategy as practice view. *Long Range Planning*, 43(1), 33–56.

Hesketh, A. (2019). Leadership of value: Leading the leading indicators for good dividends. In S. Kempster, T. Maak & K. Parry (eds), *Good dividends: Responsible leadership of business purpose* (pp. 141–158). Routledge.

Huse, M. (2007). *Boards, governance and value creation: The human side of corporate governance.* Cambridge University Press.

Huse, M. (2018). *Value creating boards.* Cambridge University Press.

International Federation of Accountants. (2020). Understanding value creation. www.ifac.org/system/files/publications/files/Understanding-Value-Creation_0.pdf.

International Integrated Reporting Council. (2013). Capitals background paper for integrated reporting. https://integratedreporting.org/wp-content/uploads/2013/03/IR-Background-Paper-Capitals.pdf.

Jensen, M. C., & Meckling, W. H. (1976). Theory of the firm: Managerial behaviour, agency costs and ownership structure. *Journal of Financial Economics*, 3(4), 305–360.

Jones, T. M., Harrison, J. S., & Felps, W. (2018). How applying instrumental stakeholder theory can provide sustainable competitive advantage. *Academy of Management Review*, 43(3), 371–391.

Kempster, S., Jackson, B., & Conroy, M. (2011). Leadership as purpose: Exploring the role of purpose in leadership practice. *Leadership*, 7(3), 317–334.

La Porta, R., Lopez-de-Silanes, F., & Shleifler, A. (1999). Corporate ownership around the world. *The Journal of Finance*, 54(2), 471–517.

Maak, T., & Pless, N. M. (2006). Responsible leadership in a stakeholder society. *Journal of Business Ethics*, 66(1), 99–115.

Maak, T., Pless, N. M., & Voegtlin, C. (2016). Business statesman or shareholder advocate? CEO responsible leadership styles and the microfoundations of political CSR. *Journal of Management Studies*, 53(3), 463–493.

Maak, T., & Pless, N. M. (2019). Responsible leadership: Reconciling people, purpose, and profit. In S. Kempster, T. Maak & K. Parry (eds), *Good dividends: Responsible leadership of business purpose* (pp. 36–41). Routledge.

Mayer, C. (2018). *Prosperity: Better business makes the greater good.* Oxford University Press.

Mayer, C. (2020). *Shareholderism versus stakeholderism—A misconceived contradiction: A comment on the 'The illusory promise of stakeholder governance' by Lucian Bebchuk and Roberto Tallarita.* Law Working Paper no. 522/2020. European Corporate Governance Institute. https://ssrn.com/abstract=3617847.

Mayer, C. (2021). The future of the corporation and the economics of purpose. *Journal of Management Studies*, 58(3), 887–901.

Paine, L., & Srinivasan, S. (2019). A guide to the big ideas and debates in corporate governance. *Harvard Business Review*, 14 October. https://hbr.org/2019/10/a-guide-to-the-big-ideas-and-debates-in-corporate-governance.

Pearce, C. L., & Conger, J. A. (2003). All those years ago: The historical underpinnings of shared leadership. In C. L. Pearce & J. A. Conger (eds), *Shared leadership: Reframing the hows and whys of leadership* (pp. 1–18). Sage.

Pearce, C., Wassenaar, C., & Mantz, C. (2014). Is shared leadership the key to responsible leadership? *Academy of Management Perspectives*, 28(3), 275–288.

Pless, N. M., & Maak, T. (2011). Responsible leadership: Pathways to the future. *Journal of Business Ethics*, 98(S1), 3–13.

Pless, N. M., Maak, T., & Waldman, D. A. (2012). Different approaches toward doing the right thing: Mapping the responsibility orientation of leaders. *Academy of Management Perspectives*, 26(4), 51–65.

Pless, N. M., Sengupta, A., Wheeler, M. A., & Maak, T. (2021). Responsible leadership and the reflective CEO: Resolving stakeholder conflict by imagining what could be done. *Journal of Business Ethics.* https://link.springer.com/article/10.1007/s10551-021-04865-6.

Plessis, J. J. du. (2016). Shareholder primacy and other stakeholder interests. *Company and Securities Law Journal*, 34, 238–242.

Plessis, J. J. du. (2017). Corporate social responsibility and contemporary community expectations. *Company and Securities Law Journal*, 35, 30–47.

Porter, M., & Kramer, M. R. (2006). The link between competitive advantage and corporate social responsibility. *Harvard Business Review*, 84(12), 78–92.

Pugliese, A., Bezemer, P.-J., & Zattoni, A. (2009). Boards of directors' contribution to strategy: A literature review and research agenda. *Corporate Governance: An International Review*, 17(3), 292–306.

Siegel, D. S. (2009). Green management matters only if it yields more green: An economic/strategic perspective. *Academy of Management Perspectives*, 23(3), 5–16.

Sjåfjell, B. (2016). Achieving corporate sustainability: What is the role of the shareholder? In H. S. Birkmose (ed.), *Shareholders' duties* (pp. 377–404). European Company Law Series. Kluwer Law International.

Stahl, G., & Sully de Luque, M. (2014). Antecedents of responsible leadership behaviour: A research synthesis, conceptual framework, and agenda for future research. *Academy of Management Perspectives*, 28(3), 235–254.

Stiles, P., & Taylor, B. (2001). *Boards at work: How directors view their roles and responsibilities*. Oxford University Press.

Stroehle, J. C., Soonawalla, K., & Metzner, M. (2019). *How to measure performance in a purposeful company? Analysing the status quo*. Future of the Corporation Series. British Academy.

Thomsen, S. (2020). Value creation and corporate governance. https://papers.ssrn.com/sol3/papers.cfm?abstract_id=3710467.

US Business Roundtable. (2019). *Statement of the purpose of a corporation*. Business Roundtable. https://opportunity.businessroundtable.org/wp-content/uploads/2019/08/BRT-Statement-on-the-Purpose-of-a-Corporation-with-Signatures.pdf.

Vandewaerde, M., Voordeckers, W., Lambrechts, F., & Bammens, Y. (2011). Board team leadership revisited: A conceptual model of shared leadership in the boardroom. *Journal of Business Ethics*, 104(3), 403–420.

van Ees, H., Gabrielsson, J., & Huse, M. (2009). Towards a behavioural theory of boards and corporate governance. *Corporate Governance: An International Review*, 17(3), 307–319.

Vasudev, P. M. (2012). Corporate stakeholders in New Zealand—The present, and possibilities for the future. *New Zealand Business Law Quarterly*, 18(2), 167–180.

Villalonga, B. (2018). The impact of ownership on building sustainable and responsible business. *Journal of the British Academy*, 6(S1), 375–403.

Waldman, D. A. (2011). Moving forward with the concept of responsible leadership: Three key caveats to guide theory and research. *Journal of Business Ethics*, 98 (S1), 75–83.

Waldman, D. A., & Galvin, B. M. (2008). Alternative perspectives of responsible leadership. *Organizational Dynamics*, 37(4), 327–341.

Waldman, D. A., & Siegel, D. S. (2008). Theoretical and practitioner letters: Defining the socially responsible leader. *Leadership Quarterly*, 19(1), 117–131.

Watson, S. (2015). How the company became an entity: A new understanding of corporate law. *Journal of Business Law*, 120(2), 1–24.

Watson, S. (2019). The corporate legal person. *Journal of Corporate Law Studies*, 19(1), 137–166.

Wilson, S., Cummings, S., Jackson, B., & Proctor-Thomson, S. (2017). *Revitalising leadership: Putting theory and practice into context*. Routledge.

6 The Role of the Board in Transitions in Corporate Control

Introduction

Our particular attention in this chapter is on the board's leadership role during the ownership transition. With the term 'transitions in corporate control', we consider initial public offerings (including privatisation), mergers, acquisitions and takeovers; that is, all strategic arrangements under which a company changes its ownership, partially or in full. The change in corporate ownership is ultimately a corporate strategy question. Decisions about ownership change strategy are, therefore, among the key decisions that a board makes, and that requires the participation of all corporate governance actors. Extensive research on the board's involvement in strategy making considers numerous topics relating to the board as a strategic decision-making group, determinants of board strategic involvement and the impact of the board on strategy (for comprehensive reviews see Judge & Talaulicar, 2017; Pugliese et al., 2009). An overarching question in all these contributions is: What role does a corporate board play in setting a company strategy?

The two cases we present illustrate two different situations in which boards demonstrated leadership during ownership transitions. The first case illustrates the position and character of the board in an unsuccessful takeover attempt of New Zealand's largest airport by an overseas financial institution (an institutional bidder). With this case we portray a divided board and highlight where a board does not represent the interests of the current shareholders. The second case tells a story of the board's active role during the preparation period for the initial public offering of a state-owned enterprise in the energy industry. Our focus here is on the board dynamics, teamwork, creativity, board-management relationships and the management of board-shareholder (government) relationship.

Initial public offering (IPO) refers to when a company issues its shares through a public flotation for the first time. This strategy is typically carried out by small and young companies aiming to raise capital for their expansion. IPOs, however, can also be carried out by well-established, privately-owned or state-owned enterprises looking for the various benefits that

DOI: 10.4324/9781003054191-6

come with being publicly traded (Lowry et al., 2017). Takeover is the situation where one company ('the bidder') makes an offer to shareholders of another company ('the target') (Farrar, 2005). For the purpose of this chapter, we focus on the literature that considers characteristics of corporate boards during these two ownership change strategies.

Our privatisation IPO (PIPO) case does not illustrate an implemented method of sale or how the share price was determined, nor does it focus on the IPO process itself. Instead, the focus is on the work of the board during the PIPO process, its structural characteristics (composition) and leadership capabilities (individual and collective). Similarly, our 'takeover case' illustrates the roles, responsibilities and dynamics of the target company's board. Although the case itself does not document legal and financial aspects of unsuccessful takeover attempts, we provide a brief explanation of a corporate governance regulatory framework, so the reader can understand the dispute between the directors, and the shareholders' consequent actions.

Consistent with the definition of responsible leadership provided in Chapter 2, responsible board leadership in the context of ownership transition refers to the board's influence on the process and outcomes of the transition through their active engagement with the company's shareholders, management and external actors. We argue that in this process the board should focus not only on short-term goals and interests of the current owners (maximisation of shareholder's wealth), but also on the benefits/costs that ownership change can bring to the company and community, and therefore, the corporate entity in the long run. In the words of Blair and Stout (1998) directors 'should be free to balance shareholders' interest against those of other stakeholders' (p. 747). We define it as the board acting in the interests of the corporate entity itself thereby benefiting shareholders and other stakeholders. In this chapter, there are three important aspects of board's responsible leadership which are considered in discussing ownership transitions. The first is the board's role and responsibilities in ownership transition. The second is the importance and interplay of the board's composition and capabilities for successful outcomes. The third is the board's responsibility in dealing with other participants in the process. The chapter then presents two case studies, Auckland International Airport and Aldridge Energy. The next section uses the lens of board's roles and responsibilities, composition, reputation and capabilities as well as interactions to explore the insights gained through responsible board leadership in the context of ownership transitions in the two cases. The last section presents conclusions.

The Board's Roles and Responsibilities in Ownership Transition

An initial public offering (IPO) is a major transformational change even for well-established organisations. As it is associated with uncertainty and risk, it requires a company's reorientation in strategies, operations and external relationships (Fischer & Pollock, 2004). Becoming public includes two major adaptations for an organisation: compliance with the formal institutional norms (regulations) regarding the ownership and governance structure, and public disclosure of its strategic intentions and financial results. According to the corporate governance literature, the board's major task during the IPO process is to align the interests of the current owners of the company with those of potential investors (Mak & Roush, 2000) and to help management to complete the transition (Kor et al., 2008).

The main question in the legal discourse on corporate governance in the situation of takeovers (Bainbridge, 2002) is about the role and responsibilities of the board of directors. According to the perspective where 'the board is not a mere agent of the shareholders, but rather is a sort of Platonic guardian serving as the nexus of various contracts that make up the corporation' (Bainbridge, 2002, p. 795), the board is given an authority to make strategic decisions on behalf of the shareholders and the company. Shareholders, however, retain the ultimate ability to control the board in the sense that the shareholders can remove the board. Our approach to responsible board leadership in the entity model requires the board to weigh up the interests of various corporate constituents held in the corporate entity and to evaluate the context in which the entity is operating in order to make decisions that are in the interests of the entity itself.

Consequently, in the process of a takeover, the board is an active agent (Bainbridge, 2002) and has a gatekeeping function (Bainbridge, 2006). The literature has consistently confirmed that 'the recommendation of target directors in takeovers is the most important variable in determining takeover outcome' (Henry, 2005, p. 131). This view is also supported by Singh and Harianto (1989) and Gaddis (1987), who further argue that the board's responsibility in evaluating takeover bids is not only to shareholders (in maximising the economic value of their investments), but also to the organisation and its management. That is, according to Gaddis (1987), the board has a moral obligation to protect the future 'productive capacity' of the organisation.

The duties and responsibilities of company directors concerning ownership transitions in general, and takeovers specifically, are different across various jurisdictions. In New Zealand, takeovers involving issuers are governed by processes and principles set out in the Takeovers Code 1993, which is based on principles of fairness for all shareholders in a takeover. In addition, the Companies Act 1993 requires directors to act in good faith and what they believe to be the best interests of the company (§131) and to exercise their powers for a proper purpose (§133). The somewhat Delphic proper purpose doctrine codified in section 133 had its origins in cases involving takeovers. Boards cannot issue new shares if their primary purpose in doing so is to thwart a takeover rather than raise new capital. New Zealand, unlike comparable jurisdictions, does not have a business judgement rule. The Courts have, however, consistently demonstrated that they are reluctant or unwilling to use the benefit of hindsight to second-guess decisions made by directors. On the other hand, in a battle for corporate control played out in a takeover, directors may use defensive tactics not in the interests of the company but to preserve their positions. The use of such tactics will mean decisions made during that period may come under more intense scrutiny.

Another element discussed in the research on corporate governance and takeovers, and relevant for the understanding of our cases is the ownership structure of the target company. The research has provided some evidence suggesting that the ownership structure of target companies has an influence on directors' decision-making regarding the takeover bids. For example, in the case of a high proportion of blockholder ownership, blockholders perform an active role during takeovers and can influence the recommendations made by the directors (Henry, 2005). The role of the board and its obligations are, however, owed to the company itself not its current shareholders and any particular grouping of them.

Board Composition, Reputation and Capabilities

Capacity and capability of a board are interrelated categories. In a well-designed board, board members have an appropriate balance of knowledge, experience and skills which fit the current company's situation and strategy. To be responsive to the needs of an organisation, the board composition needs to enable directors' active contribution to the company's strategy.

In the case of IPOs, because of their 'liability of market newness', companies aim to signal their legitimacy to potential investors (Certo, 2003, p. 433) by establishing a sound governance structure. This includes appropriate governance arrangements (such as the board committees and a governance charter) and prestigious boards of directors (Certo, 2003; Mizruchi, 1996). Several studies have confirmed the importance of directors' reputations in attracting tangible and intangible resources to a company (Eraković & Goel, 2008; Hillman & Dalziel, 2003; van Ees et al., 2008). Therefore, the appointment of prominent directors to the company whose strategic intent is to attract market investors contributes to the board and corporate reputation.

As Certo (2003) rightly put it, board reputation resides in the subjective evaluation (by others, for example, investors) of directors' objective characteristics such as skills, experiences and social connections. Board reputation has two major facets. The first is associated with the board's structural characteristics. It refers to established (and expected) governance structure and processes, and usually includes attributes such as size, independence, CEO/chair duality, tenure, diversity, directors' expertise and experience, and number and structure of board committees. The second is related to directors' capabilities; that is, the skills, experience, knowledge and networks that individual directors bring to the decision-making process of the board.

Research in structural characteristics has shown that relatively larger boards populated with independent, long-tenured and well connected outside directors, positively influence perceptions of board effectiveness/effective monitoring (Certo et al., 2001; Garcia-Meca & Palacio, 2018; Musteen et al., 2010). For example, according to Musteen et al. (2010), 'greater representation of outside directors on the board can represent an important, visible and well-understood signal of effective governance' (p. 501) as well as indicate a company's potential advantage to access scarce resources and gain insights from different industries.

Thus, it could be anticipated that in preparation for ownership transition (especially PIPOs) companies will appoint highly reputable individual directors to the board; that is, well-educated individuals with significant knowledge of the industry and/or previous experience in IPOs. Such individuals are expected to actively interact with various external participants throughout the process and help management to prepare a sound IPO strategy. Adding directors with financial expertise is of special importance in this regard. Individuals with connections to key stakeholders or with significant interlocking directorships are also desirable members of the board during ownership transitions (Certo, 2003). The research has also demonstrated that in highly regulated industries or in the context where the government has a significant impact, the appointment of board members with political experience (former high governmental officials) is a common practice (Lester et al., 2008; Zattoni et al., 2017).

The literature is inconclusive on the importance of composition of the board for the outcome of takeovers. Studies conducted in the USA and UK (O'Sullivan & Wong, 1998; Shivdasani, 1993) have indicated that the board's composition (that is, the proportion of independent directors, directors' tenure and leadership structure) has an impact on takeover success. On the other hand, research conducted in Australia, which is the most comparable context considering the market for corporate control to New Zealand, has suggested an absence of a significant relationship between board composition characteristics and the outcome of takeovers (Henry, 2004, 2005). The main reason for these differences in findings, as suggested by Henry (2004), is the distinction in legal and institutional frameworks of corporate governance and takeover regulations in these countries.

The second facet, related to board capability, is less visible and more difficult to evaluate (and investigate). Individual capabilities reside in an individual's human and social capital. Individual director's capabilities include their motivation, processing ability, personal networks, skills and knowledge that directors bring to the board and organisation. To perform their task effectively, boards also need to have organising, relationship-building, integration and reconfiguration capabilities (Klarner et al., 2021). Or, in other words, they need to have a collective capability (that is, board 'chemistry'), which will help them govern strategic activities. Each director brings a unique combination of knowledge, skills and experience, but it is a collective effort of the group to utilise knowledge and skills of different individuals on the board. In regard to collective capabilities, the research by Nicholson et al. (2017) has demonstrated that effective boards need to balance supportive and critical director behaviours in the boardroom and build a socialised sense of accountability. Other researchers claim that a good functioning board follows a team production model (Kaufman & Englander, 2005; Machold et al., 2011).

Two assumptions are raised here. First, board members' individual capabilities should complement each other and their joint efforts (working together as a team) would create value for the company (Huse & Gabrielsson, 2012). Second, the board is seen as 'a trustee for the firm as a whole' and, therefore, their major task is to lead and coordinate the work of all organisational participants (Blair & Stout, 1999). Hence, the board is *a nexus of leadership-in-governance* (Cikaliuk et al., 2020).

Interactions between the Board and Other Actors

The ownership transition, be that an IPO or takeover, is a process that involves multiple interactions between the board and numerous internal and external actors. The interactions during this process are omnidirectional and intensive, and include dealings with management, shareholders, external advisers (to the board and the company), government officials, industry experts and key stakeholders. The board holds a formal decision-making authority, but this wide range of actors influence the board's decisions through their agendas, status, dispositions, preferences and biases (Welch et al., 2020) in various stages of the process.

The corporate governance research considering ownership transitions does not pay sufficient attention to these interactions and contexts. The research usually overemphasises the role of the board and CEO as the locus of decisions. It also overlooks the roles and interactions of other actors whose actions, interventions and decisions may influence the outcomes of the transition process. Our privatisation IPO case illustrates how changes in the government decision on the listing sequence of three energy companies caused major pressure and uncertainty for the board.

The work and intensity of building and orchestrating relationships from the perspective of the board also needs to be observed. Here, we specifically draw attention to within-group interactions (i.e. work allocation and interactions within the board) and between-group interactions (i.e. interactions between the board and management; between the board and internal committees; between the board and external adviser groups; between the board and blockholders). The situation of ownership transition, which involves complex tasks and time constraints, requires effective task coordination, efficient exchange of information and critical discussion of alternatives and concerns among the board members. IPOs and takeovers are not regular board tasks (such as monitoring and advice) and, therefore, need intensive informal and formal interactions within the board (Macus, 2008).

Research (and our cases) have demonstrated that interactions between the board and other actors in the ownership transition are a balancing act. This act requires a strong presence and involvement of all board members and constant negotiation efforts with different groups. Within these groups of actors, some are more powerful than others. While the government in privatisation IPOs (or a company founder in a typical IPO) and blockholders in takeovers play the major role, the other actors, such as management and external advisers, can also play an important role in providing information, performing specific activities and evaluating prospective ideas. The board's task is to interpret and audit the information, coordinate their actions, and integrate the ideas.

Case Studies

In this section, two cases illustrate ownership transitions and how they play out for each of the companies through board led responsible leadership. The first case features Auckland International Airport and the takeover attempts. This is followed by Aldridge Energy and its partial privatisation.

Case Study 6.1 Auckland International Airport Takeover Quandary 2006–2007[1]

On 20 November 2007, John Maasland, board chair of Auckland International Airport (AIA), threaded a route through the 800 shareholders and a throng of reporters towards the podium for the annual general meeting. Efforts of board led responsible leadership in governance had not quelled the speculation about the status of the third takeover attempt in four months.

Critics, including block shareholders, were sceptical that a foreign investor with controlling ownership would act in the best interest of stakeholders in New Zealand's gateway to the world. Maasland adjusted his eyeglasses, glanced towards the aspiring shareholder nominee directors who had taken up positions in the front row seats, and launched into his presentation. Even an experienced board chair like Maasland did not see the perils ahead.

Auckland International Airport: Brief History

For a decade, the company operated as a state-owned enterprise, until being privatised in 1998. Major shareholders, Auckland City and Manukau City, retained their block hold of shares with 12.7 per cent and 9.5 per cent. Institutional investors, UBS Nominees Pty Limited and the Commonwealth Bank Group, held 9.7 per cent and 9.5 per cent as of June 2005.

As a top 10 listed company, AIA was a major player in the tourism/transportation industry. The airport, with its 278 operating staff, maintained its status as the second busiest for international passengers in Australasia. Inbound tourism was the most critical value driver of the company with nearly three-quarters of all international passengers transiting through the airport.

Board of Directors (2006)

In August 2006, John Maasland joined the four other independent, non-executive directors and accepted the role as board chair two months later. With his experience as a lawyer, coupled with years of corporate leadership and board governance experience, Maasland brought strategic insight and commercial acumen. Maasland held a number of senior executive positions with Wilson & Horton, a news and media company, including chief executive officer from 1996 to 1998. In 1998, he was appointed to the board of Carter Holt Harvey, Australasia's largest woods product producer of pulp, paper and packaging. He became board chair in 2003 until the company was acquired in 2007.

Anthony Frankham, appointed in 1994, was a chartered accountant with special financial consulting experience, which he brought to the role of director for 14 listed companies, four of which he had served as chair. As a life member and past president of the Institute of Chartered Accountants of New Zealand, Frankham's track record extended to a role on the Takeovers Panel, a government initiative established under the Takeovers Act, which ensured that shareholders had adequate information to assist their decision-making for control-change transactions, such as takeovers and allotments or acquisitions of parcels of shares.

Joan Withers was chief executive officer of Fairfax, New Zealand's largest media company. Following her appointment to the board in 1997, Withers served as a director for publicly listed companies, privately held companies, and state-owned enterprises prior to taking the helm once again in the media industry.

Michael Smith, appointed in 1998, had 29 years of experience with Australasia's largest food and beverage company, Lion Nathan, as an executive and then as a director for the parent company. Smith, founding director of two private equity funds and chair/director of both publicly listed firms and foundations, added to the board's competencies in finance and accounting practices, business development and strategy.

Dr Keith Turner joined the board in 2004. Turner, chief executive officer of Meridian Energy, had experience with major industry reform initiatives in transforming New Zealand's energy sector into a market-driven industry. Along with insight into the political process of reforming industry, Turner added planning and business development expertise to the board.

Becoming New Zealand's Airport (2006–2007)

The board and management reviewed research for an assessment of the company's business model and performance. Their efforts reaffirmed that the company was a key part of the country's economy as well as tourism and transportation infrastructure. To create long-term value for its shareholders, the board sought to reposition the company as New Zealand's airport, as Maasland explained:

> While we remain absolutely committed to the growth of the Auckland region, we also have a significant opportunity and obligation to contribute further to the growth of New Zealand tourism, our country's single largest industry and export earner. We have extended our vision beyond Auckland towards a strongly New Zealand-based positioning. We have adopted a new vision of representing our country.

Seeking a Strategic Partner (2007)

The board created an *ad hoc* committee to examine options for AIA to deliver long-term growth. Smith and Frankham represented AIA in the opportunities being considered, including parties acquiring an ownership interest and supporting AIA's strategic development.

Smith confirmed that the board had been in discussion with parties since May 2007. He explained:

> Some of them have come to us and we have gone out to some of them. We think, depending on who the parties are, that there are some value-enhancing opportunities. That is what we are turning our minds to—people who could bring other things to the party beyond money.

Prior to receiving any formal offers, the board had sought out and received exploratory inquiries from local and international parties. In May 2007, Australia's Macquarie Airports Limited attempted to increase its ownership stake by offering to buy shares. Around the same time, the Canadian Pension Plan Investment Board (CPPIB) had approached block shareholders, Manukau City Investments and Auckland City, with an exploratory offer to purchase their shares. The board issued a 'do not sell' announcement. Shareholders rejected both offers, and CPPIB stated that it did not intend to proceed at that time.

On 10 July 2007, AIA, persistently the subject of takeover speculation for months in the press, confirmed that prospective bidders were conducting due diligence. Smith, who described his role as 'the one fronting most of the negotiations with people', could not release the identity or number of parties involved because non-disclosure agreements were in place.

Transformational Transaction Offers (2007)

DUBAI AEROSPACE ENTERPRISE'S OFFER

On 23 July 2007, Maasland ended the speculation and announced a proposal for Dubai Aerospace Enterprise (DAE) to take a controlling stake in AIA. The day prior to Maasland's announcement, the board had unanimously recommended that shareholders accept, barring a better bid. Smith crafted the press release for the deal which would be voted on at the annual general meeting (AGM) in November. The bid was conditional on a 75 per cent shareholder acceptance and government clearance through the Overseas Investment Office.

The board had commissioned an independent report by a corporate finance advisory firm on the proposed transaction. A copy of the report, the amalgamation proposal, a prospectus, and an investment statement would be released to shareholders in October 2007 in advance of the AGM. Maasland commented, 'We look forward to discussing further details about the merits of this proposal with shareholders and other stakeholders in the weeks ahead'.

AWARENESS-RAISING FOR THE DAE BID

Shareholders' concerns about foreign ownership of strategic assets emerged. Faced with the prospect of the Dubai bid for control of AIA, long-term block shareholder for Manuaku City, Mayor Barry Curtis, disagreed with the board's strategy: 'I am personally totally opposed to a foreign company obtaining a controlling interest in our domestic and international airport'. Curtis explained:

> I treasure our 10.05 per cent stake in the company ... This matter is of major importance to the people of Manukau City, the Auckland region, and New Zealand and I have no hesitation in expressing my opposition to a foreign company taking a controlling interest in our airport. Who knows where this could finish up?

Mayor Curtis explained that he would talk to another block shareholder, incumbent Auckland City Mayor Dick Hubbard, to jointly oppose the bid. With a shareholder threshold approval of 75 per cent required for the deal to proceed, the two shareholders could effectively block the transaction with their combined share ownership.

The strong public reaction did not come as a surprise to Maasland. He acknowledged, 'There was bound to be a bit of concern voiced. One has to accept people will have concerns, but we have to work through it. Let's get the issues out in front now and we'll work through those'.

With local government elections scheduled for October 2007, a month prior to the anticipated shareholder vote, the DAE bid became part of the political discussion. Both Auckland City and Manukau City councils initiated consultations of their residents on the proposed sale of AIA shares. As Auckland Mayor Hubbard pointed out:

> This isn't just about a Dubai-based company, it's whether we sell all or part of our shares. There is no rush, and we will wait until we have all the information and the views of the people before decisions are made.

At the national level, the reaction was similarly negative. Concerns about foreign ownership of assets, monopoly pricing, and profits flowing to overseas investors were raised. Political leaders from the left and right were unified in their objections. The governing Labour Party (a centre-left party) attempted a neutral stance given its obligation to be an impartial regulator of the airport with little success. Trade Minister Phil Goff explicitly gave the Government's backing to those opposed to the deal: 'The Government's view is very much in line with that of 80 per cent of the Auckland public. They don't want to see key public utilities—the airport and the ports authority, the shares in those bodies—sold off'. Prime Minister Helen Clark acknowledged public opposition to the privatisation of such assets and agreed with her Trade Minister's statements. She identified the potential risk that foreign ownership would not be in New Zealand's interest given that 'we are not well positioned to be a major international hub'.

In September 2007, DAE withdrew its bid amid opposition from politicians, block shareholders and the public. Auckland City Council had decided not to sell. On 6 September 2007, after a five-day required 'good faith' consultation between DAE and AIA, the parties agreed that they had no alternative but to terminate the proposed sale.

Manukau City Mayor, Curtis, pointed out that 'The withdrawal of Dubai Aerospace at the end of the day has done us all a favour'. He explained:

> My best advice to the company and its directors is to pay due and proper respect to the significant shareholding of the two local government units and do not take them for granted. I was very surprised by the position they adopted and think the public reaction has been a huge learning curve for the airport company and its directors.

CANADA PENSION PLAN INVESTMENT BOARD (INITIAL OFFER)

Another prospective bidder, Canada Pension Plan Investment Board (CPPIB), submitted a proposal. A majority of the directors did not believe that pursuing the proposal would be in the best interests of shareholders or the company, and they would not recommend the proposed transaction. The board had no intention of making the proposal available to shareholders or the public. Maasland explained the board's position on transparency of the offer for strategic fit and value-add: 'It's the job of the directors to recommend or reject an offer. We're not in the business of just putting it out into the marketplace and saying, "you take a look at it"'.

The sole dissenting director, Smith, believed the proposal was in the best interest of shareholders and should have been put to them with a positive recommendation. The constructive engagement of directors appeared to fall short of expectations. As one director explained:

> There was quite a lot of unease around the board table about the way the chair was handling the whole process. The basic debate about what is right for the shareholder, the process of assessment, and management of the whole takeover bid did crystallise vigorous debates with one end saying, 'long term value' and the other end saying, 'best price for the stock today, sell it'. That debate did not ever really get resolved around the Dubai bid before the Dubai bid was pulled. So, it was still there in the CPPIB bid.

CANADA PENSION PLAN INVESTMENT BOARD (SECOND OFFER)

Undeterred by its initial failure to make a deal with AIA, CPPIB launched a second formal attempt. CPPIB had 'received strong encouragement from Auckland Airport shareholders' that investors wanted to evaluate the proposal.

CCIPB sidestepped the board and sent a new simplified proposal to investors directly. The board repeated its 'don't sell' advice, proposing that shareholders wait for the board's recommendation and an independent adviser's report before acting. With the formal bid in place, the board asked its investment advisers, First NZ Capital and Credit Suisse, to actively solicit other better proposals. 'While we have had discussions with more than 10 parties over the past 18 months, covering a range of local and international entities, these discussions were largely on the basis of a restructuring rather than a takeover', Maasland explained.

Shareholders Step Forward (2007)

The prospective change in ownership of AIA drew the ire of some shareholders. Efforts to communicate with shareholders appeared to cause disappointment. Shareholders were kept informed through the annual report, the interim report, an annual meeting of shareholders, information provided to analysts during regular briefings, disclosure to the NZX and ASX in accordance with AIA's disclosure and communications policy, and AIA's website. Directors considered the disclosure of additional information, 'But much of this information was price sensitive, and because AIA was listed, there was certain information we could not pass on without breaching both NZX's listing rules and the Securities Act', one director explained.

With the local government elections completed, the newly elected Mayor of Auckland, John Banks, believed that the airport's capital structure needed an overhaul: 'The balance sheet is not delivering us the kind of benefits we could otherwise expect as a shareholder in a major international utility and the return on investment of between 2 per cent and 3 per cent is not great', Banks concluded. 'That board needs a big shakeup'.

Following the announcement of the DAE bid, Infratil, an infrastructure investment firm, had increased its AIA holdings to a strategic 6.2 per cent through a joint investment with the New Zealand Superannuation Fund. Lloyd Morrison expressed concern that the board was undermining the value by mixing their objectives. He explained:

> But what has not been clear is what their objectives are—whether they are selling control or whether they are bringing in someone strategically. I think that confusion has destroyed a reasonable part of the value in terms of the outcomes. I think it has deterred the interest of some parties who may have been put off.

Formation of the New Board: Who Would Best Serve Shareholders' Interests?

In preparation for the upcoming AGM on 20 November 2007, block shareholders decided to propose their own nominees for the board for the first time since the company had been listed. Smith, as anticipated, had announced that he would not be standing for re-election following the collapse of the DAE bid and the board's rejection of the initial CPPIB proposal.

Long-standing director Withers was scheduled to offer herself for re-election by the shareholders. Withers was aware that the largest shareholder, Auckland City Council, publicly opposed her standing again. Critics confirmed that Auckland City Council would not support her re-election because 'We don't think the board has run a particularly good process'. She was also aware that Manukau City, the third-largest shareholder, would support her election. Withers personally questioned whether her previous directorship with the financially troubled Feltex, a New Zealand carpet maker, would prevent her re-election. Withers went forward as an independent, non-executive candidate, knowing that she had the unanimous support of the board.

The board was concerned that directors nominated by block shareholders would be beholden to those shareholders and their specific interests. The board decided not to make any recommendations about the shareholder nominee directors because the board 'had no part in finding them'. The decision would be up to the shareholders as to who would best serve shareholders' interests broadly. After all, any shareholder nominee would need to win the majority support of the voting shareholders to be elected.

Lloyd Morrison stepped forward as a prospective non-independent, non-executive director nominated by Infratil. He was chair of Infratil Airports Europe (the holding company of Infratil's European airports) and a director of TrustPower, Infratil Energy Australia and Wellington Airport. His desire to seek a board seat was discouraged by the AIA board. Maasland explained:

> I think Lloyd Morrison has a conflict of interest. We have made that point to him. He disagrees. One thing is he is a director of Wellington Airport, which is not a complementary airport. We do compete. And then there's Whenuapai. He tells me that is also complementary but, frankly I believe our second runway should be where we are going to put it [at Auckland International Airport], not out at Whenuapai.

Morrison publicly refuted the claims, pointing out any potential conflicts could be dealt with appropriately and were 'insignificant compared to the substance of what I can offer'.

John Brabazon offered himself for election. As an investment banker, he had chaired Manukau City Investments, the council's vehicle which held around a 10 per cent stake in the airport. The board classified his nomination by Manukau City as a non-independent, non-executive candidate.

Richard Didsbury was also a new independent, non-executive candidate whose nomination was backed by Auckland City Council. Didsbury, the co-founder of Kiwi Income Property Trust, a publicly listed company that owned and managed retail and commercial property investments, was a director for the former Infrastructure Auckland.

Ushering in Winds of Change

Maasland deftly led the 2½-hour AGM, fielding resolutions for director remuneration, auditors' remuneration, and the re-election and election of directors. Responses to questions raised by shareholders concerning CPPIB's second bid would be limited, Maasland pointed out, because the offer was under review with the board's appointed finance advisers.

RE-ELECTION AND ELECTION OF DIRECTORS

Maasland invited each of the prospective directors to deliver a presentation to the voting shareholders. Withers, seeking re-election, acknowledged shareholder discontent with the board's decision to reject the CPPIB offer following DAE's withdrawal. She stated:

> I realise those who were unhappy with that decision may choose to exercise their views by not supporting my re-election to this board. But personally, I would rather face the prospect of losing my board seat for making what I believe was the right decision rather than keep that seat by making a popular one.

In his presentation, Morrison made the case for securing the 'right cornerstone shareholder' for AIA, acknowledging that NZ businesses had been 'undersold in the past'. He stated that he was 'crystal clear' that he would act in the interests of all shareholders. Morrison announced he would resign from the Wellington Airport board if elected. He stated that any conflict over an investment to transform the military airport at Whenuapai into a civilian airport could be dealt with, if it should materialise.

In Brabazon's presentation to the 800 gathered voting shareholders, he pointed to his ability to exercise independent judgement, 'My responsibility, if elected, is to act in the best interests of all shareholders'. 'Any board that ignores the legitimate concerns of its shareholders does so at its peril'. He noted, 'The status quo is unsustainable. Significantly improved returns to shareholders may be possible'. He pointed out, 'The board should pro-actively lead a restructuring process. A number of operational issues need to come under the microscope as improvements may be possible'.

Didsbury, promoting himself as a 'team player' in his presentation, pointed to a future where AIA property assets could generate 60 per cent of the company's revenue, exceeding aeronautical revenue. He stated that the board's handling of the CPPIB concerned him: 'It may also be true that they did the best they could in the circumstances. It is very easy to criticise'.

CEO RESIGNATION (2007)

Maasland confirmed that he had accepted Don Huse's resignation as CEO, having held the position for five years. For his final presentation at the AGM as CEO, Huse outlined the status of major projects. As one director explained, 'Huse tended to leave the takeover issues to the board and regarded that his function was to keep the company running whilst this diversion was taking everyone else in different directions'.

BOARD ELECTION RESULTS (2007)

All four candidates seeking board seats had been elected. The now seven-member board chaired by Maasland consisted of a combination of long-serving directors, including Frankham, Turner and Withers along with the newly elected directors, Didsbury, Brabazon and Morrison. Maasland shared his thoughts about the effect of the election outcome on board cohesiveness and performance:

> I am delighted with Richard Didsbury. I think he will be a superb addition to the board. I will reserve my decision on John Brabazon. John has very strong views. I hope he will be a good team player. So far as Lloyd Morrison is concerned, and while clearly there will be some conflicts … I think he will bring some good qualities.

He further explained, 'A board can cope with a lot of different opinions once you get the teamwork going and the thing flowing. I'm quite content we'll get a solid board'.

BOARD CHAIR RESIGNATION (2007)

On 27 November 2007, a week after the disclosure of the AGM director election results, Maasland resigned effective immediately. On Maasland's departure, a director stated, 'It was John Maasland's decision to resign but I think it's fair to say that the winds of change were blowing, and he probably took attitudes into account in making his decision'.

After 13 months in the role, Maasland stated, 'It is a very different board and in consequence I feel like I'm a relic of the past. It's not the board I was appointed to and I think there will be some quite different thoughts going forward now'. Maasland noted that the election of 'three particularly strong directors representing major shareholders [present a challenge because] that's going to be their interest'.

Maasland admitted that the failed takeover offers from DAE and CPPIB and internal board dynamics contributed to his decision to step down:

> I think it is better that someone else can take the consensus going forward and does not quite have some of the baggage that I may have in terms of the other bids … it's a new board, it's better for them to start off with a new structure. They were happy to see me go, and at the same time, I am happy to go—I guess it is a meeting of minds in that respect.

The Board's Key Challenges: Where to Go from Here?

The board's strategy to create long term growth by positioning the company for takeover had encountered resistance from multiple stakeholders, including opposition from shareholders. The directors would need to appoint a new board chair, deal with the CPPIB offer, and select a new

CEO. Perhaps more importantly, the directors would need to rebuild confidence with shareholders and other stakeholders that the board could, once again, responsibly lead.

Case Study 6.2 Aldridge Energy Partial Privatisation[2]

It was early April 2014, Stephanie Bennett, chair of Aldridge Energy and the directors gathered to celebrate the company's first day of trading. The initial public offering saw share ownership change significantly while the Crown kept its 51 per cent as planned. With more stakeholders than ever before, Bennett recognised that board led responsible leadership in governance would be needed to shape future corporate performance.

A Brief History (1999–2009)

Aldridge Energy had come a long way from its beginning as a regional, state-owned enterprise following a major reform in the electricity industry in 1999. Over the next decade, the company built capacity to match consumer demand. The company cemented its reputation as a reliable provider for electricity with its non-weather-dependent fossil fuel generators that fed into the transmission grid. The company traded electricity with other power producers to ensure service was not interrupted. It built a client base of electricity and gas customer accounts. By 2009, the company's 30 per cent electricity retail market share was among the largest in the country.

Revised Performance Expectations and a New Chair Appointed

In 2009, the Crown introduced a set of initiatives to strengthen commercial performance, transparency and oversight. Although the Crown owned all the shares in the company, the government expected Aldridge Energy, like other state-owned enterprises, to be as profitable and efficient as comparable private-sector businesses. The company established its own policies for social value-enhancing objectives in line with expectations for state-owned enterprises.

A new board chair, Stephanie Bennett, was appointed by government to bring about these changes. At the time, Bennett was the chair of companies operating in the financial sector and construction industry. She also served as director of an investment savings and insurance company in addition to health- and education-related associations and trusts. Bennett brought relationship building skills, strategy expertise and an extensive network of contacts to the role.

In her first full year as board chair, Bennett worked with the eight, independent non-executive directors and the CEO, Owen Hillman, to map a strategy that would introduce a new strategic direction for the company. Hillman, appointed as CEO in 2008, drew on his extensive domestic and international political, regulatory and environmental management experience to help to shape the plan with the directors. With nearly 20 years of operational, management and leadership experience in heavy industry, including oil and gas, mining and power, Hillman brought a combination of strategic, operational and technical insights to the board's strategy discussions.

In 2010, discussions with the board for the government-directed acquisition of hydro generation assets wrapped up. The company now owned a hydro power scheme, taking Aldridge Energy from a regional to a national company. Its offshore oil and gas joint venture was also fully underway with commercial production. The company adjusted its coal-fired generation capacity to comply with new environmental targets. With these changes to its generation, trade and retail capacity, the company launched a campaign to attract new customers.

Government Signals a Change in Ownership (2011–2012)

In May 2011, the government confirmed it would go ahead with an initial work programme to prepare Aldridge Energy for mixed model ownership. The Treasury accepted the lead for government. Many facets of the mixed ownership programme needed consideration: sequencing, estimated proceeds, offer instrument, offer structure, governance, ownership, scale of share sale, selling syndicate structure, maximising investor participation, marketing and communications, programme management and risk monitoring.

A scoping study, conducted by a Crown-appointed investment firm, identified gaps between the current status of the company and its IPO-readiness status. With the scoping study report in hand, the board and Hillman worked to resolve governance and operational issues. Hillman restructured the executive team. A new chief financial officer with experience in publicly listed companies took over, and a new role as general manager of strategy and business development began. The company upgraded its financial reporting systems, streamlined procured engineering services, and extended a customer-centric orientation throughout its business activities.

The board already supported the governance principles and code, as set out in best practice guidelines for listed companies. From that perspective, selective policy and procedural changes were necessary. The board established a charter that described its specific role and responsibilities, and set out the values, principles and practices that informed its function.

The board did not yet have a nominations committee, because the Crown had handled identification, selection and appointment of directors. The Crown would continue to appoint the board chair and deputy chair. The board had already taken a leading position among listed companies by including gender diversity in its annual report. The company was ready for the next phase of the IPO.

Define the Best Interests of the Company

While the government had concluded that partial privatisation was the best path for Aldridge Energy, the board needed to reach its own conclusion. As directors, they were formally separate from the Crown, and they needed to consider whether, on balance, a partial listing was in the best interests of the company. As one director explained, 'This was essentially a compliance listing, not a capital raising. It was a listing of existing shares, which provides liquidity to shareholders but does not in any way change the capital resources of the company'.

Bennett was highly conscious that every director had to be comfortable with the process, willing to participate, and able to contribute. Using a legal framework, the board worked though 'a logical process for thinking through the question of whether it was acting in the best interests of the company and what that meant', one member of the senior management team explained. A director elaborated on the decision process:

> The most difficult question that you ask is, is it the right thing for the company? That was at the core of everything, and we had to keep addressing it. Stephanie Bennett brought it up a whole series of times over the year before because that is the key question you have to ask. The shareholders make their own decision whether it is in the best interest of them or the citizens of this country. That is not our point. We are there for the company.

Preparation of an IPO

THE IPO DIRECTOR-APPOINTED COMMITTEES (2013–2014)

In 2013, Aldridge Energy entered the IPO preparation phase. Two key committees were established. An IPO Steering Group began working with Bennett as co-chair and Hillman as a member. As the governance committee of the IPO process for Aldridge Energy, the Steering Group was responsible for bringing about the success of the IPO and achieving the best possible outcome. It advised, monitored, reviewed and approved material for the IPO. It received notice of any delays, and it resolved issues that the Due Diligence Committee had escalated or the government had forwarded.

An IPO Due Diligence Committee began with Philippa Mills as co-chair and Craig Taylor as a member. The Due Diligence Committee led the process to ensure that the prospectus had proper preparation—that it was accurate, verified and there were no material omissions. The oversight and coordination included legal, business, financial and accounting due diligence among others. Mills, recognised nationally for her expertise in accounting, brought an ability to look at the numbers and assess the big picture as a director in listed companies, non-profit organisations and professional associations. Taylor, appointed to the board in 2012, added his financial acumen, extensive IPO experience and general management experience to the committee.

ROLE OF THE BOARD IN RELATION TO IPO COMMITTEES

The board recognised that greater IPO preparation would occur if each director contributed, including those who were not directly involved in IPO-related committees. Following IPO committee meetings, the full board received briefings on outstanding issues, helping to identify and reduce risks. 'You cannot get to the end of the IPO process and have directors saying they did not understand', an executive team member commented. Directors had a real appetite and discipline for the IPO process, and they stayed at the centre of it. Hillman pointed out:

> The board as a whole was active. It consumed everything that was generated. I have never seen a board do that before in my experience. You always get somebody that skates along. It read everything we gave it, even the debates when the Due Diligence Committee had to come back to the board for overall board agreement or approval.

Issues before the Board

The board faced three key decisions to position the company for the IPO:

- define its assets;
- define its stance towards investors; and
- define its stakeholder relationships (iwi).

DEFINING ITS ASSETS

As a soon-to-be listed company, Aldridge Energy's financial performance would face greater scrutiny from independent analysts. 'The glare of the public eye means that if you say you are going to deliver a number and you miss it, it is a very big problem', explained one director.

> The IPO process forced management, in particular, to really consider what they were doing well, what they could do better, which assets maybe weren't as good as historically they had been, what were the sacred cows. They really had to get them out all onto the table before the IPO, because you did not want to have something suddenly turn up after the event and be a big surprise.

The scoping study singled out the oil and gas field joint venture, noting it was 'not sure' whether to keep it as part of the company. The board needed clarity in defining the nature of its assets for the IPO. It acquired detailed financial information from management about scenarios with/without the oil and gas joint venture. While the oil and gas field was initially developed for thermal generation fuel security, the role had evolved. The board clarified that the oil and gas joint venture was a strategic investment contributing one third of the company's earnings. The Crown, which could have directed its divestiture, agreed. The oil and gas joint venture stayed.

DEFINING ITS STANCE TOWARDS INVESTORS

Initially, the board planned to produce a conventional prospectus statement. Mills, co-chair of the Due Diligence Committee, learned of a simplified disclosure prospectus for potential investors. Bennett and Mills discussed the different approaches: an innovative investment statement (short form) and a traditional prospectus (long form). Both contained information about what the company did, its strategy, capital structure, share offering details and consolidated financial information. They differed significantly on risk information.

Once Bennett and Mills became aware of this option, they took it to the board. The Crown's legal advisers opposed this approach, pointing out that 'the Crown did not want to test or innovate in the market'. From a market point of view, the new short-form investment statement was attractive, but the Crown remained indecisive. Bennett concluded that the whole prospectus issue was a matter of judgement, and that the board would have the final word.

The prospect of stepping outside of the conventional approach to adopt an innovative model 'weighed heavily on the mind of the board'. 'The board was balancing government regulation and political requirements with making sure it got the right outcomes for the company', one executive explained. The debate among the directors concerned what was in the best interest of the company for the prospectus. The 'directors had a strong view that was well informed on both the knowledge of the market and the quality of the asset as an offering into the market—its unique value proposition', which informed the debate. 'It was a big move', another director commented. 'This is where the leadership of Bennett in particular really helped us all to see the bigger picture', a director explained. 'It was a point of difference for us because we could nicely summarise into 60 or 70 pages, what otherwise had taken 400 pages to do. We believed that would definitely appeal to retail investors'. After several meetings, it was unanimous that the board would use that innovative investment statement.

DEFINING ITS STAKEHOLDER RELATIONSHIPS (IWI)

One of the most sensitive issues the board faced was its relationships with iwi. The company operated its generation activities throughout the country. It had to balance its business activities with economic, environment and social issues. The types of relationships that the company had with iwi were many and varied.

In 2009, Bennett had embarked on renewed efforts to build constructive relationships. While looking for a resolution to a protracted case about resource consent issues, Bennett heard the phrase: 'It is a matter of the willingness and the meeting of minds'. It became an important concept for Bennett in working with her team to develop a solution and to end a legal dispute. The approach involved looking beyond the conventions of the situation and asking, 'what was the right thing to do?' Others adopted this approach, and the board soon realised that by doing the right thing, it ended up doing the most effective thing too. Hillman was resolute that the IPO would not affect the relationships that had developed:

> We believed we could still be a commercial outfit and still deal with people honestly and fairly. It was getting over that hesitation that suddenly we were going to become something different than what we were. One of the most sensitive things was getting the board to accept that what had worked for us in the past was still going to work for us in the future.

'A lot of our time, if we can invest in relationships that then allow us to be commercially effective, we do that', Bennett commented. The board decided to 'step up its stakeholder engagement'. A director explained:

> One of the key concerns of iwi in particular was once the IPO had gone through, would we still have the same chair. There was a concern because of the goodwill and the relationships that had been built pre-IPO with the chair and the CEO and senior management, that this IPO process might involve looking for a new chair or CEO, and therefore, undo all the good work that had been done. So, it was giving reassurance that this was a company that stood behind its objectives around stakeholder engagement. Finding ways to reinforce that message is what we did pre- and during the IPO, and post-IPO.

Bennett pointed out, 'The relationship issue is enormously important'. Developing and maintaining relationships with iwi and the local communities in which the company operated allowed for a different risk profile in the investment statement.

Engagement throughout IPO Planning and Preparation

BOARD–MANAGEMENT RELATIONSHIP

Throughout the planning and preparation phases of the IPO, the board and management worked together closely. An experienced IPO project manager joined the process: 'He lived and breathed the IPO, day in and day out'. Initially, Hillman explained, 'We were not able to turn stuff around as quickly as the board would have liked, because we were still trying to run the business. Once we got the project manager in, it became much easier to do that, and then the board engagement became completely different'.

Over time, the dual priorities taxed directors and management. Bennett pointed out, 'The workload was enormous. Running a big company and running a due diligence process across a long period of time like that, it did put a strain on the executive and on the directors'. It was important to ensure that 'business as usual did not falter and still make sure the company was performing properly'.

The directors were mindful of constructive communication, mutual support, and openness to new ideas as leadership practices that sustained board-management collaboration while delivering a successful IPO:

> There were times they had adopted a very conventional approach to a number of the work streams that they were tasked with during the IPO. The board gave them the confidence to then come back and perhaps try different approaches.... As an overall team, the board and senior management, we were very solid and tight knit. Obviously with the robust debate as a given, that is what helped us get through relatively smoothly. That could not have happened without the strong leadership of the board.

CHAIR–CEO–CROWN RELATIONSHIPS

During the preparation phase, a lot of the focus was on the boundary between the shareholder responsibilities and shareholder actions, and the board and company responsibilities and actions. It involved 'ensuring that we had a good interchange between those two parties and that they were both acting appropriately in the interests of everyone', as one director explained. It involved 'leadership that was prepared to push the boundaries but at the same time ensure that there was the technical oversight to ensure compliance'. Another director pointed out, the 'communication with Treasury and government about how things were going was led by Stephanie Barrett with Owen Hillman'.

The approach reflected the long-standing relationship between Barrett and Hillman. Barrett explained: 'My relationship with the chief executive is critical, and I spend a lot of time with him'. She elaborated: 'A chair and her role with a chief executive is not to do the chief executive's job, but to work out if there are things that may strategically either hold the company back, or sometimes is it just a matter of encouraging the chief executive to consider different approaches'.

Barrett and Hillman's leadership approach extended to the board and the IPO committees and how they engaged with the Crown. Hillman explained the mindset of the IPO process:

> We started from the premise that they own the shares. They are selling their shares; they are not mine. I must figure out how I am going to help them do this, minimise the disruption and get the best outcome for them and us at the same time.

To bring about the alignment of goals, a director pointed out, 'We worked more closely and more aligned and saw the government as a partner rather than as antagonists. We operated on the basis that we want to get this thing done; we both have the same agenda'. Another director commented, 'It was our reputations on the line; we wanted them to sell it well, and we wanted it to go well'.

The board and management used leadership processes to influence the IPO process where it made sense. 'Treasury drove a process. We influenced it. We made things simple. Every time a problem came up, we fixed it, and we did not complain about it'. One director pointed out, 'as a result, it did tend to take our thoughts and continually asked for suggestions as to what could be done better'. Bennett pointed out:

> Apart from two or three particular legal elements that the Crown took total responsibility for—around pricing for example—they sought our advice … While they were responsible for some of those calls, there were still high levels of engagement both with the board and myself, in our forming a view. It also occurred with Owen Hillman and myself in engaging with the Crown and relaying that view. So, of the cast of thousands of advisers in those discussions, it was down to one or two of the key Treasury people, and sometimes one or two of the external people.

The board recognised that the rationale for the intense scrutiny during each facet of the process was, in part, due to the nature of the shareholder, as a director explained:

> It is a government process: they need to make sure that everything is done right because they have an opposition sitting in Parliament, and it is going to pick on the smallest detail. They are forced into a process which is ticking every box two or three times.

The IPO Transaction

SIZE AND STRUCTURE OF IPO

Consistent with public statements at the outset of the mixed model ownership programme, Crown ownership was set at 51 per cent, no investor could hold more than 10 per cent of shares, and domestic investors would hold 85 per cent of shares.

SEQUENCE

The government set the sequence for the listing of the energy companies. The board did not know the overall order. This uncertainty created additional work and expense, as one director explained:

> We had to wait in queue, which cost money because we appointed advisers and we prepared; we missed out on being number one. Then we prepared to be number two; we missed out. Government should have told us we were number three. It did not.

Uncertain if Aldridge Energy would be first, second or third among the companies being listed by government, the board maintained a constant state of readiness.

MARKETING THE IPO TO ATTRACT INVESTORS

The board was mindful that the marketing of the share sale needed to appeal to prospective retail and institutional investors. The board wanted a 'very clean message and a very consumer-oriented story' that highlighted the strengths, strategy, market opportunity and why Aldridge Energy was a good investment opportunity. In the promotional phase, Hillman, the chief financial officer, and the investor relations manager travelled throughout February, March and April 2014 to meet prospective domestic and international shareholders.

The IPO was a success. In early April 2014, the company welcomed new investors on the first day of trading, which was among the highest number of shareholders for any company in the country. The Crown had to invoke share ownership limits so that investors did not miss out on the over-subscribed new issue. The energy company had successfully transitioned from a state-owned enterprise to mixed model ownership.

The Board's Next Steps

Bennett and the directors were mindful that the celebration of the company's listing would soon give way to the realities of new shareholders' expectations and stakeholders' interests in the performance of the energy company. Bennett recognised that responsible leadership in governance would be needed to continue the collaboration among the directors, senior management, and stakeholders in the pursuit of Aldridge Energy's transformation.

Discussion

With these two cases, we aimed to draw attention to the issues of responsible board leadership in the context of ownership transitions (PIPO and takeover). Both cases deal with strategic leadership by the board and demonstrate the boards' active role in the strategic decision-making process. Although these two cases illustrate different scenarios and outcomes of ownership transitions and different dynamics on two boards, there are several important lessons that can be learned from both studies.

First, the most important question of corporate governance is the fiduciary duty of directors or *the responsibility of directors—to the company and shareholders*. In our corporate governance model where the company is seen as an entity, directors should act in the best interest of a company, as the company is more than a shareholder fund (see more in Cikaliuk et al., 2020). Both our cases illustrate situations in which the boards faced a dilemma in whose interest to serve. From the outset, the board of the energy company considered the interest of the company. Although there was some ambiguity and disagreements in relationships between the board and shareholder (government) during the process, in general, the interests of the company and shareholders were aligned—successful initial public offering. For the airport company, the question of the board's responsibility was detrimental. Throughout the course of multiple takeover offers, there were two major issues in this regard. First, it was not clear that the board and block shareholders had the same interests. Second, the board itself was divided in making recommendations—some members of the board focused on the long-term, strategic needs of the company whereas others were looking at what was right for the shareholders in terms of their control retention. The whole takeover saga resulted in a crisis, the resignation of two board members who were the major actors in the process and formation of the new board (the block shareholders proposed their own nominees for the board). In this case, the shareholders exercised their ultimate right of control over the company's affairs (Hansmann & Kraakman, 2001).

Second, the *composition of the board is not a sufficient indicator* that the board is an effective organisational body. In the introduction we emphasised the importance of a board's structural characteristics, as well as individual and collective capabilities in the process of ownership transitions. Our two cases demonstrate that the collective capability, or the right match within the board, is significant in the situation when the board faces a novel and complex situation with long-term consequences. A number of interconnected factors inform a decision on ownership transition and board members, individually and as a group, need to be able to sense, process and openly communicate all issues. The presence of board members with appropriate knowledge and experience may signal to potential investors, as suggested by some research (Certo, 2003), that the organisation has been efficiently governed, but it does not mean that the board has the right leadership skills and internal processes for the job at hand. The PIPO case in the energy company shows that the board was carefully designed with a clear charter. The new CEO and chair were appointed in 2008/2009 to introduce new strategic directions for the company (SOE) and to make it profitable. In preparation for an anticipated PIPO, they 'handpicked' new board members selecting those who had credentials, motivation and skills to contribute to the company's IPO. The division of labour and coordination of activities on the board were clear from the outset. The chair's major concerns were external stakeholders and advisers, the deputy chair was guiding and coordinating all board and management IPO activities, and other members of the board were working on specific tasks with management. The board and executive management were functioning as a team and all decisions were made by consensus.

On the other hand, the first case which illustrates the board's handling of a takeover situation in the airport company shows a lack of integration and sense of common interest on the board. The composition of this board was sound—a high percentage of outside, reputable directors with past and current appointments in multiple publicly listed firms. However, an assumed heterogeneity of interests represented in the board and the absence of mechanisms for regulating conflicts between shareholders' interests and the board undermined the board's ability to resolve the takeover quandary.

Third, *the board's use of knowledge and skills* (individual capability) and *teamwork* (collective capability) are important conditions in anticipating what potential investors and current shareholders are looking for. Sensing the vibe of the capital market, dealing with uncertainty, knowing the company's operations, building a community of interests and openly sharing information, past experience and concerns all lead to the board's effectiveness in dealing with their major task—leading the ownership transition process. In creating long-term value for their shareholders and the company, the board needs to demonstrate adaptability to alternative scenarios, timeliness in their actions and decisions, and integrative and innovative thinking. In the PIPO process of the energy company, the special board committee and chair convinced the whole board to offer innovative, non-standard final offering documents (the prospectus) to potential investors, even though the external adviser opposed the idea, and the main shareholder was hesitant.

Fourth, *the board is a locus of interactions* between a multitude of actors in the ownership transition. In early stages of IPO/takeover preparations, the board needs to be aware of the various agendas of all actors involved, including management and directors. And they need to clearly communicate all concerns explicitly and implicitly voiced. It is evident from both cases how the board's encounters (or lack of) with various actors had implications on the activities, decisions and the final outcomes. The PIPO case illustrates how active the board was, regularly interacting with all parties involved—from the government as the shareholder and regulator to a number of external agencies and internal *ad hoc* committees. The takeover case, however, demonstrates how the target company's commercially-oriented board missed an opportunity to purposefully interact with their public-sector blockholders. If they did, they would have been mindful of the shareholders' potential (and real) opposition to foreign bidders. The board is an independent governance body, but in creating long-term value for the company and its owners, the board needs to work interdependently with the shareholders, management and a range of relevant stakeholders.

Fifth, *board and management are in this together.* Preparing a company for the first public offering or selling it partially or as a whole to another company requires from the board and management team a massive joint effort. The responsibility for the decision of the ownership transition ultimately rests with the board (and shareholders), but at a practical level the board does not always know enough detail about the company's operations. For that very reason, boards must work in partnership with management, whose capabilities comprise an important factor in ensuring the success of this strategy. This strategic partnership is reflected in relationships with internal and external stakeholders that they each develop to achieve the best deal for the company and its shareholders.

Conclusion

Ownership transition represents one of the most important and powerful strategic changes faced by boards of directors. They are highly significant considerations undertaken by the board which can have long-term effects on the social and economic objectives of the company. Despite the attention paid to the relationship between performance outcomes and ownership structure, few have examined the board's roles and responsibilities, board characteristics and interactions in effecting changes in share ownership structure. In this chapter, we examined the board's roles and responsibilities and board composition, reputation and capabilities with interactions undertaken by the board to bring about an ownership change. We develop the argument that boards of directors differently enact responsible leadership which enable and hinder ownership transitions. By highlighting both successful and unsuccessful changes in ownership, we distil insights for researchers of boards of directors and those that support and interact with them. We underscore the need for further studies to link board led responsible leadership with ownership transitions.

Notes

1 This case study was written with the cooperation of the Auckland International Airport board. All data are based on field research and public sources. The research underpinning this case study included in-depth interviews with directors appointed in the period 2006–2007. The material produced by the company included the company's annual reports, press releases and notices of annual general meetings, among others. It also featured material produced by third party sources which included newspaper articles and reports, among others.

2 This case study was written with the cooperation of the Aldridge Energy board. All data are based on field research and public sources. The research

underpinning this case study included in-depth interviews with the chair, directors, CEO and executive management appointed in the period 2009–2015. The material produced by the company included the company's IPO prospectus, annual reports, press releases and notices of annual general meetings, among others. It also featured material produced by third party sources which included newspaper articles and reports, among others.

References

Bainbridge, S. M. (2002). Director primacy in corporate takeovers: Preliminary reflections. *Stanford Law Review*, 55(3), 791–818.

Bainbridge, S. M. (2006). Director primacy and shareholder disempowerment. *Harvard Law Review*, 119, 1735–1758.

Blair, M. M., & Stout, L. A. (1998). Team production in business organizations: An introduction. *Journal of Corporate Law*, 24, 743–750.

Blair, M. M., & Stout, L. A. (1999). A team production theory of corporate law. *Virginia Law Review* 85(2), 247–328.

Certo, S. T. (2003). Influencing initial public offering investors with prestige: Signalling with board structures. *Academy of Management Review*, 28(3), 432–446.

Certo, S. T., Daily, C. M., & Dalton, D. R. (2001). Signaling firm value through board structure: An investigation of initial public offerings. *Entrepreneurship Theory and Practice*, 26(2), 33–50.

Cikaliuk, M., Eraković, L., Jackson, B., Noonan, C., & Watson, S. (2020). *Corporate governance and leadership: The board as the nexus of leadership-in-governance*. Elements in Corporate Governance Series. Cambridge University Press.

Companies Act 1993 (New Zealand). https://legislation.govt.nz/act/public/1993/0105/latest/DLM319570.html#DLM319572.

Eraković, L., & Goel, S. (2008). Board–management relationships: Resources and internal dynamics. *Management Revue*, 19(1–2), 53–69.

Farrar, J. (2005). *Corporate governance: Theories, principles and practice* (2nd ed.). Oxford University Press.

Fischer, H. M., & Pollock, T. G. (2004). Effects of social capital and power on surviving transformational change: The case of initial public offerings. *Academy of Management Journal*, 47(4), 463–481.

Gaddis, P. O. (1987). Taken over, turned out. *Harvard Business Review*, 65(4), 8–22.

Garcia-Meca, E., & Palacio, C. J. (2018). Board composition and firm reputation: The role of business experts, support specialists and community influential. *Business Research Quarterly*, 21(2), 111–123.

Hansmann, H., & Kraakman, R. (2001). The end of history for corporate law. *Georgetown Law Journal*, 89, 439–468.

Henry, D. (2004). Corporate governance and ownership structure of target companies and the outcome of takeovers. *Pacific–Basin Finance Journal*, 12(4), 419–444.

Henry, D. (2005). Directors' recommendations in takeovers: An agency and governance analysis. *Journal of Business Finance & Accounting*, 32(1–2), 129–159.

Hillman, A. J., & Dalziel, T. (2003). Boards of directors and firm performance: Integrating agency and resource dependence perspectives. *Academy of Management Review*, 28(3), 383–396.

Huse, M., & Gabrielsson, J. (2012). Board leadership and value creation: An extended team production approach. In T. Clarke & D. Branson (eds), *The Sage handbook of corporate governance* (pp. 233–253). Sage.

Judge, W. Q., & Talaulicar, T. (2017). Board involvement in the strategic decision making process: A comprehensive review. *Annals of Corporate Governance*, 2(2), 51–169.

Kaufman, A., & Englander, E. (2005). A team production model of corporate governance. *Academy of Management Perspectives*, 19(3), 9–22.

Klarner, P., Yoshikawa, T., & Hitt, M. A. (2021). A capability–based view of boards: A new conceptual framework for board governance. *Academy of Management Perspectives*, 35(1), 123–141.

Kor, Y. Y., Mahoney, J. T., & Watson, S. (2008). The effects of demand, competitive, and technological uncertainty on board monitoring and institutional ownership of IPO firms. *Journal of Management & Governance*, 12(3), 239–259.

Lester, R. H., Hillman, A., Zardkoohi, A., & Cannellar Jr., A. A. (2008). Former government officials as outside directors: The role of human and social capital. *Academy of Management Journal*, 51(5), 999–1013.

Lowry, M., Michaely, R., & Volkova, E. (2017). Initial public offerings: A synthesis of the literature and directions for future research. *Foundations and Trends in Finance*, 11(3–4), 154–320.

Machold, S., Huse, M., Minichilli, A., & Nordqvist, M. (2011). Board leadership and strategy involvement in small firms: A team production approach. *Corporate Governance: An International Review*, 19(4), 368–383.

Macus, M. (2008). Board capability: An interactions perspective on boards of directors and firm performance. *International Studies of Management & Organization*, 38(3), 98–116.

Mak, Y. T., & Roush, M. L. (2000). Factors affecting the characteristics of boards of directors: An empirical study of New Zealand initial public offering firms. *Journal of Business Research*, 47(2), 147–159.

Mizruchi, M. S. (1996). What do interlocks do? An analysis, critique, and assessment of research on interlocking directorates. *Annual Review of Sociology*, 22(1), 271–298.

Musteen, M., Datta, D. K., & Kemmerer, B. (2010). Corporate reputation: Do board characteristics matter? *British Journal of Management*, 21(2), 498–510.

Nicholson, G., Pugliese, A., & Bezemer, P. J. (2017). Habitual accountability routines in the boardroom: How boards balance control and collaboration. *Accounting, Auditing & Accountability Journal*, 30(2), 222–246.

O'Sullivan, N., & Wong, P. (1998). The impact of board composition and ownership on the nature and outcome of UK takeovers. *Corporate Governance: An International Review*, 6(2), 92–100.

Pugliese, A., Bezemer, P.-J., Zattoni, A., Huse, M., Van den Bosch, F. A. J., & Volberda, H. W. (2009). Boards of directors' contribution to strategy: A literature review and research agenda. *Corporate Governance: An International Review*, 17 (3), 292–306.

Shivdasani, A. (1993). Board composition, ownership structure and hostile takeovers. *Journal of Accounting and Economics*, 16(1), 167–198.

Singh, H., & Harianto, F. (1989). Management–board relationships, takeover risk, and the adoption of golden parachutes. *Academy of Management Journal*, 32(1), 7–24.

van Ees, H., van der Laan, G., & Postma, T. J. (2008). Effective board behaviour in the Netherlands. *European Management Journal*, 26(2), 84–93.

Welch, X., Pavićević, S., Keil, T., & Laamanen, T. (2020). The pre–deal phase of mergers and acquisitions: A review and research agenda. *Journal of Management*, 46 (6), 843–878.

Zattoni, A., Witt, M. A., Judge, W. Q., Talaulicar, T., Chen, J. J., Lewellyn, K., & van Ees, H. (2017). Does board independence influence financial performance in IPO firms? The moderating role of the national business system. *Journal of World Business*, 52(5), 628–639.

7 CEO Succession

Introduction

From the perspective of responsible leadership, one of the most important 'how' questions concern how companies and their boards of directors responsibly lead to create sustainable business success. The 'how' of responsible leadership extends beyond the actions and decisions of boards of directors to create a diverse and inclusive environment examined in the previous chapter to CEO succession. In this chapter, we focus on CEO succession and responsible leadership processes that boards of directors can mobilise to select CEOs who are able to lead stakeholders inside and outside of the company to achieve its purpose or improve its capability to achieve its purpose.

The past two decades or so have been characterised by an evolving number of tasks performed by boards of directors as companies have coped with a rapidly changing environment. Pressures from the new global environment, changes in regulation, and developments in technology have resulted in boards of directors looking to CEOs to integrate elements and practices of employee standards, environmental protection, product sustainability, inclusive value creation and ethical business practices.

Amidst the shifting environment, ensuring the continuity of organisational functioning and enabling a smooth CEO transition remain the two key tasks for the board of directors (Khurana, 2001; Biggs, 2004). Studies that examine the preparedness of boards of directors for CEO selection, whether it is an anticipated or unexpected change in the top executive position, suggest that more than half of the boards need to improve their succession planning (Castañón Moats & DeNicola, 2021; for a review see Harrell, 2016). The significant corporate resources involved and the limited preparedness by boards for CEO succession has prompted some boards of directors to explore how they can be more effective in fulfilling one of its most important tasks. This raises an interesting question: what factors distinguish between more and less effective boards of directors for CEO succession and selection?

Central to this undertaking is the recognition that the process of CEO selection requires long-term preparation and engagement of the whole

DOI: 10.4324/9781003054191-7

board, particularly the chair and outgoing CEO. The process itself has internal and external facets. Internally, it involves complex formal and informal consultations between the chair, outgoing CEO, other board members, and potential internal candidates. Externally, the process includes the majority shareholder and other important stakeholders who need to be informed (if not engaged) about the change in the company's leadership. In this chapter, we consider how responsibly led boards of directors' behaviours and actions affect the CEO succession and selection process, paying special attention to the psychological and knowledge-based pathways mobilised by boards in the performance of this task.

This chapter is structured into five sections. The first section examines responsible leadership and executive succession. In the second section, we examine psychological and knowledge-based pathways of responsible leadership mobilised by boards of directors in the conduct of board tasks focusing on CEO succession. We then examine the responsible leadership role of the board chair in relation to CEO succession and board dynamics. In the next section, we present a case study. We conclude with a discussion of theoretical and practical implications.

Responsible Leadership, Influence Pathways and Board Tasks: CEO Succession

Although responsible leadership has emerged only recently as a construct in the leadership literature, there is broad agreement that responsible leadership leads to improved firm performance in some way, such as creating stakeholder relationships (Doh & Stumpf, 2005; Maak et al., 2016), improving economic, environmental and social value (Waldman, 2011; Waldman et al., 2020) to realise an ethically sound shared business vision or purpose (Maak & Pless, 2006; Waldman & Galvin, 2008). Responsible leadership literature frames these performance improvements, in part, through the decision-making processes of those at the apex of the company (Maak & Pless, 2006; Pless et al., 2012; Waldman & Galvin, 2008; Waldman et al., 2020). The board, in its decision-making capacity for the entity, balances relationships with legitimate stakeholders over time.

Responsible leadership has been the focus of an emergent theoretical and conceptual literature, but few empirical analyses have explored the processes or pathways of responsible leadership in large, listed companies by boards of directors through CEO succession planning and selection. Our approach, which draws on Doh and Quigley (2014), underscores the importance of deliberate influence pathways, such as psychological and knowledge-based processes, in a stakeholder approach to affect organisational and board dynamics involving CEO succession planning and selection and, in so doing, shape firm outcomes.

The psychological and knowledge-based pathways include an array of responsible leadership behaviours and actions that influence outcomes at four levels: individual, team, organisational and societal. As a multilevel construct, the psychological and knowledge-based pathways of responsible leadership coexist and interact, as opposed to operating as separable, mutually exclusive processes (Doh & Quigley, 2014). This perspective allows us to place the board of directors at the centre of the discussion on responsible leadership in governance. It also means, following on from Pearce et al. (2014, p. 284), that we recognise CEO 'selection is perhaps the single most important action that can foster responsibility'.

The topic of executive succession holds an important place in corporate governance and management literature in general. Researchers have mainly focused their investigations on the insider versus outsider CEO succession (e.g. Boeker & Goldstein, 1993; Cannella & Lubatkin, 1993; Clutterbuck, 1998; Zhang & Rajagopalan, 2010), the effects of succession on corporate performance (e.g. Carroll, 1984; Zajac, 1990; Shen & Cannella, 2002; Lee, Phan & Yoshikawa, 2008), post succession senior executive turnover (e.g. Friedman & Saul, 1991; Shen & Cannella, 2002) and pitfalls in CEO searches (e.g. Khurana, 2001; Biggs, 2004).

The existing literature tends to be focused on the *context* (i.e. conditions and antecedents) and the *outcome* of the succession process (i.e. decision and effects), but does not convincingly elaborate on the succession *process* itself. Even after some decades of research on the topic, only a handful of scholarly studies specifically address the board's CEO succession process (Weisbach, 1988; Zajac & Westphal, 1996; Ocasio, 1999).

Our approach in this chapter supports growing research on boards of directors that has moved beyond formal, static and impersonal legal models, based primarily on agency theory, to multidimensional understanding of board roles as an organisational mentor, leader, motivator, and value creator (see for example, among others, Huse, 2007; Minichilli et al., 2009; van Ees et al., 2009; Vandewaerde et al., 2011; Yar Hamidi & Gabrielsson, 2014). In order to generate fresh ideas and gain a better understanding of the complexities inherent in board task performance, contemporary research highlights a need by responsibly led boards for processes that critically reflect on the relevance of current CEOs, the necessity for change, and the eventual realisation of CEO transition. To date, researchers have not explored psychological and knowledge-based pathways of responsible leadership in the context of CEO succession planning and selection by boards of directors, overlooking ways that boards can promote responsible leadership and firm performance.

Psychological Pathway and CEO Succession

The psychological pathway of responsible leadership involves understanding human behaviour and mental processes and the way in which these interactions are affected by an individual's psychology, mental state, and external environment (Defillippi & Ornstein, 2003; Doh & Quigley, 2014).

Psychological pathways extend the responsible leadership literature by examining three processes through which leader inclusivity of stakeholders' perspectives can bring about positive outcomes for stakeholders and organisations (Doh & Quigley, 2014). The three subprocesses are trust, psychological ownership, and commitment.

Recent empirical research that examines the psychological pathway of responsible leadership has seen increased empirical support (for a review see Stahl and Sully de Luque, 2014). Empirical studies in this research stream document significant and persistent differences among companies with stakeholder inclusive approaches in employee commitment (Fragouli & Alhaider, 2020) and talent retention (Doh et al., 2011). However, when it comes to the creation and adjustment of firm level strategies and decisions senior executives and boards play a particularly critical responsible leadership role (Waldman et al., 2020; Waldman & Balven, 2014; Maak et al., 2016).

In an empirical study of business leaders and entrepreneurs of for-profit and non-profit organisations from different industries and countries, Pless et al. (2012) found that the meaning of responsibility varied with the breadth of the stakeholder groups considered and the degree to which accountability towards others was narrow or broad. To the two classic orientations, economist and idealist, they added integrative and opportunity-seeker orientations (the latter relabelled as instrumental orientation, see Maak et al., 2016) of responsible leadership, thereby expanding views about the purpose of the firm, the relevance of stakeholder groups and the meaning of value creation.

Related empirical research in CEO succession planning and selection does not adopt a responsible leadership approach *per se* but does examine the influence of the board of directors' processes and organisational practices on firm performance. Three subprocesses are associated with the psychological pathway: trust, psychological ownership, and commitment.

Trust

Although much has been written about the structural elements of boards including rules, procedures, composition, and committees in relation to the conduct of tasks, a key intangible asset is trust. Trust is critical to promote transparency and accountability both of which are necessary for responsible leadership (Waldman et al., 2020; Maak et al., 2016) and effective board dynamics (Huse et al., 2005; Ogunseyin et al., 2019; van Ees et al., 2008; van Ees et al., 2009). Board members need to trust each other that board decisions, once made, will be supported, confidentiality will be respected, and directors will be consistent and honest in their actions and behaviours (Huse et al., 2005). The board-CEO relationship is another relationship in which reciprocal trust is important to effective task performance. The board must trust the CEO to bring full disclosure and transparency to interactions with stakeholders internal and external to the company. The CEO must trust the board to provide timely and informed confidential response. Support for these arguments comes mainly from research that examines how trust and emotions affect the effectiveness of boards in its interactions with external and internal stakeholders, and how board roles are influenced (Huse, 1998; Huse & Zattoni, 2008).

Psychological Ownership

Psychological ownership suggests a state in which people feel as though they have a stake in a job or organisation (Pierce et al., 2001; Dawkins et al., 2017). In contrast to formal share ownership as a mechanism to control opportunistic behaviour (i.e. solve the 'agency problem'), psychological ownership broadly refers to evoking a feeling that decisions by employees should be made in the long-term interest of the company by acting *as if* they own the company. In this way, stakeholders develop a sense of efficacy, self identity, belonging and accountability towards a purpose, job, team or organisation (Avey et al., 2009; Pierce et al., 2001). Governance research supports a positive relationship between board task performance and directors' self identification with the organisation (Hillman et al., 2008; Veltrop et al., 2018). Recent empirical work has extended psychological ownership from the individual to the collective or shared mindset, linking team attitudes and behaviours (for a review see Dawkins et al., 2017). In a related stream, the conceptual model of shared leadership in the board (see Vandewaerde et al., 2011) suggests that directors of boards enact leadership collectively for decisions made in the best interest of the entity.

Commitment

Distinct from psychological ownership and its sense of 'it's mine/ it's ours' (i.e. possessiveness), organisational commitment refers to membership. That is, it is a personal commitment or desire to remain affiliated with an organisation and contribute to the achievement of that organisation's objectives motivated by beliefs, values, and security (for reviews see Bodjrenou et al., 2019; Cioca et al., 2021). Leadership that fosters stakeholder autonomy, participation, and development through self direction is associated with positive work outcomes, including employee intention to stay (Kim & Beehr, 2018) and job satisfaction (Amundsen & Martinsen, 2015), because it promotes intrinsic motivation, positive feeling about and attraction to the work and workplace by employees. In a similar vein, empirical research on board commitment and motivation supports a positive relationship with task performance (Huse et al., 2005; Minichilli et al., 2009).

Knowledge-Based Pathway and CEO Succession

The second pathway by which responsible leadership can influence outcomes is knowledge-based. In this pathway, responsible leaders encourage knowledge sharing within and across boundaries of the organisation among stakeholders. The knowledge-based pathway extends the responsible leadership literature by examining processes through which leader inclusivity of stakeholders' perspectives increases the stock of knowledge created or acquired and expands the extent to which knowledge is shared and mobilised across the company (Doh & Quigley, 2014). The knowledge-based subprocesses are options, creativity, and knowledge sharing.

Recent related research on boards' service task has focused on directors' specialised knowledge and social connections to help firms gain access to valuable resources. One means to achieve this goal is through diverse boards of directors. Studies of board composition find positive relationships between knowledge diversity of board members and board service task performance (for a review see Åberg et al., 2019). Another related research stream examines board capital in relation to boards' performance of its service task. Boards need to possess both human capital, which refers to board members' expertise, knowledge, reputation and skills, and social capital which involves the social ties of directors (Carter & Lorsch, 2004; Jiang et al., 2021; Kiel & Nicholson, 2002) to effectively fulfil its tasks. Both the amount and richness of knowledge available to boards of directors provide benefits which, we maintain, are critical for CEO succession and selection. Related empirical research associated with the three subprocesses of the knowledge-based pathway—options, creativity and knowledge sharing—are examined.

Options

Options provide boards of directors with the opportunity for analysis to gain insight into the merits of potential action before commitments are made. The increased knowledge accessible by boards through diverse perspectives offers the prospect to validate a choice by evaluating the risks and benefits to identify which option seems best suited to the interests of the entity itself at any time. A substantial literature on the contributions of different perspectives (i.e. cognitive conflict) to board task performance reaches varied conclusions, in part, due to definitional differences (for a meta-analysis of this literature see Heemskerk, 2019). The empirical results are mixed. In general, the studies suggest a somewhat positive association between cognitive conflict and board task performance, but the overall effect is too small to confirm (Heemskerk, 2019). When considered in terms of strategic and complex decision making, boards may benefit from a combination of preparation, participation and analysis (i.e. effort norms), the use of directors' knowledge and skills along with differences of perspective for effective task performance (Åberg et al., 2019; Heemskerk, 2019; Huse, 2009).

Creativity

Creativity refers to the generation of fresh ideas and concepts for changing products, services and processes to better achieve an organisation's goals

(Amabile, 1998). In an organisational context, creativity is often associated with inspirational thought, cognitive leads and intuitive insights which occur at the individual, team, and organisational level and have the potential for a breakthrough that is appropriate, useful and actionable (for a review see Anderson et al., 2018). In short, creativity brings the originality needed for organisational innovation. At an individual level, creative capability is conceptualised as expertise, creative thinking and motivation (Amabile, 1998). Considerable research has focused on factors that promote and hinder creativity and innovation in organisations among employees including leadership (Anderson et al., 2018; Zhang & Bartol, 2010) and firm ownership (Liu et al., 2017). Among boards of directors, the provision of advice and counsel to the CEO and executive management for strategic decision making may be considered as a creative capability in order to realise the organisation's purpose (Hendry et al., 2010; Pugliese et al., 2009; Stiles & Taylor, 2001).

Knowledge Sharing

Knowledge sharing refers to the provision of task-related information and knowledge with others to solve problems and improve outcomes (Doh & Quigley, 2014). Knowledge sharing is a type of activity (i.e. knowledge exchange) that involves processes applied in practice to create value (for a review see Ahmad & Karim, 2019). Knowledge sharing of task-relevant ideas, information, and suggestions that directors bring to the role is a recognised contribution of the board (Carter & Lorsch, 2004; Nicholson & Kiel, 2004). Empirical research finds a positive relationship between board members' use of knowledge and skills and service task performance (Åberg et al., 2019; Heemskerk, 2019). In an early process-oriented model that identified boards as strategic decision-making groups, Forbes and Milliken (1999) proposed that effective task performance involved, in part, the knowledge and skills of directors who integrated and built on the contributions of others. Huse (2005, 2007) has reiterated this point by arguing that directors work as a group, despite being elected or appointed to the board because of individual skills and knowledge, and that the final outcome of the task is the result of their joint efforts.

Role of the Board Chair and CEO Succession

Discussions of effective board task performance and leadership frequently consider the role of the board chair as central and critical (Carter & Lorsch, 2004; Cikaliuk et al., 2018, 2020; Gabrielsson et al., 2007; Leblanc, 2005) (for a review see Banerjee et al., 2020). Several key elements of the chair's work involve developing high quality relationships with others (Huse, 1998; Leblanc & Gillies, 2005), creating board cohesiveness (Forbes & Milliken, 1999), and enacting leadership (Banerjee et al., 2020). Although empirical studies of responsible leadership by board chairs are rare, in terms of our current discussion the psychological and knowledge-based pathways may be mobilised by board chairs to support effective performance of board tasks, including CEO succession.

In a value-creating board, as Huse et al. (2009) point out, the board chair must perform a range of tasks: build trusting relationships among board members and with the CEO, support the board members to help them become effective team members by motivating and providing them with all the information they might need, encourage open communications within and outside the boardroom, facilitate robust discussions at board meetings, and actively develop and refine governance structures and processes. For the board to perform effectively, the board chair needs to be enthusiastic, be highly capable in managing processes, possess high levels of integrity, be highly respected, and be thoroughly prepared for meetings.

In a study of the behavioural aspects of board chairs, Gabrielsson et al. (2007) argued that the attributes of an effective board chair include having the ability to motivate and use the competence of each board member (e.g. coach effectively and emphasise the attributes of high-performance teamwork), having an open and trustful leadership style, working well with the CEO, and developing the working structures and processes of the board continually. These behaviours are conceptually highly relevant for responsible leadership enacted by board chairs in relation to CEO succession and selection. Board chair literature suggests that board chair behaviour involves increased consideration of internal and external stakeholders' interests and objectives to be balanced in the best interest of the company (Banerjee et al., 2020). The following case study of three iterations of CEO succession at Air New Zealand helps to illustrate these insights.

Case Study

Case Study 7.1 CEO Succession at Air New Zealand[1]

John Palmer, board chair for Air New Zealand, felt positive about stepping down after 12 years. Board led responsible leadership had revitalised the once troubled company through three successful CEO appointments. 'The appointment of the right CEO is the most important decision that as a director you will ever make', Palmer explained. Now, with his planned departure at hand, Palmer anticipated the board's CEO succession process would again reap the expected performance for this world top 40 airline group.

Airline Acquisition Fiasco and Bailout: 2000–2001

In 2001, Air New Zealand's 60-year history of practical, fast, and economic transport for people and goods was in jeopardy. Its aggressive acquisition of Australian-based Ansett Airlines in 2000 threatened to ground the carrier less than one year later. Faced with a loss of US$605 million in 2001, the biggest loss by a public company in the corporate history of New Zealand, Air New Zealand had exhausted its credit and its options. Trading in its shares was halted on the New Zealand Exchange on 13 September 2001 due to the company's financial crisis. In early October the Air New Zealand board, its major shareholders, and the New Zealand Government announced a proposal for a substantial capital injection. By December 2001, Air New Zealand shareholders had approved the proposal and accepted a US$382 million equity rescue package from the New Zealand Treasury. Consequently, the government acquired 83 per cent ownership of the company. Through necessity rather than by design, the airline became New Zealand's first stock exchange listed state-owned enterprise.

The Art of the Rebuild (2002)

A clean break amid crisis meant a new board and CEO—terms set by the Crown as part of its rescue package. Following a search, the responsible shareholding minister identified and approved John Palmer as a board chair-designate and director. As an experienced board chair, Palmer faced two urgent and major tasks at the outset—rebuilding the board and appointing a new CEO. He began the board rebuild by selecting independent directors with expertise in fields ranging from international business, finance, information technology, marketing, engineering, and labour relations gained outside of the airline industry. Palmer invited to the board two directors from the previous board, four new directors, and the acting CEO (who was also a board member). Palmer agreed with the majority shareholding minister, prior to his appointment, that the minister would have a veto right on any proposed director, but would have no part in the search process. Each hand-picked director was approved by the shareholding minister and subsequently ratified at the annual general meeting. To preserve the board's independence, none of the initial directors was a government appointee despite the Crown being the largest shareholder.

Responsible leadership by the board demanded a shared vision: Palmer did that. The directors on the board all shared a commitment to restoring the airline to its place of pride in New Zealand and the world. Unlike most boards, this newly formed board had limited experience in understanding the specific drivers and dynamics of the airline industry. Importantly, though, they had candour, commitment, and a wealth of domestic and international experience and knowledge to engage in the turnaround. Along with building a motivated board, Palmer tackled the pressing issue of finding a chief executive officer. He understood that the next few months—and subsequent years—would demand responsible CEO leadership.

Naming a Chief Executive Officer

In early December 2001, the board appointed an international recruitment firm and constituted a new three-member CEO selection subcommittee, consisting of Palmer, a director reappointed from the previous board, and the acting CEO and deputy chair. As the new search began, the *ad hoc* subcommittee soon confronted barriers. 'No one wanted to be the CEO of a company that had just lost US$605 million ... also September 11 was very fresh and raw'.

Faced with mounting pressure to choose between two applicants, the selection committee met, and each director independently arrived at a similar conclusion. Palmer made the tough but courageous call: neither of the candidates was selected. He was 'prepared to walk away [from either candidate] because it was more than considering who is the best person without actually asking the question, "Is this the right person for the job?"'. The search would have to start over, and the interim CEO and director might need to stay on for an additional six months.

Then the CEO search took an intriguing turn. To the surprise of his fellow directors, Ralph Norris, one of the directors on the subcommittee, decided that he would apply for the position of CEO. Following a discussion with the board, he was required to adhere to the same process as other candidates. He was fast-tracked through the psychological assessment and interviewed in only two days. Within a week the board approved his appointment.

When Norris joined the board in 2001, prior to the financial collapse of the airline, he had no intention of becoming its CEO. He had recently retired as CEO of ASB Bank, a bank owned by the Commonwealth Bank of Australia. Norris pointed out, 'At the high level, I had a good understanding of the business and the industry; when it got down to the operational areas I was obviously not as well equipped'. As an experienced CEO, Norris was acutely aware that 'the appointment of the chief executive is the most critical decision that any board makes. The company will thrive or wither on the quality of the performance of the chief executive and the team the chief executive builds around him or her so that is really critical'. On that basis, he applied—and was chosen—for the job.

Defined Departure

Over the next 36 months (2002–2005), Norris and the board focused on stabilising and then revitalising the company. Norris invested in laying the foundation for a new culture—one that embraced innovation, technology, and customer service. They overhauled the business plan and reconfigured domestic operations. In June 2003, Air New Zealand reported a profit—its first in four years.

An Outsider Inside

The board and Norris agreed his primary key performance indicator (KPI) during his last two years was to find, recruit, and mentor a potential successor. No one among the executive management team offered the complete package. He needed an external prospect.

Norris tapped into his network and found two potential candidates. One of them was Rob Fyfe, whom Norris once tried to recruit for the ASB Bank. He approached Fyfe and offered him the role of chief information officer—a new position created within the executive management team. Fyfe accepted the position with an upfront understanding he would be a contender for the CEO role.

Developing and Field-Testing a Candidate

Like Norris, Fyfe gained his experience in banking and telecommunications, although he had also worked for the Royal New Zealand Air Force. Norris explained that banking and aviation shared common traits—both were network, global, mass-customer businesses with a high reliance on information technology (Knibb, 2004).

Over the next 18 months, Fyfe engaged in a series of development opportunities including a strategic review of Air New Zealand's business. The outcome 'demonstrated Fyfe's ability to work with people and established his credibility across the organisation', stated Norris. While this activity proceeded with a view to getting Fyfe 'up the learning curve quickly as possible', of equal importance was the strategy the board was developing for the airline.

The Search for the Next CEO (2005)

With the announcement of Norris's departure, the board did not consider the appointment of Fyfe to the role of CEO a *fait accompli*. The board was committed to following a process that would validate their appointment of the 'right' person. Fyfe would be expected to apply for the job like anyone else.

Palmer explained an organised succession planning process 'started well in advance of the appointment of a CEO'. It involved establishing board ownership of the process with the whole board engaged in regular annual discussions of the plan, including updates on talented leaders within the company. Palmer relayed the questions the board wrestled with: 'firstly, how do we identify people inside the business? And how do we have discussions to work out whether there is enough capability in some people that with some assistance, that they can become genuine candidates?' In the absence of promising CEO talent among the executive members, what measures do we take 'to get some people inside the business to give them a feel for the airline that they can build on or do we run the risk of appointing the capability from outside?'

For a successful CEO transition, the board re-affirmed its need to agree on the requisite capabilities to lead the airline. Between 2005 and 2006, the company faced tough strategic, workforce, and workplace decisions which included layoffs. An unprecedented 44 per cent rise in the price of jet fuel forced the company's profitability down 47 per cent. Net profit after tax was US$62 million for 2006. It was an apt time for the board to again exercise its leadership, set a vision, set future direction, and align the capabilities of the next CEO to achieve the airline's goals.

They assessed the airline's current market position, the achievements realised in technology, customer service focus, and culture shift. The board next identified a constellation of qualities, characteristics, and experience for the future CEO. For some directors, the next CEO needed to be a change agent, people-oriented, commercially astute and bring a strong customer service ethic. Others sought a CEO with experience in leading innovation and transformation. Collectively, these attributes defined the responsible leadership needed by Air New Zealand for its next CEO.

With the desired CEO profile in hand, a selection firm conducted a global search. The board convened an *ad hoc* sub-committee with two directors and the chair, who developed a short list of three candidates—two external and one internal (Fyfe). The whole board interviewed the candidates with questions posed by the directors. Following the final interview, the board discussed the strengths and talents of each candidate. Each director assessed the relative risks connected with each potential appointment as Palmer posed a series of questions. One external candidate without airline experience was determined to be a high risk despite a demonstrated record of accomplishment leading change in large organisations. The other external candidate was a seasoned aviation professional, someone who could 'come in and run the airline, not a problem, but would he really transform it?' queried one director. And then there was Fyfe: he had gained 18 months' aviation experience under the mentorship of Norris. He knew the strategy, the desired culture, and the people. He was aware that 'we have got to try new things and if they don't work, adapt, adjust, withdraw and try something else' (Le Pla, 2006). Although some directors initially expressed concern over his potential appointment, this concern was not shared by Norris. He recalled, 'When I left, I made it very clear to the board Fyfe was the right candidate for the job'. Following robust discussion and considerable deliberation the board ultimately selected Fyfe.

Beginning a Fresh Search for the Next CEO (2011)

By 2011, Fyfe had transformed Air New Zealand financially, operationally and culturally. He exemplified leadership that instilled the desired culture among employees, managers, and supply chain partners. He initiated and achieved open and lateral communication within the company; the absence of knowledge-sharing had prevented cross departmental collaboration in the past. He also developed a personal practice of working one day a month in roles such as baggage handler, service call operator, and food server aboard aircraft. Together with the chair, they initiated a similar annual practice for directors.

The relationship with Fyfe and the board was 'about having a safe environment at the board table', which grew and evolved over Fyfe's tenure. For the board, clarity of role and responsibility was vital to their collective leadership action. The contributions of board members and Palmer's leadership style enabled Fyfe to do his job—lead the company— 'in a way that some other boards would not have probably been prepared to risk'. Fyfe and Palmer had a respectful professional relationship and Fyfe 'would never make any significant decision without talking to the board about it and making sure that Palmer was across things'.

Another Defined Departure

After seven years in the role, Fyfe notified the board of his desired departure by December 2012, providing the board with an 18-month timeline for transition. The board once again embarked on a recruitment process for the next CEO. The same recruitment firm initiated a search for prospective candidates internationally and domestically.

A New Outsider-Inside

In May 2010, Christopher Luxon, then CEO of Unilever Canada and a New Zealander, attended a presentation in Toronto about non-executive directorship given by a global expert from an international search firm. Luxon and the search expert chatted about the country where they both grew up. Subsequently in December 2010, the search expert contacted Luxon and indicated that Air New Zealand was looking for new promising executive talent. The idea of returning to New Zealand took hold; Luxon had found a fit between his values and the chair's, relishing an opportunity to model responsible leadership in his native country. With the understanding that the role of CEO was not pre-ordained, Luxon took the job as group general manager for the international division of Air New Zealand but nurtured the hope that he would be a candidate for the top job.

Developing and Field-Testing Internal Candidates

Luxon arrived in New Zealand in May 2011 to take up his new role. Luxon drew on his international experience with start-ups, turnarounds, and realignments gained through job rotations within Unilever. To facilitate Luxon's transition, a 46-year 'veteran' of the executive management team accompanied the new general manager to all the ports and markets, looking at all the different functions. Luxon met with employees on the front line as well as with management. By August Luxon was solely responsible for turning around the international division at a time when it was losing US$2 million a week. Luxon's focus paid off. The restructured long-haul services returned to the black for the first time in five years.

After these initial successes and with eight months' experience gained at Air New Zealand, Luxon was well positioned as an inside candidate when Fyfe formally announced his resignation in January 2012. Palmer met with Luxon and confirmed he was a candidate for the position. He joined a pool of two other internal candidates that Fyfe had identified.

The Board's Formal Process

The faces around the boardroom table had been relatively consistent for the past seven years while Fyfe transformed the airline and its culture. Because the board initially emerged from a 'blank sheet of paper' in 2002, some directors were set to step down simultaneously as they reached the preferred nine-year term limit. Palmer provided a strong lead to the board by choosing prospective independent directors. The five new directors, approved by the shareholding minister and formally appointed at shareholder meetings between 2006 and 2013, boosted competencies in finance, accounting, marketing, strategy, and tourism. In alignment with the airline's trans-Tasman strategy, an Australian became a director. All others were New Zealanders.

As in previous appointments to the board, the new directors delivered a range of expertise gained outside of the airline industry. Consistent with the board's initial composition, all directors were independent non-executive directors; the government chose none of them. Collectively, these features added expertise, youth, and internationalism while maintaining a core of financial, marketing, and general business experience.

Aligning Desired Capabilities with Strategy

Although the composition of the board may have changed, the new and seasoned directors shared a commitment to find the right CEO. Collectively, the directors decided the airline needed to enhance its profit-making capability through its distribution and sales channels, signalling a shift away from the cultural transformation focus of the past decade. After the directors agreed and committed to the strategic direction, the board recognised they needed a different type of candidate from the incumbent CEO.

Creating the CEO Profile

The board returned to the same white board exercise they had used in the past, beginning again with a blank slate. They first agreed that the new

CEO was not to be a clone of Rob Fyfe. Directors canvassed all angles to determine the attributes and characteristics of the desired CEO. Ultimately, three top essential attributes and nine desirable qualities coalesced from robust discussion. Most board members agreed that the position demanded emotional intelligence and agility. Various directors of the board favoured as essential people skills and team-builder skills coupled with being numbers- and value-driven.

The right CEO required emotional, physical and mental stamina. This cluster translated into resilience. The board also recognised the importance of the right cultural fit between the airline and its future CEO through the qualities of kiwi spirit and values. A results-focus was described as deal and alliance savvy. 'We were looking for different people management characteristics to give this harder commercial edge to the business now that the culture and technology had been really well developed', the board chair explained. Industry and international experience, change management and customer understanding made it onto the list along with high energy, self-awareness, and flexibility. These qualities were ranked as desirable but not essential. 'In an airline sense globally', the chair pointed out, the profile emerged from 'very unconventional thinking'.

Although less than a year had passed since the search that had brought Luxon to Air New Zealand, the same consulting firm was re-engaged with a new brief to scan internationally and domestically.

Scanning Widely and Benchmarking Candidates

The board established a small *ad hoc* CEO selection subcommittee with Palmer and a director. The search firm identified external candidates, and the subcommittee winnowed the list to a select few who best matched the CEO profile.

The board reviewed external prospects against the three internal candidates and set the outsiders aside. They were simply not as strong as the internal candidates. While board members were well-acquainted with the candidates through their quarterly presentations to the board, visits made by directors to site specific operations, and participation at strategy sessions, Palmer and Fyfe ensured the board had 'visibility' of all inside contenders. Candidates were encouraged to participate in standing committees to gain experience and so that the board could see their development.

Managing the Internal Competition

All internal candidates completed the assessment administered by the selection firm. Subsequently, one of the candidates withdrew. Two candidates, including Luxon, remained in the running. Managing potentially destructive competition between them was essential. This time was an economically difficult period for the airline and it could ill-afford unwanted tensions within the business. The carrier earlier that year had announced plans to reduce its staff of 11,500 by 440 after recording a 71 per cent plunge in half-year profit. The airline cited a weak global economy and the high cost of jet fuel (Perry, 2012).

Considering the Candidates

Both candidates made a presentation to the board, explaining why they wanted the job and what they would do if they got it. Following each presentation, individual board members posed questions about the value drivers needing to be sharpened, changed, and created for the next phase of the airline's growth. The board also sought assurance that each candidate understood the culture and values that needed to be maintained. During the break between the two presentations, the directors were discouraged from talking with each other about the presentations. Each director was to make an initial personal decision about who was the ideal candidate.

Selecting the Successor

The board reconvened later that same day. Three short questions were posed by the chair. Palmer went around the table and asked each director, 'Are either of the candidates worthy of appointment, yes or no'? All confirmed 'Yes, we have an appointable candidate'. He followed up with his second question, 'Is there a preferred candidate, yes or no?' There was an unequivocal affirmative response from the directors. Finally, he proceeded around the table one last time and asked each director for the name of their preferred candidate. It was Luxon. The chair contacted Luxon and offered him the position of CEO of Air New Zealand.

Presenting a Transition Recommendation

At a subsequent meeting, the board discussed the timing of Fyfe's departure. The chair proposed a six-month transition. The board was not unanimous about the six months: it was 'quite a tense subject around the board as to how it should be run' explained one director.

Given the tremendous confidence the board had in selecting Luxon as the next CEO, several directors queried the rationale for the delay. They preferred a clean sharp break so that there was no confusion about the line of command for people. It risked fostering uncertainty, rumours, and politicisation of employees with loyalty to the outgoing CEO while the new CEO-designate led a corporate restructuring process.

These directors also thought about the role of the chair in this transition. According to one director, the nature of the risk required Palmer to 'keep his nose right in there to make sure it was not creating issues below'. Such operational involvement ran counter to the clearly defined roles for the board and management. Other directors had no reservations about the transition period. As directors, they were familiar with the personalities of the outgoing and incoming CEO and believed the two would make it work. Following two meetings of vigorous and open debate about the transition, the board was ready to move forward. Palmer made it clear there was only one CEO: the incumbent Fyfe. Accountability for business performance and delivery of the key performance indicators resided with Fyfe during the transition. The board met monthly with Fyfe. They also met with Luxon on specific projects, including his plan for restructuring the company.

Designing and Implementing the Transition

The transition period allowed Luxon to continue to gather data and develop a new organisational structure. Fyfe and Luxon met with Air New Zealand partner organisations, such as the CEOs of Star Alliance, and began to transition Fyfe's relationships to the incoming CEO. With the internal restructuring completed and new executive team appointments made within the first five months by the CEO-designate, 'the day Luxon started as CEO he was going 100 per cent'. According to the chair:

> Businesses lose traction, sometimes lose focus, and in many cases lose value in the transition of a CEO because there is a hiatus while the new CEO either changes things or comes up to speed. Both can be very damaging. I think the way we did it has shown that there would have been concern in the market and in the public saying, 'How are you going to replace Rob Fyfe, a very high profile, very successful CEO?' The reality is the business never missed a beat.

Celebrating 75 Years of Aviation and CEO Succession

CEO succession is about the future. A director pointed out:

> While we have been successful in appointing three great CEOs, we made our own success. With Norris we got a little lucky probably. But in the case of Fyfe and in the case of Luxon we made our own luck; we had taken a lot of time to think clearly about the skill sets and attributes that we wanted for the CEO at that point in the Airline's evolution.

The chair echoed succession planning as a leadership responsibility for realising a shared vision. According to Palmer, a wise board appoints 'the right person, not the best person, and gives them the tools and the capability to deliver what they promised'.

Discussion

In the case study, we wanted to feature the pathways that can be taken by the board to provide responsible leadership for CEO succession. The case study demonstrates that the board developed and used psychological and knowledge-based processes to benefit the CEO selection process as the company evolved from a crisis to become a top performing company. We have identified four ways in which the board sought to fulfil its task through responsible leadership in governance for CEO succession.

The board of directors *brought trust, a sense of ownership and commitment to bear on its decisions* for CEO succession planning and selection. The board members' strong motivation to save the national flag carrier and emotional attachment to the organisation created an obligation to care about the organisation's wellbeing. Through their interactions, the board balanced a need for trust, closeness and distance, as well as dependence and interdependence (Åberg et al., 2019) which facilitated effective task performance. The commitment shared among the directors to select the 'right' candidate for the executive position in each instance was motivated, in part, by a desire to fulfil the board's vision of the business and its future potential performance. The board's performance of responsible leadership extended to prospective CEO candidates who were provided with an exploratory, pre-CEO experience to learn and acquire company-specific knowledge and skills and, perhaps equally important, gain a feel for the company and its culture. These types of trust-based activities and relationships with stakeholders helped the board to be effective in protecting the interests of the company and establish norms and standards.

The board of directors *promoted options, creativity and knowledge-sharing in the design and implementation* of its CEO succession and selection task that was participative, innovative, and collaborative. In all three scenarios, the directors participated early on in designing the process, determining desirable CEO characteristics, identifying and mentoring people inside the business, evaluating capabilities of external candidates, and deciding the appointment. The board was creative and courageous in finding solutions to major strategic problems. The board of directors engaged in skilful, intentional dialogue and debates at the board meetings to leverage different knowledge and skills to create a CEO succession and selection process that became part of the company's operating practice. Our case study demonstrated that participative relationships embedded in teamwork help to foster knowledge-sharing, constructively leverage differences of perspective, encourage flexibility and learning which were critical for effective board task performance in the CEO succession and selection task.

The board chair *demonstrated an integrative orientation of responsible leadership* in this case study (Pless et al., 2012; Maak et al., 2016) who combined strategic thinking and a sense of the economic bottom line with stakeholder interests. This orientation had implications for strategy, decision making and stakeholder engagement for board task performance. He brought clarity to the CEO selection process by developing processes and procedures that allowed structured interactions at board meetings and enabled directors to creatively and constructively share differences. To be able to perform these tasks, the chair needs to bring together rational/analytic thinking with a concern for stakeholders' emotions, keep a sense of independence of mind along with the ability to work through tensions, possess high levels of integrity, coach effectively and emphasise attributes of high-performance teamwork along with broader accountability than shareholder's interests (Banerjee et al., 2020). The chair's ability to develop trustful relationships between all governance actors promoted engagement additionally facilitated the effective functioning of the board.

The board's *decisions on new CEO appointments were not influenced by its largest shareholder*, the government. All three CEO succession processes were undertaken independently of any consultation with the shareholding ministry. Given the government's substantial block ownership, we would expect that the government would want to exercise its monitoring rights to influence decisions on the board. The government, however, did not appear to distort governance processes in the pursuit of its own special nonfinancial objectives. The government opted not to even appoint any of its own directors to the board. Like other investors, the government has a focus on value creation and mitigating market risk and can effectively realise these objectives in the absence of direct involvement with board decision-making (Pargendler, 2012). The board is the ultimate defender of the company's mission (Useem, 2006) and its decision-making should be autonomous (and well-informed) even when the decision, such as the selection of a new CEO, has important consequences for the company.

Conclusion

Responsibly led boards of directors are driven by purpose to realise the best interest of the company by balancing the interests of stakeholders internally and externally in the conduct of CEO succession and selection. In the performance of this task, the board mobilises two complementary pathways that extend from an initial idea through to the eventual realisation of CEO transition. Throughout the task, the board must demonstrate capability in mobilising processes that foster trust, commitment, and a sense of ownership as aspects of the psychological pathway of responsible leadership. In the knowledge-based pathway, they must also exhibit behaviours and actions consistent with openly sharing knowledge, welcoming new ideas, and constructively leveraging differences in perspectives.

The pathways, which were examined independently for clarity and conciseness in this chapter, illustrate how the board developed, implemented, and managed a succession process for three CEOs that was sound in design and achieved its desired benefits. The case also shows the collaborative relationships developed between the board and the CEO; open and informed communications within the boardroom; the chair's responsible leadership role and the hands-off relationship of the majority stakeholder. The responsible leadership exercised by boards of directors suggests that board task performance in relation to CEO succession provides further understanding of how succession may shape firm outcomes in pursuit of its purpose.

Note

1 This case study was written with the cooperation of the Air New Zealand board. All data are based on field research and public sources. The research underpinning this case study included in-depth interviews with chairs, directors and CEOs appointed in the period 2002–2013. The material produced by the company included the company's annual reports, press releases and notices of annual general meetings, among others. It also featured material produced by third party sources which included newspaper articles and reports, among others. A previous version of this case was published (see Cikaliuk et al., 2018).

References

Åberg, C., Bankewitz, M., & Knockaert, M. (2019). Service tasks of boards of directors: A literature review and research agenda in a new era of governance practices. *European Management Journal*, 37(5), 648–663.

Ahmad, F., & Karim, M. (2019). Impacts of knowledge sharing: A review and directions for future research. *Journal of Workplace Learning*, 31(3), 207–230.

Amabile, T. M. (1998) How to kill creativity. *Harvard Business Review*, 76(5), 77–87.

Amundsen, S., & Martinsen, Ø. L. (2015). Linking empowering leadership to job satisfaction, work effort, and creativity: The role of self-leadership and psychological empowerment. *Journal of Leadership & Organization Studies*, 22(3), 304–323.

Anderson, N., Potocnik, K., Bledow, R., Hülsheger, U., & Rosing, K. (2018). Innovation and creativity in organizations. In D. S. Ones, N. Anderson, C. Viswesvaran & H. Kepir Sinangil (eds), *Handbook of industrial, work & organizational psychology: Managerial psychology and organizational approaches*, vol. 3 (pp. 161–186). Sage.

Avey, J. B., Avolio, B. J., Crossley, C. D., & Luthans, F. (2009). Psychological ownership: Theoretical extensions, measurement and relation to work outcomes. *Journal of Organizational Behaviour*, 30(2), 173–191.

Banerjee, A., Nordqvist, M., & Hellerstedt, K. (2020). The role of the board chair: A literature review and suggestions for future research. *Corporate Governance: International Review*, 28(6), 372–405.

Biggs, E. L. (2004). CEO succession planning: An emerging challenge for boards of directors. *Academy of Management Executive*, 18(1), 105–107.

Bodjrenou, K., Xu, M., & Bomboma, K. (2019). Antecedents of organisational commitment: A review of personal and organisational factors. *Open Journal of Social Sciences*, 7(5), 276–289.

Boeker, W., & Goldstein, J. (1993). Performance and successor choice: The moderating effects of governance and ownership. *Academy of Management Journal*, 36 (1), 172–186.

Cannella, A. A., & Lubatkin, M. (1993). Succession as a sociopolitical process: Internal impediments to outsider selection. *Academy of Management Journal*, 36(4), 763–793.

Carroll, G. R. (1984). Dynamics of publisher succession in newspaper organizations. *Administrative Science Quarterly*, 29(1), 93–113.

Carter, C. B., & Lorsch, J. W. (2004). *Back to the drawing board: Designing corporate boards for a complex world*. Harvard Business Press.

Castañón Moats, M. & DeNicola, P. (2021). How the best boards approach CEO succession planning. https://corpgov.law.harvard.edu/2021/09/20/how-the-best-boards-approach-ceo-succession-planning/.

Cikaliuk, M., Eraković, L., Jackson, B., Noonan, C., & Watson, S. (2018). Leadership in governance: Women board chairs. In L. E. Devnew, J. Le Ber, M. Torchia & R. J. Burke (eds), *More women on boards: An international perspective* (pp. 269–283). Information Age.

Cikaliuk, M., Eraković, L., Jackson, B., Noonan, C., & Watson, S. (2020). Board leadership and governance for clear-sighted CEO succession at Air New Zealand. *Journal of Management and Organization*, 26(5), 774–797.

Cioca, I., Wietrak, E., Barends, E., & Rousseau, D. (2021). *Organisational commitment: An evidence review—Scientific summary*. Chartered Institute of Personnel and Development.

Clutterbuck, D. (1998). Handing over the reins: Should the CEO's successor be an insider or an outsider? *Corporate Governance: An International Review*, 6(2), 78–85.

Cunningham, G. B. (2006). The relationships between commitment to change, coping with change and turnover intentions, *European Journal of Work and Organizational Psychology*, 15(1), 29–45.

Dawkins, S., Tian, A. W., Newman, A., & Martin, A. (2017). Psychological ownership: A review and research agenda. *Journal of Organizational Behaviour*, 38(2), 163–183.

Defillippi, R., & Ornstein, S. (2003). Psychological perspectives underlying theories of organisational learning. In M. Easterby-Smith & M. A. Lyles (eds), *The Blackwell handbook of organizational learning and knowledge management* (pp. 19–37). Blackwell.

Doh, J. P., & Quigley, N. R. (2014). Responsible leadership and stakeholder management: Influence pathways and organizational outcomes. *Academy of Management Perspectives*, 28(3), 255–274.

Doh, J. P., & Stumpf, S. A. (2005). Towards a framework of responsible leadership and governance. In J. P. Doh & S. A. Stumpf (eds), *Handbook on responsible leadership and governance* (pp. 3–18). Edward Elgar.

Doh, J. P., Stumpf, S. A., & Tymon, W. G. (2011). Responsible leadership helps retain talent in India. *Journal of Business Ethics*, 98(s1), 85–100.

Forbes, D. P., & Milliken, F. J. (1999). Understanding boards of directors as strategic decision-making groups. *Academy of Management Review*, 24(3), 489–505.

Fragouli, E., & Alhaider, M. (2020). The influence of responsible leadership on talent retention. *Business and Management Review*, 11(1), 306–318.

Friedman, S. D., & Saul, K. (1991). A leader's wake: Organization member reactions to CEO succession. *Journal of Management*, 17(3), 619–642.

Gabrielsson, J., Huse, M., & Minichilli, A. (2007). Understanding the leadership role of the board chairperson through a team production approach. *International Journal of Leadership Studies*, 34(2), 11–36.

Harrell, E. (2016). Succession planning: What the research says. *Harvard Business Review*, 94(12), 70–74.

Heemskerk, K. (2019). Promising avenue or dead end street? A meta analytic review of the Forbes and Milliken model of board behaviour. *Corporate Governance: The International Journal of Business and Society*, 19(3), 471–489.

Hendry, K. P., Kiel, G. C., & Nicholson, G. (2010). How boards strategise: A strategy as practice view. *Long Range Planning*, 43(1), 33–56.

Hillman, A. J., Nicholson, G., & Shropshire, C. (2008). Directors' multiple identities, identification, and board monitoring and resource provision. *Organization Science*, 19(3), 383–396.

Huse, M. (1998). Researching the dynamics of board–stakeholder relations. *Long Range Planning*, 31(2), 218–226.

Huse, M. (2005). Accountability and creating accountability: A framework for exploring behavioural perspectives of corporate governance. *British Journal of Management*, 16, S76–S79.

Huse, M. (2007). *Boards, governance and value creation: The human side of corporate governance*. Cambridge University Press.

Huse, M. (ed.). (2009). *The value creating board: Corporate governance and organizational behaviour*. Routledge.

Huse, M., Minichilli, A., Nordqvist, M., & Zattoni, A. (2005). Board tasks in small firms: The importance of motivation and evaluations. *Singerie*, 75(8), 17–36.

Huse, M., & Zattoni, A. (2008). Trust, firm life cycle, and actual board behaviour: Evidence from 'one of the lads' in the board of three small firms. *International Studies of Management and Organization*, 38(3), 71–97.

Jiang, H., Xia, J., Devers, C., & Shen, W. (2021). Who will board a sinking ship? A firm-director interdependence perspective of mutual selection between declining firms and director candidates. *Academy of Management Journal*, 64(3).

Khurana, R., (2001). Finding the right CEO: Why boards often make poor choices. *MIT Sloan Management Review*, 43(1), 91–95.

Kiel, G., & Nicholson, G. (2002). *Boards that work: A new guide for directors*. McGraw Hill.

Kim, M., & Beehr, T. A. (2018). Empowering leadership: Leading people to be present through affective organizational commitment? *The International Journal of Human Resource Management*, 31(16), 2017–2044.

Knibb, D. (2004). Ralph Norris: Down to business. *Airline Business*, 20(5), 34. www.flightglobal.com/ralph-norris-down-to-business/54153.article.

Leblanc, R. (2005). Assessing board leadership. *Corporate Governance: An International Review*, 13(5), 654–666.

Leblanc, R., & Gillies, J. (2005). *Inside the boardroom: How boards really work and the coming revolution in corporate governance*. Wiley.

Lee, S. H., Phan, P. H., & Yoshikawa, T. (2008). The role of the board and its interaction with the successor's human capital in the Asian family enterprise. *Multinational Business Review*, 16(2), 65–88.

Le Pla, R. (2006). Rob Fyfe: Blue sky thinking behind the clouds. *New Zealand Management Magazine*, 53(8), 48–51.

Liu, D., Gong, Y., Zhou, J., & Huang, J. (2017). Human resource systems, employee creativity, and firm innovation: The moderating role of firm ownership. *Academy of Management Journal*, 60(3), 1164–1188.

Maak, T., & Pless, N. M. (2006). Responsible leadership in a stakeholder society. *Journal of Business Ethics*, 66(1), 99–115.

Maak, T., Pless, N. M., & Voegtlin, C. (2016). Business statesman or shareholder advocate? CEO responsible leadership styles and the microfoundations of political CSR. *Journal of Management Studies*, 53(3), 463–493.

Minichilli, A., Zattoni, A., & Zona, F. (2009). Making boards effective: An empirical examination of board task performance. *British Journal of Management*, 20(1), 55–74.

Nicholson, G., & Kiel, G. C. (2004). Breakthrough board performance: How to harness your board's intellectual capital. *Corporate Governance: The International Journal of Business in Society*, 4(1), 5–23.

Ocasio, W. (1999). Institutionalized action and corporate governance: The reliance on rules of CEO succession. *Administrative Science Quarterly*, 44(2), 384–416.

Ogunseyin, M. A., Farquhar, S. S., & Machold, S. (2019). The determinants of trust in the boardroom. In J. Gabrielsson, W. Khlif & S. Yamak (eds), *Research handbook on boards of directors* (pp. 49–75). Edward Elgar.

Pargendler, M. (2012). State ownership and corporate governance. *Fordham Law Review*, 80(6), 2917–2973.

Pearce, C., Wassenaar, C., & Mantz, C. (2014). Is shared leadership the key to responsible leadership? *Academy of Management Perspectives*, 28(3), 275–288.

Perry, N. (2012, June 19). Air NZ's new CEO Christopher Luxon sees growth opportunities in Asia, US. http://globalnews.ca/news/257764/ap-interview-air-nzs-new-ceo-christopher-luxon-sees-growth-opportunities-in-asia-us.

Pierce, J., Kostova, T., & Dirks, K. (2001). Toward a theory of psychological ownership in organizations. *Academy of Management Review*, 26(2), 298–310.

Pless, N. M., Maak, T., & Waldman, D. A. (2012). Different approaches toward doing the right thing: Mapping the responsibility orientation of leaders. *Academy of Management Perspectives*, 26, 5–65.

Pugliese, A., Bezemer, P.-J., & Zattoni, A. (2009). Boards of directors' contribution to strategy: A literature review and research agenda. *Corporate Governance: An International Review*, 17(3), 292–306.

Shen, W., & Cannella, A. A. (2002). Revisiting the performance consequences of CEO succession: The impacts of successor type, postsuccession senior executive turnover, and departing CEO tenure. *Academy of Management Journal*, 45(4), 717–733.

Stahl, G., & Sully de Luque, M. (2014). Antecedents of responsible leadership behaviour: A research synthesis, conceptual framework, and agenda for future research. *Academy of Management Perspectives*, 28(3), 235–254.

Stiles, P., & Taylor, B. (2001). *Boards at work: How directors view their roles and responsibilities*. Oxford University Press.

Useem, M. (2006). How well-run boards make decisions. *Harvard Business Review*, 8 (11), 130–140.

Vandewaerde, M., Voordeckers, W., Lambrechts, F., & Bammens, Y. (2011). Board team leadership revisited: A conceptual model of shared leadership in the boardroom. *Journal of Business Ethics*, 104(3), 403–420.

van Ees, H., Gabrielsson, J., & Huse, M. (2009). Towards a behavioural theory of boards and corporate governance. *Corporate Governance: An International Review*, 17(3), 307–319.

van Ees, H., van der Laan, G., & Postma, T. J. (2008). Effective board behaviour in the Netherlands. *European Management Journal*, 26(2), 84–93.

Veltrop, D., Molleman, H., Hooghiemstra, R., & van Ees, H. (2018). The relationship between tenure and outside director task involvement: A social identity perspective. *Journal of Management*, 44(2), 445–469.

Waldman, D. A. (2011). Moving forward with the concept of responsible leadership: Three key caveats to guide theory and research. *Journal of Business Ethics*, 98 (s1), 75–83.

Waldman, D. A., & Balven, R. M. (2014). Responsible leadership: Theoretical issues and research directions. *Academy of Management Perspectives*, 28(3), 224–234.

Waldman, D. A., & Galvin, B. M. (2008). Alternative perspectives of responsible leadership. *Organizational Dynamics*, 37(4), 327–341.

Waldman, D. A., Siegel, D. S., & Stahl, G. K. (2020). Defining the socially responsible leader: Revisiting issues in responsible leadership. *Journal of Leadership & Organizational Studies*, 27(1), 5–20.

Weisbach, M. S. (1988). Outside directors and CEO turnover. *Journal of Financial Economics*, 20(C), 431–460.

Yar Hamidi, D., & Gabrielsson, J. (2014). Developments and trends in research on board leadership: A systematic literature review. *International Journal of Business Governance and Ethics*, 9(3), 243–268.

Zajac, E. J. (1990). CEO selection, succession, compensation and firm performance: A theoretical integration and empirical analysis. *Strategic Management Journal*, 11 (3), 217–230.

Zajac, E. J., & Westphal, J. D. (1996). Who shall succeed? How CEO/board preferences and power affect the choice of new CEOs. *Academy of Management Journal*, 39(1), 64–90.

Zhang, X., & Bartol, K. M. (2010). Linking empowering leadership and employee creativity: The influence of psychological empowerment, intrinsic motivation, and creative process engagement. *Academy of Management Journal*, 53(1), 107–128.

Zhang, Y., & Rajagopalan, N. (2010). CEO succession planning: Finally at the centre stage of the boardroom. *Business Horizons*, 53(5), 455–462.

8 Diversity and Inclusion

Introduction

Our primary intention in this chapter is to illustrate and explain the importance of the board's active role in promoting diversity at the governance and organisational levels. Our case study and initial comments focus on gender diversity, but we expand our discussion to other key aspects of diversity. We argue that board of directors' attitude towards diversity issues is central not only for corporate governance practice (that is, board and executive team's compositions), but also for the organisation's approach and actions in relation to diversity and inclusion. From a business case point of view, in today's highly competitive and uncertain environments, diverse views can provide a better understanding of the current and future trends and can improve the quality of board decisions (Bennett & Lemoine, 2014; Horney et al., 2010). Our case study demonstrates how diverse human capital in the top echelon of the organisation plays a critical role in enhancing new strategy development and organisational performance.

We start this chapter by unfolding the meaning of diversity and inclusion in organisational groups. Then, we examine three areas of prior research that have been shown to be critical in diversity and inclusion strategies: board attitudes and composition, corporate strategy and role modelling. Next, we present the Bank of New Zealand case study. This is followed by discussion and conclusions.

Defining Diversity and Inclusion

In group and organisational settings, diversity is a multidimensional construct which in general involves four different but related categories: demographic, cognitive, affective and organisational (Harrison et al., 2002; Hassan & Marimuthu, 2018; Milliken & Martins, 1996). *Demographic dimensions*, such as gender, age, race, ethnicity, religion, nationality and sexual orientation, are observable, inherent, surface-level characteristics of diversity. These dimensions, single or in combination, are the most

DOI: 10.4324/9781003054191-8

commonly researched predictors of diversity in corporate governance literature (Kagzi & Guha, 2018). An important assumption here is that 'people of diverse demographic backgrounds really are *different* in some meaningful way' (Broome et al., 2010, p. 805). *Cognitive dimensions* (deep-level, job-related or acquired attributes) may include educational level, functional background, industry experience, tenure, reputation and socio-economic roots (Hassan & Marimuthu, 2018; Milliken & Martins, 1996). These dimensions influence an individual's identification and interpretation of problems, and recognition and formulation of potential solutions (Dallas, 2002; Hambrick & Mason, 1984). The assumption is that the board's cognitive heterogeneity (depth and breadth of directors' knowledge and experience) is beneficial for organisations operating in dynamic and uncertain environments. Recent studies have supported this assumption (see Melkumov & Khoreva, 2015; Torchia et al., 2015) demonstrating that cognitively diverse boards make high quality decisions in situations of complex problems.

Affective dimensions also present deep-level, less visible attributes which refer to diversity in personality and may include values, attitudes and beliefs (Harrison et al., 2002). Chattopadhyay et al. (1999), in their research on upper-echelon executive beliefs, have emphasised the importance of normative beliefs for organisation performance. Normative beliefs relate to the perceived importance of various organisational goals (Chattopadhyay et al., 1999). In the context of a corporate board, a normative belief may relate to a director's position on how important it is for an organisation to achieve marketplace-based reputation (product quality, customer-centric) in contrast to share-market-based reputation (share price, shareholder-centric). Or, in other words, it may relate to a director's stakeholder-shareholder orientation. *Organisational dimensions* relate to diversity in organisational memberships and roles. The assumption is that an individual's associations with other organisations (such as cross-organisational directorships or involvement in governance/executive bodies in organisations from different sectors) may affect a director's behaviour in board processes.

The above diversity dimensions are interrelated and making a clear difference between them is rather difficult (for example, categorising *cognitive* and *affective* dimensions is empirically blurry). Notwithstanding this challenge, all dimensions influence the way individuals think and behave in a group/organisation setting and all of them affect group/organisation performance. The most recent studies of corporate boards have demonstrated close links between various diversity dimensions and performance across governance, social and environmental matters (Chen & Eraković, 2019; Garcia, 2018). Diversity of perspectives at the governance level sets the foundation for a robust process of strategy formation (Estélyi & Nisar, 2016; Miller & Triana, 2009), promotes productive relationships with non-shareholder stakeholders (Bear et al., 2010; Harjoto et al., 2015), increases creativity and innovation (Miller & Triana, 2009; Tuggle et al., 2010) and may enhance financial performance (Erhardt et al., 2003; Taljaard et al., 2015).

Inclusion in organisation and groups literature is a related but distinctively different category to diversity. While diversity denotes 'differences, similarities and related tensions' (Thomas, 2004, p. 3), that can positively or negatively contribute to group effectiveness, as explained above, inclusion involves actions and practices which enable 'the full participation of all relevant [diversity] elements' (Hayles, 2014, p. 55). Or, while diversity efforts promote *representation* of 'historically unrepresented groups' (Winters, 2014, p. 205), inclusion necessitates arrangements (*structures*) and actions (*behaviours*) that increase the engagement and contribution of these groups. The evolving literature on inclusion discusses a number of macro and micro conditions (see Ferdman & Dean, 2014; Gallegos et al., 2020; Winters, 2014) for the development of inclusive environments and actions in organisations. To facilitate the analysis of our case study, we outline three key preconditions of inclusion in the group setting: established norms—respect for and value of diverse opinions; equal access to and value of information; and possibility to actively participate (especially in decision making).

First, inclusion must be an integral part of an organisation's culture, value system and strategy (Wasserman et al., 2008). Organisations should establish a set of norms regarding diversity and inclusion that guide organisational behaviour in all aspects of organisational processes. Wasserman et al. (2008) emphasise the importance of leaders in creating a culture of inclusion. This undertaking places a demand on the leader to integrate the quest for increased diversity and inclusion into the company's long-term competitive strategy. Second, inclusion assumes an open exchange of information that is noticeably different among group members. Effective groups should develop 'critical norm conditions' where each piece of information has an equal value and is assessed and validated according to 'objective' standards and individual thought (Postmes et al., 2001). The third condition, the possibility of active participation, includes creating an environment where individuals feel included (Shore et al., 2011). In such an atmosphere 'differences are considered opportunities for both individual and organizational learning' (Chrobot-Mason & Thomas, 2002, p. 324). Alternative points of view and 'unshared information'(Galinsky & Kray, 2004) reduce groupthink and improve the quality of the decision-making process.

Diversity as a Goal and Diversity as a Means towards a Goal

The literature on diversity in governance and organisational settings published in the last two decades has largely targeted gender as a single equality category (Baker et al., 2020). Some authors have studied a broader range of diversity dimensions trying to explain whether board and senior management team diversity enhances organisational, financial and social performance (see Bear et al., 2010; Erhardt et al., 2003; Perryman et al., 2016). Although the empirical research is still inconclusive on this subject, a number of studies have emphasised certain tangible and intangible benefits of diversity in executive and governance suites. We focus on three major research propositions in the next sections.

Board Diversity Contributes to Better Board Functioning

Research has demonstrated that heterogeneous boards, because of variety in directors' experiences, knowledge and perspectives, may be more effective executing monitoring tasks (see Huse et al., 2009), can make better informed decisions (see Nielsen & Huse, 2010) and are likely to be more innovative and creative in strategy development (see Kor, 2006; Miller & Triana, 2009). However, research (see Rhode & Packel, 2014) has also suggested that demographic diversity does not necessarily bring diversity in perspectives (i.e. diversity of thought). For example, similar occupational and socio-economic backgrounds of demographically different board members may not ultimately improve decision-making processes and their outcomes (see Nielsen & Huse, 2010; Post & Byron, 2015; Singh, 2007).

The research on deep-level diversity has suggested that directors' diverse experiences and personalities may enhance board creativity and cognitive conflict (i.e. work-related differences in opinions) (Torchia et al., 2015). The cognitive dimensions of diversity ('use of knowledge and skills') have also a predictive effect on task performance (Minichilli et al., 2012). Melkumov and Khoreva (2015) have also found support for the argument that cognitive diversity on boards provides value to directors' monitoring and resource provision tasks. They have shown that directors' knowledge of the focal company and its industry, including professional and international experience, positively and strongly impact directors' involvement in monitoring tasks as well as their engagement as boundary spanners and mentors.

In relation to the board's advisory tasks, Tuggle et al. (2010) have paid particular attention to how cognitive dimensions of board diversity could be 'a potential source of creative thinking about new opportunities for growth' (p. 550). They have suggested that boards with greater heterogeneity associated with directors' industry experience, output-oriented background and tenure focus more attention on entrepreneurial issues at board meetings.

In a nutshell, the research has shown that demographic characteristics (surface-level diversity) of directors, based on gender, age and ethnicity, do matter. However, demographic diversity is not a sufficient factor to ensure better board functioning. Other studies, focusing on 'cognitive variety' (Eisenhardt et al., 2010), draw attention to those attributes of diversity (deep-level diversity) which have much greater impact on board effectiveness and organisations.

Diverse Boards Add Value to the Organisation's Strategy

The board's role in corporate strategy formation is emphasised in numerous publications (see Huse, 2008; Pugliese et al., 2009; Weitzner & Peridis, 2011). Scholars and practitioners acknowledge that the board cannot play this role without the presence of diversity around the board table. As 'a strategy shaping governance body' (McNulty & Pettigrew, 1999), the board considers a big picture and governs strategic activities. Therefore, the diversity of views, experiences, expertise, connections and backgrounds may strengthen the board's contribution to corporate strategy.

It has been found that the board's demographic diversity may directly and indirectly benefit corporations in their responses to environmental challenges (Bear et al., 2010; Dallas, 2002). Gender diversity scholars have argued that women on boards, in particular, may positively influence a company's performance through their active involvement in strategy process (see Adams, 2016; Levi et al., 2014; Post & Byron, 2015). Although the literature is inconclusive on female directors' direct contributions to more effective corporate strategy and firm performance, there is evidence of their indirect, positive influence through board processes (especially those through which they make decisions) (see Elstad & Ladegard, 2012; Kim & Starks, 2016; Nielsen & Huse, 2010).

Researchers have also engaged with other aspects of board diversity and their influence on strategy. For example, several studies have found that directors' multiple directorships can be seen as a contributing factor to effective board task performance (Bøhren & Strøm, 2010; Estélyi & Nisar, 2016; Shropshire, 2010). Directors tied to other companies can bring new ideas to the focal firms and add value to strategy development. Furthermore, the research in this vein has demonstrated that diverse boards show greater concern for corporate social responsibility and long-term sustainability (Harjoto et al., 2015; Post et al., 2011) and make efforts in strengthening relationships with various stakeholders (Broome et al., 2010; Cikaliuk et al., 2019).

A Diverse Board Acts as a Role Model for the Rest of the Organisation

The board does not work in isolation from the rest of the organisation. To paraphrase the title of Hambrick and Mason's (1984) seminal article: *The organization is a reflection of its top managers*, the board's composition similarly resonates the organisation's mission, strategic intentions and identity. According to Broome et al. (2010), board diversity may demonstrate to an organisation's employees the value the board places on diversity. It is likely that organisations with (demographically) diverse boards will also have diverse management teams (Joy, 2008) and employee-friendly policies (Fairfax, 2005). Diverse boards may also moderate relationships with management and contribute to a more effective exchange of information and ideas between the two groups (Broome et al., 2010).

The board and executive team should be the leaders of diversity and inclusion in every organisation (Gallegos et al., 2020; Wasserman et al., 2008). Hence, the board and management with demographically diverse members and inclusive practices serve as a role model for building a diverse workforce and an inclusive working environment. They develop the norms, provide access to information and empower diverse groups. Accordingly, representation and inclusion of different interests (employees, investors, customers, community, etc.) must be a component of the board and management's strategic vision. The organisation's leaders need to demonstrate long-term commitment to diversity, foster collaboration at inter-group levels and invest in their own learning to become inclusive leaders (Gallegos et al., 2020). The following Bank of New Zealand case study helps to illustrate these insights.

Case Study

Case Study 8.1 Bank of New Zealand Diversity Initiatives[1]

It was late Thursday afternoon of August 2016 and the Bank of New Zealand board just closed their regular meeting. This was a unique meeting at which the board farewelled their long-standing female director, Susan Macken, and welcomed a new chair of the bank's Diversity Council, Martin Gaskell. The occasion provided a good opportunity for board members and executives to discuss the process that the board, the executive leadership team and bank managers undertook in the last several years while developing an initial diversity strategy. It was also a convenient moment to start conversations around future steps for crafting multidimensional diversity initiatives. Although it was still too early to evaluate the contribution of the gender diversity strategy to the bank's financial figures, the board of directors felt confident their strategic diversity imperative would remain a key differentiating factor for years to come.

Brief History of the Bank of New Zealand

The Bank of New Zealand is the oldest, continuously operating bank in New Zealand. It was incorporated in 1861 and became the country's first national bank. From its first woman clerk in 1915, Miss Ivy Lillian Waters, to its bank services 'for women by women' in 1958, women took many roles in the bank as it continued to expand its operations and adapt to changes in the economy and society.

Governance Framework: Bank of New Zealand as a Subsidiary of National Australia Bank

Over the decades, the bank had shifted between private, government and public ownership. In 1992, the National Australia Bank (NAB) purchased the shares of the Bank of New Zealand, which became a member of the NAB Group as a wholly owned subsidiary.

The NAB Group consisted of financial and insurance service companies operating in Australia and New Zealand, Asia, the United Kingdom and the United States. As a subsidiary, the Bank of New Zealand operated with a high level of autonomy. It established an independent board of directors, board charter and committees. Their responsibilities aligned with those of the NAB Group board. The Bank of New Zealand board consisted of seven to nine directors. Two board members were typically appointed from NAB.

Bank of New Zealand Diversity Strategy (2010): Early Initiatives

Andrew Thorburn, managing director and CEO of Bank of New Zealand, learned that the NAB Group had made progress in targeting a diversity initiative. NAB had engaged in background research, conducted an audit and set targets for October 2010. The parent company recognised that a long-term approach to diversity, talent development and capability building required an unwavering commitment across its subsidiaries. Thorburn and the board were keen to adapt NAB's commitment for the Bank of New Zealand.

In early 2010, the Bank of New Zealand board and executive leadership team participated in an annual strategy session. It was Thorburn's opportunity to engage fully with the board and management and to gain their strategic insights and contributions. In one of the activities, a board member and HR director co-delivered a diversity presentation on the changing demographics for Auckland and New Zealand.

By 2010, New Zealand had one of the highest immigration rates in the world and was well on its way to becoming the fifth most ethnically diverse country in the OECD (see Chen, 2015). A pronounced trend in immigration saw the biggest increases coming from Chinese, Indian and Filipino ethnic groups. Auckland, the gateway city for most immigrants, had not been exempt. A large indigenous Māori population, coupled with a large Pacific community, made Auckland distinct domestically and internationally. In time, presenters proposed, demographic changes would require a business transformation for the bank to compete effectively. They addressed implications for staff recruitment and retention, which they encapsulated in the phrase, 'It is not a diversity strategy; it is a business strategy'.

The presentation landed well. It adopted a multidimensional orientation to diversity, expanding the bank's historical gender diversity focus. The board discussed how to position its initial efforts in leading the transformation. Some directors believed that the demographic shifts compelled a multidimensional ethnic and cultural orientation as the starting point. Other directors saw a substantial upside for beginning with gender diversity. With the different perspectives around the boardroom table, the directors knew they broadly shared a commitment to acting on gender diversity.

In April 2010, with the board-senior management strategy session still fresh in their minds, Thorburn and Louise Harvey-Wills, HR director, commissioned a review of the bank's systems, policies and processes regarding gender diversity. Having reviewed the consultant's report, Thorburn and Harvey-Wills were keen to lead the charge. In October 2010, while alert to demographic trends, Thorburn, with the BNZ board's endorsement, committed to initial gender targets with NAB.

Between February and August 2011, the bank conducted further research on gender. Debbie Teale, the consultant who produced the initial 2010 report, returned with a focus on identifying the systemic issues. The assessment revealed that the bank did not differ significantly from other financial institutions with its low retention of women and under-representation of women in senior management.

The small working group guided by Harvey-Wills recognised that a major transformation, like the one they envisaged for the bank, would demand a compelling business logic. They needed to demonstrate the commercial case not only to their own board and employees, but also to NAB. The board encouraged the adoption of a commercial case orientation to the strategy to temper criticism that the initiative was 'just a human resource thing or a political correctness thing'.

The board acknowledged that Thorburn would have to reach widely and dig deeply into all aspects of the operations to effect a strategic transformation while remaining committed to its vision and values in an increasing competitive marketplace. The all-encompassing transformation would demand board and CEO leadership, collectively and individually, to engage employees and encourage them to achieve their potential to the fullest.

Based on the commercial case, they gave their commitment to support Thorburn on this ambitious journey. With that assurance in place, this small working group, with external support from Teale, crafted a plan to provide the foundation for the Bank of New Zealand to capitalise on its emerging diversity and inclusion strategy.

Creation of a Diversity Council (2011)

By December 2011, a gender diversity strategy was presented to the Bank of New Zealand board. One of the key recommendations of the report that the board adopted stated that this initiative should not reside within the Human Resources department despite the groundwork that unit had done. The report called for board and CEO to lead the strategy and a separate body, the Diversity Council, to implement it.

The board also determined that the chair of the Diversity Council would report informally to the chair for the People and Remuneration Committee of the board. This second key decision established an informal (dotted line) reporting relationship to ensure the board was well informed. The

Diversity Council was accountable to the CEO (Thorburn). Senior executives from each of the bank's business divisions, including Asian and Migrant banking and Māori banking, joined the Diversity Council for their capability to effect change in the units they led.

A third key decision was that someone other than Thorburn would chair the Diversity Council. The board believed that separating the roles of CEO and chair of the Diversity Council would allow the requisite attention for this transformation effort. The board also considered employees' and other stakeholders' reactions to this decision, as a great deal was at stake. The board wanted to add to the bank's overall image, reputation and performance, not risk it.

Thorburn believed that Anthony Healy was an ideal candidate to chair the Council given his operational experience as the leader of the bank's business banking division, BNZ Partners. Healy also brought strategic vision, teambuilding expertise and mentoring capability. From Healy's perspective, it was a good fit because he brought a fresh set of eyes to the bank and a passion for change. His rock-solid commitment developed, in part, because of familial insight into the challenges and the few effective ways to fuel positive change. He explained:

> The reason I got involved was partly living the experience through my wife's eyes of being a professional and the challenges she faced—many of which were not conscious to the organisation or to the people that she was working with. So partly it was important to me from a justice sense. Thirdly, what does flexible working mean? Because my wife went for a three-and-a-half-day week in her law firm and she ended up working 80 hours a week and getting paid for three and a half days, so that doesn't work. So, I helped her manage through all that.

The board's fourth key decision was to create a specific mandate for the Diversity Council. It 'leads the Bank of New Zealand Diversity Agenda, sets strategic priorities and oversees performance related to diversity'.

To build a coordinated view among the directors and gain alignment with management, the board accepted the recommendation for gender diversity as a starting point with a proviso for the development and implementation of a multidimensional diversity strategy, including ethnicity and culture. Healy committed to aggressive timelines. This fifth key decision by the board, in combination with the others, set the trajectory for bank's strategic transformation through its diversity strategy.

Implementing the Strategy

In its communication efforts, a challenge for the Diversity Council was to move employees from being interested to becoming actively engaged.

DEVELOPING RECEPTIVITY FOR CHANGES

With the strategy developed and refined through engagement with the board, the Diversity Council decided not to launch any programmes immediately. Instead, it opted to develop company-wide receptivity for change by organising a series of galvanising workshops. While the business case and macro trends affecting the future of the bank appeared clear, the goal of the 'Unconscious Bias' workshops was to make them personal for each employee.

The workshop launched with the executive leadership team and cascaded through the organisation. Between the introduction of the first session in 2012 and 2014, the top 500 ranked employees participated in the workshops. During this period, the Diversity Council rebranded the workshops to 'Unconscious Knowledge' acknowledging that each individual has unconscious knowledge which can impact the decision-making process in positive and negative ways.

EARLY INITIATIVES

In 2012, following the launch of the 'Unconscious Bias' workshops, the Diversity Council introduced a series of targeted initiatives aimed at a cultural and business transformation. The multi-pronged initiative included identification of flexible career pathways, personal professional development for leadership, mentoring and sponsorship. The Diversity Council adapted a programme from NAB, 'Realise', to strengthen the talent pipeline of women for the top three layers of management.

The Diversity Council also set a goal to reclassify all positions in the bank as 'flexible'. It established a policy that all jobs could use flexible work arrangements, such as job sharing and working from home. While the bank accepted this in principle, actual practice lagged. Policy revisions ensued. Managers gained the discretion to opt out with an explanation of the exception. The 'adopt or explain' principle increased the flexibility option to 60–70 per cent of all advertised positions.

Board of Directors Commits to Modelling the Way

UNCONSCIOUS BIAS WORKSHOPS

As the board of directors learned more about the initiatives the Diversity Council had spearheaded, the programmes attracted the directors who wanted to model the way. In 2013, intrigued by the executive team's experience in the 'Unconscious Bias' workshop, one director joined a session.

In 2014, the full board participated in an 'Unconscious Bias' workshop. With expectations riding high, this session did not initially have the desired impact. The facilitator elected to walk through the learning objectives and programme changes. This did not sit well with the directors, who wanted to learn from their shared experience. The board engaged in a second workshop with directors and senior executives later that year. As one of the directors pointed out, 'I think it has actually brought to light some unconscious biases that people were a bit surprised about'.

OTHER PROGRAMMES AND INITIATIVES

The board created and implemented an annual plan of activities and events to expand their input, knowledge and skills on diversity. The directors participated in at least two rounds of Te Reo Māori language training. They went to a Marae with a group from the Māori cadetship programme. Following a meeting with the interns, the board set a target goal set for selection and retention of interns.

On an individual level, members of the board championed the leadership development program, 'Realise'. One of the directors, Macken, played a strong personal leadership role in her sponsorship, mentorship and connection with women in the programme who aspired to senior leadership roles.

The alignment of the board members' individual and collective commitment did not go unnoticed. As one member of the executive leadership team stressed, 'It was really important they had shown that they were committed to role modelling diversity as well as interest in the whole programme around what the board commissioned'.

DIVERSITY OF THE BOARD ITSELF (2008 TO 2015)

Having joined the board in June 2005, Dr Susan Macken was credited with leveraging her experience as an economist at the World Bank and as a senior manager in high-profile, publicly listed companies, and as an experienced director. Her initial three-year appointment was renewed. Healy lauded Macken's commitment to diversity in the workplace where she played a strong personal leadership role not only in her role as board director, but also candidly sharing her successes and challenges.

In 2008, Dr Andrew Pearce accepted the invitation to join the board. With Pearce's professional qualifications as an environmental scientist, he valued the board's willingness to seek out directors who were not like-minded individuals. In his previous role, Pearce introduced a 'women-as-scientists' initiative and held directorships with local government as well as the elected body of Ngai Tahu in commercial operations and infrastructure companies.

In 2008, Stephen Moir's appointment brought a people-focused, bottom-line profitability orientation he acquired, in part, through his work experience in banking in Southeast Asia and South Africa. In 2009 the board welcomed Prudence Flacks, the second female director. Having honed her commercial law acumen in one of New Zealand's largest law firms, Flacks brought expertise in corporate and regulatory matters, corporate finance, capital markets, securitisation and business restructuring to the boardroom. In 2011, Doug McKay, an experienced international CEO and director, was approached. He joined the board in 2013. In 2015, McKay accepted the appointment as board chairman.

Meanwhile, changes also came from the NAB Group. In 2011, a NAB executive, Gavin Slater, was appointed as a BNZ non-executive director. Michaela Healey, the NAB Group Executive People Communications and Governance, replaced the outgoing NAB Group CEO Clyne on the BNZ board in 2014. She was the third female director appointed. The change in BNZ leadership introduced an additional change to the BNZ board. Anthony Healy, the chair of the Diversity Council, became managing director and CEO of the Bank of New Zealand.

Consistent with its selection criteria, the board recommended that Mai Chen join it in April 2015 as the bank's sixth independent director and the fourth women on the board since 2008. Prior to her appointment Chen had initiated the Superdiversity Centre aimed at increasing awareness of the legal and policy implications of the demographic changes facing New Zealand's businesses, governments and citizens. This initiative combined Chen's legal expertise as New Zealand's pioneer in the practice of public law.

The directors' appointments affirmed their collective commitment to diversity. As one director explained:

> You cannot have people on the board just to tick a box. They must be able to contribute. Boards these days do not have passengers. Shareholders are not prepared to pay for that. At the end of the day, you have to run a bank so you must have the skills that you need around the table.

The board cultivated a culture that encouraged meaningful contribution as stated by one director:

> It is extraordinary to be on a board like this because it makes you feel able to contribute fully; not to self-censor to stay on side and to be the same—but you feel encouraged to be different, which allows you to maximise your contribution.

Another director elaborated:

> You cannot make up a perfect board. What you want is diversity of experience in different types of industries. There are some 'must haves'. I do not think you can have a bank board without a lawyer, and someone deeply experienced in financial services.

The board's approach to identifying and attracting new directors seemed to pay off in terms of board leadership in positioning the bank as an international trail blazer for gender diversity.

Board of Directors Sets and Monitors Strategic Diversity and Inclusion Direction

The board's commitment to setting direction matched its commitment to monitoring, evaluating and revising the implementation of the diversity initiative.

BOARD'S ROLE IN SETTING AND REVISING STRATEGIC DIRECTION THROUGH DIVERSITY COUNCIL

The board delegated authority to the CEO working through the Diversity Council to set targets. The Chair of the Diversity Council, Healy, would then 'bring it to the board, the board reviewed it, pushed it around, changed it, challenged it. The product ended up better'. The challenges Healy faced when presenting the targets to the board were two sides of the same coin. One set of questions queried whether the bar was high enough. The others concerned whether the strategy was achievable without a drain on their resources.

BOARD'S ROLE IN MONITORING PERFORMANCE

With the board's commitment to strengthening the bank's fitness for the future the directors also made it clear that performance counts. The board championed that the bank 'do it with hard measures' from the outset. To capture employees' attention that this transformation was a collective effort, Thorburn incorporated diversity performance objectives for every formal leader in the bank.

DELIVERING AWARD-WINNING GENDER DIVERSITY AND RECORD-BREAKING FINANCIAL RESULTS

The approach to diversity as a strategy seemed to have paid off. In 2014, the Bank of New Zealand earned international and national recognition for its efforts. The United Nations recognised the Bank of New Zealand's corporate leadership as the supreme winner for gender equality and its progress in implementing the UN Women's Empowerment Principles. The bank won Deloitte's Top 200 inaugural diversity award. The Asia-Pacific Economic Cooperation forum (APEC) also recognised it as one of the top 50 companies for women to work among 21 Pacific Rim economies.

The Bank of New Zealand's vision to be New Zealand's most respected bank, enabled by its campaign 'Be Good with Money', also guided another year of successful financial performance. In 2015, cash earnings exceeded US$700 million for the first time as part of its ongoing commitment to balance sheet strength.

Board Considers Next Options (Beyond Gender) for Diversity and Inclusion Initiative

With the 'maturing of the strategy' some directors were keen to move ahead with the next phase of the diversity strategy.

SEGMENTED CUSTOMER BASE

A 'Superdiversity Stocktake', financed in part by the Bank of New Zealand, laid out the sweeping changes that the financial service industry faced, including demographic shifts of consumers. As one director pointed out:

> The Diversity Council is trying to go beyond just gender, which is important, but frankly, it is the battle that we should have won by now, and we should be moving on especially in Auckland where we are almost 50 per cent Māori, Asian and Pasifika. We really do need to address ethnicity. It is a burning platform for companies.

The Diversity Council had launched a series of pilot initiatives beyond gender which delivered promising results. The bank was trying to grow by initiating specialised business units aimed at Asian, Māori, Indian and Pasifika clients. As one director explained, 'If our banking business is going to succeed, we need to be able to relate to all new types of customers'.

With a multi-lingual team in place, the Asian and Migrant banking unit actively reached out to high value niches which included investor and highly skilled migrants and groups to understand their priorities. By building relationships among the growing, diverse Asian community, the bank aimed to capture the increasing trade and capital flows between New Zealand and China and other Asian countries.

While one dimension of the bank's strategy targeted migrants coming to Auckland, the bank took a country-wide approach to building relationships among individual and business-led Māori clients through its Māori banking unit. Following the Crown-treaty process, the bank anticipated that 35–40 per cent of the GDP for New Zealand would have some Māori ownership by 2030. With the growth potential for banking among Māori businesses, trusts and individuals, the bank was keen to grow its 22 per cent market share.

The tailored approaches seemed to resonate with Asian and Māori consumers and led to specifically designed initiatives with Indian clients and staff. Internally, the heads of the businesses collaborated to ensure a few key objectives: they worked to minimise silos among business units, share lessons learned in recruitment and retention, and underpin their activities with compelling commercial cases.

HIRING TALENT

With pressure to identify, attract and recruit talent from a wide range of backgrounds, adaptations emerged. In terms of gender diversity, the bank implemented gender-balanced selection criteria. To build a talent pipeline, they started Māori cadetship and graduate programmes. To expand the multi-lingual talent pool based on evolving demographics, graduate recruitment targeted Mandarin-speaking Chinese.

The Diversity Council introduced a 'cultural ambassadors' initiative for employees of similar ethnic and cultural backgrounds to connect, network and share experiences. A member of the Diversity Council traced the emergence of one aspect of this initiative: 'A Samoan/Pacific Island workgroup talked about inclusion—being able to bring all of yourself to work—to attract, retain and make staff feel better'.

RETAINING AGING WORKFORCE TALENT

Undertaking initiatives to balance an aging workforce with attracting new prospects earned the bank further distinction among its competitors. Healy elaborated:

> The retention initiative was based around helping mature employees plan for the next phase in their lives. It takes a holistic view of the mature employee and considers their identity, financial aspirations, career, health and relationships as part of their employment agreement with the bank.

Board's Key Challenges: Where to from Here?

It was still early days for the multidimensional diversity initiative. The board members' mindsets converged around the gender issue, but they were still not clear on the implications the multiple dimensions of diversity would have for the transformation of Bank of New Zealand. As one director explained, 'It was a combination of a whole lot of fine-grained practices that changed the game with gender. So where to from here is a little more difficult'.

While the board considered strategic direction, it also grappled with the accountability of the Diversity Council. With Healy's promotion to CEO in 2014, he no longer embodied the separation between CEO and chair of the Diversity Council as set out by the board. The board's renewed commitment to the diversity and inclusion strategy seemed to warrant scrutiny of the Diversity Council's composition and role.

As chair, McKay reinforced the board's commitment to sustaining its record of profitability and growth. He explained Bank of New Zealand would focus on its competitive diversity strategy for the future:

> It is critical, it is at the heart of our strategy. But it is all about how you implement and how you give effect in the organisation. Because we all intellectually understand the evidence base—that is, building globally around diversity in organisations leads to better long-term financial performance. We look at every decision we make from a diversity perspective. We do not always reach the high standards we set ourselves and occasionally we fall back a bit on some of the key measures we would like to be continually driving. There is no conversation that is not influenced by a diversity outcome, because a good diversity outcome is a good business outcome.

Discussion

With this case study, we aimed to draw attention to board leadership and support in setting a strategic initiative that aligns diversity and performance as a long-term corporate strategy. Although the case study illustrates how the management of the bank, with encouragement and active engagement of the board, developed a gender diversity strategy as part of their corporate strategy, our intention in discussing the case study goes beyond this topic. First, we argue that a responsible board should consider diversity in a wider sense in the context of strategy development. Second, we maintain that strategic change efforts that involve diversity must be purposefully put into practice. These and other relevant points are discussed below.

Untraditional Thinking for Untraditional Challenges

Boards and organisations are facing major challenges due to uncertain and disruptive environments. Therefore, organisational decision-makers are becoming more open to thinking about challenges in non-traditional ways. Accordingly, organisations need to recruit people who can embrace where the world is going and who have the motivation and ability to engage with different types of people with different value sets. This also means that boards and management need to clearly understand the demands and influence of present and future stakeholders beyond shareholders.

In the case of the bank, the board and management focused on two aspects of diversity strategy: the business case and the social case. In the former, they formulated a diversity strategy as part of their overall corporate strategy. Specifically, they considered specific areas where a diversity strategy could contribute to their corporate goals. For example, they looked at the changing demographics of New Zealand and the bank's current and potential market share conceiving and evaluating different strategic approaches to different groups of customers. In the latter, the board and management focused on social goals and performance. Here, their attention centred on the bank's employees and their career development. The board and management initiated programmes for these employees to acquire new skill sets to benefit them personally as well as the bank.

An important question for responsible boards is how to achieve and balance business and social performance. Having directors with different demographic and educational backgrounds, personal and professional experiences, and organisational affiliations would help boards and organisations to better embrace the idea of social performance as a core business issue (Dentchev, 2004). This calls for directors who grasp new strategic challenges and understand the needs of an organisation's internal and external constituencies. The need for strategic transformation in a changing environment and an increasing importance of various non-shareholder stakeholders are key conditions for diversity in the boardroom and the organisation.

The Importance of Diversity at the Board Level

There are two dimensions of board diversity which should be pointed out in this case. The first is an observable one—the compositional, demographic dimension. The appointment of directors of different gender and backgrounds, however, will not necessarily result in better board workings. Some boards are doing well at getting diversity on boards, but they might be less successful at getting diversity out of boards (Chen & Eraković, 2019). At the time, the BNZ board was the most diverse corporate board in New Zealand; half of the board members were women and there were three different nationalities on the board. Demographic diversity was not implemented for the sake of diversity, but it did, in fact, serve the interests of the bank as explained in the first point. In addition, research indicates that more women and different nationalities may increase the diversity of perspectives, which in turn can direct a board's attention to consumers and international markets, and ultimately contribute to the company's competitive advantage (see Dallas, 2002; Erhardt et al., 2003; García-Meca et al., 2015).

The second dimension of board diversity for this case is affective. This dimension played an important part in capturing directors' genuine interest and support for the bank's gender diversity strategy. Four prominent members of the board, including the chair and CEO, faced situations through which they became aware of diversity issues (e.g. poverty, visible minority). Through these experiences, they became open to and proactive in supporting diversity initiatives. Their lived diverse challenges also helped them to better understand and develop empathy for the bank's customers, employees and other stakeholders' needs and foster commitment to the bank's social objectives.

Strong Board–Management Relationships

The board–management relationship, including processes of building and nurturing this relationship, is a key aspect of governance. For these relationships to be productive, directors and executives individually and collectively should be able to question their own thinking; that is, reflect on what they think and why, and collectively understand the implications of exercising leadership. The board's diversity, or lack of it, can have a substantial effect on this relationship-building task. According to research (Broome et al., 2010; Dezsö & Ross, 2012; Landaw, 2020), diverse boards have greater expectations of insight from management and are more involved with management in exploring new ideas, trends and business opportunities. In the current, diverse environment, directors, as well as management, should be able to communicate and work with multiple organisational constituents.

The Change Model: Attitudinal versus Structural Changes

The above points reiterate an important question from the practice and theory of change management: What and how to prioritise—attitudinal or structural changes? One line of thought assumes that structural changes, such as new organisational roles and responsibilities, cause a shift in attitudes and individual behaviours (see Beer et al., 1990). The opposing approach argues that without a change in culture (that is, underpinning beliefs and assumptions) implementation of organisational changes (those related to social structure dimensions) are not possible (Powell & Posner, 1980; Waldersee & Griffiths, 2004).

To address this question, the change management that was followed by the bank's leadership commenced by analysing developments outside the organisation. They primarily focused on the changing face of Auckland and its cultural diversity. Next, they undertook a global research of best practices in organisation diversity. Finally, they engaged in a bank-wide study of career development and talent management. The board supported 'culture shaping actions', prioritising changes in values and beliefs of management at all levels (attitudinal changes). Their position was that these changes were the precondition for new structures, systems, policies and procedures (structural changes) to work effectively in the context of its gender diversity strategy.

In the later stage, the board was more focused on structural elements; that is, specific areas (e.g. positions, business units, systems) where diversity initiatives could contribute to the bank's corporate strategy. The board emphasised the importance of market share ('different approach to different groups'), financial and non-financial measures, and links between diversity initiatives and innovation (i.e. creation of new products).

Conclusion

This chapter examined three research areas that have been shown to be critical in the process of developing diversity and inclusion in organisations: board attitudes and composition, corporate strategy and role modelling. These dimensions of diversity and inclusion help to understand how inclusive board culture and directors' individual interests and concerns about gender (and beyond) diversity issues have contributed to strengthening the bank's capabilities for future environmental challenges. This suggests that responsibly led boards regard diversity and inclusion as a strategic asset and as a source of economic and social performance. Future developments will benefit from continuing a dialogue between research and practice that can further explore the ways in which responsibly led boards promote diversity in all of its dimensions.

Note

1 This case study was written with the cooperation of the Bank of New Zealand board. All data are based on field research and public sources. The research underpinning this case study included in-depth interviews with the chair, directors, CEO, executive management and management appointed in the period 2005–2015. This case was developed with the use of interviews along with publicly available resources. The material produced by the company included the parent company's annual reports, press releases and notices of annual general meetings, among others. It also featured material produced by third party sources which included newspaper articles and reports, among others.

References

Adams, R. B. (2016). Women on boards: The superheroes of tomorrow? *The Leadership Quarterly*, 27(3), 371–386.

Baker, H. K., Pandey, N., Kumar, S., Haldar, A. (2020). A bibliometric analysis on board diversity: Current status, development, and future research directions. *Journal of Business Research*, 108(January), 232–246.

Bear, S., Rahman, N., & Post, C. (2010). The impact of board diversity and gender composition on corporate social responsibility and firm reputation. *Journal of Business Ethics*, 97(2), 207–221.

Beer, M., Eisenstat, R. A., & Spector, B. (1990). Why change programs don't produce change. *Harvard Business Review*, 68(6), 158–166.

Bennett, N., & Lemoine, G. J. (2014). What a difference a word makes: Understanding threats to performance in a VUCA world. *Business Horizons*, 57(3), 311–317.

Bøhren, Ø., & Strøm, R. Ø. (2010). Governance and politics: Regulating independence and diversity in the board room. *Journal of Business Finance & Accounting*, 37(9–10), 1281–1308.

Broome, L. L., Conley, J. M., & Krawiec, K. D. (2010). Dangerous categories: Narratives of corporate board diversity board diversity and corporate performance: Filling in the gaps. *North Carolina Law Review*, 89, 759–808.

Chattopadhyay, P., Glick, W. H., Miller, C. C., & Huber, G. P. (1999). Determinants of executive beliefs: Comparing functional conditioning and social influence. *Strategic Management Journal*, 20(8), 763–790.

Chen, M. (2015). Superdiversity stocktake: Implications for business, government and New Zealand. www.chenpalmer.com/wp-content/uploads/Superdiversity_Stocktake.pdf.

Chen, M., & Eraković, L. (2019, June). *Diverse thinking in New Zealand boardrooms:. Looking through rose-coloured glasses* [paper presentation]. EURAM Conference, Lisbon, Portugal.

Chrobot-Mason, D., & Thomas, K. M. (2002). Minority employees in majority organizations: The intersection of individual and organizational racial identity in the workplace. *Human Resource Development Review*, 1(3), 323–344.

Cikaliuk, M., Eraković, L., Jackson, B., Noonan, C., & Watson, S. (2019). Board of directors: Building relationships with non-shareholder stakeholders. In J. Gabrielsson, W. Khlif & S. Yamak (eds), *Research handbook on boards of directors* (pp. 209–228). Edward Elgar Publishing.

Dallas, L. (2002). New managerialism and diversity on corporate boards of directors. *Tulane Law Review*, 76(5–6).

Dentchev, N. A. (2004). Corporate social performance as a business strategy. *Journal of Business Ethics*, 55(4), 397–412.

Dezsö, C. L., & Ross, D. G. (2012). Does female representation in top management improve firm performance? A panel data investigation. *Strategic Management Journal*, 33(9), 1072–1089.

Eisenhardt, K. M., Furr, N. R., & Bingham, C. B. (2010). Microfoundations of performance: Balancing efficiency and flexibility in dynamic environments. *Organization Science*, 21(6), 1263–1273.

Elstad, B., & Ladegard, G. (2012). Women on corporate boards: Key influencers or tokens? *Journal of Management & Governance*, 16(4), 595–615.

Erhardt, N. L., Werbel, J. D., & Shrader, C. B. (2003). Board of director diversity and firm financial performance. *Corporate Governance: An International Review*, 11 (2), 102–111.

Estélyi, K. S., & Nisar, T. M. (2016). Diverse boards: Why do firms get foreign nationals on their boards? *Journal of Corporate Finance*, 39, 174–192.

Fairfax, L. M. (2005). The bottom line on board diversity: A cost-benefit analysis of the business rationales for diversity on corporate boards. *Wisconsin Law Review*, 2005(3), 795–854.

Ferdman, B. M., & Deane, B. (eds). (2014). *Diversity at work: The practice of inclusion.* Jossey-Bass.

Forbes, D. P., & Milliken, F. J. (1999). Cognition and corporate governance: Understanding boards of directors as strategic decision-making groups. *The Academy of Management Review*, 24(3), 489–505.

Galinsky, A. D., & Kray, L. J. (2004). From thinking about what might have been to sharing what we know: The effects of counterfactual mind-sets on information sharing in groups. *Journal of Experimental Social Psychology*, 40(5), 606–618.

Gallegos, P. V., Wasserman, I. C., & Ferdman, B. M. (2020). The dance of inclusion. In K. M. Thomas (ed.), *Diversity resistance in organizations* (pp. 165–177). Routledge.

Garcia, A. (2018). Director skills: Diversity of thought and experience in the boardroom. https://corpgov.law.harvard.edu/2018/10/10/director-skills-diversity-of-thought-and-experience-in-the-boardroom/.

García-Meca, E., García-Sánchez, I.-M., & Martínez-Ferrero, J. (2015). Board diversity and its effects on bank performance: An international analysis. *Journal of Bank & Finance*, 53(April), 202–214.

Hambrick, D. C., & Mason, P. A. (1984). Upper echelons: The organization as a reflection of its top managers. *The Academy of Management Review*, 9(2), 193–206.

Harjoto, M., Laksmana, I., & Lee, R. (2015). Board diversity and corporate social responsibility. *Journal of Business Ethics*, 132(4), 641–660.

Harrison, D. A., Price, K. H., Gavin, J. H., & Florey, A. T. (2002). Time, teams, and task performance: Changing effects of surface- and deep-level diversity on group functioning. *The Academy of Management Journal*, 45(5), 1029–1045.

Hassan, R., & Marimuthu, M. (2018). Bridging and bonding: Having a Muslim diversity on corporate boards and performance. *Journal of Islamic Accounting and Business Research*, 9(3), 457–478.

Hayles, V. R. (2014). Communicating about diversity and inclusion. In B. M. Ferdman & B. R. Deane (eds). *Diversity at work: The practice of inclusion* (pp. 55–90). John Wiley & Sons.

Heilman, M. E. (2012). Gender stereotypes and workplace bias. *Research in Organizational Behavior*, 32, 113–135.

Horney, N., Pasmore, B., & O'Shea, T. (2010). Leadership agility: A business imperative for a VUCA world. *People & Strategy*, 33(4), 323–328.

Huse, M. (2007). *Boards, governance and value creation: The human side of corporate governance*. Cambridge University Press.

Huse, M. (2008). *The value creating board: Corporate governance and organisational behaviour*. Routledge.

Huse, M., Nielsen, S., & Hagen, I. (2009). Women and employee-elected board members, and their contributions to board control tasks. *Journal of Business Ethics*, 89(4), 581–597.

Joy, L. (2008). Advancing women leaders: The connection between women board directors and women corporate officers. www.catalyst.org/wp-content/uploads/2019/01/Advancing_Women_Leaders_The_Connection_Between_Women_Board_Directors_and_Women_Corporate_Officers_0.pdf.

Kagzi, M., & Guha, M. (2018). Board demographic diversity: A review of literature. *Journal of Strategy and Management*, 11(1), 33–51.

Kim, D., & Starks, L. T. (2016). Gender diversity on corporate boards: Do women contribute unique skills? *American Economic Review*, 106(5), 267–271.

Kor, Y. Y. (2006). Direct and interaction effects of top management team and board compositions on R&D investment strategy. *Strategic Management Journal*, 27 (11), 1081–1099.

Landaw, J. (2020). How diverse is your board, really? *Harvard Business Review*, 11 June. https://hbr.org/2020/06/how-diverse-is-your-board-really.

Levi, M., Li, K., & Zhang, F. (2014). Director gender and mergers and acquisitions. *Journal of Corporate Finance*, 28, 185–200.

McNulty, T., & Pettigrew, A. (1999). Strategists on the board. *Organization Studies*, 20(1), 47–74.

Melkumov, D., & Khoreva, V. (2015). The effect of board capital and conflict on the tasks of the board of directors. *International Studies of Management & Organization*, 45(1), 60–79.

Miller, T., & Triana, M. D. C. (2009). Demographic diversity in the boardroom: Mediators of the board diversity–firm performance relationship. *Journal of Management Studies*, 46(5), 755–786.

Milliken, F. J., & Martins, L. L. (1996). Searching for common threads: Understanding the multiple effects of diversity in organizational groups. *Academy of Management Review*, 21(2), 402–433.

Minichilli, A., Zattoni, A., Nielsen, S., & Huse, M. (2012). Board task performance: An exploration of micro- and macro-level determinants of board effectiveness. *Journal of Organizational Behavior*, 33(2), 193–215.

Nielsen, S., & Huse, M. (2010). Women directors' contribution to board decision-making and strategic involvement: The role of equality perception. *European Management Review* 7(1), 16–29.

Perryman, A. A., Fernando, G. D., & Tripathy, A. (2016). Do gender differences persist? An examination of gender diversity on firm performance, risk, and executive compensation. *Journal of Business Research*, 69(2), 579–586.

Post, C., & Byron, K. (2015). Women on boards and firm financial performance: A meta-analysis. *Academy of Management Journal*, 58(5), 1546–1571.

Post, C., Rahman, N., & Rubow, E. (2011). Green governance: Boards of directors' composition and environmental corporate social responsibility. *Business & Society*, 50(1), 189–223.

Postmes, T., Spears, R., & Cihangir, S. (2001). Quality of decision making and group norms. *Journal of Personality and Social Psychology*, 80(6), 918–930.

Powell, G. N., & Posner, B. Z. (1980). Managing change: Attitudes, targets, problems, and strategies. *Group & Organization Studies*, 5(3), 310–323.

Pugliese, A., Bezemer, P.-J., Zattoni, A., Huse, M., Van den Bosch, F. A. J., & Volberda, H. W. (2009). Boards of directors' contribution to strategy: A literature review and research agenda. *Corporate Governance: An International Review*, 17 (3), 292–306.

Rhode, D., & Packel, A. K. (2014). Diversity on corporate boards: How much difference does difference make? *Delaware Journal of Corporate Law* 39(2), 377–426.

Shore, L. M., Randel, A. E., Chung, B. G., Dean, M. A., Holcombe Ehrhart, K., & Singh, G. (2011). Inclusion and diversity in work groups: A review and model for future research. *Journal of Management*, 37(4), 1262–1289.

Shropshire, C. (2010). The role of the interlocking director and board receptivity in the diffusion of practices. *The Academy of Management Review*, 35(2), 246–264.

Singh, V. (2007). Ethnic diversity on top corporate boards: A resource dependency perspective. *The International Journal of Human Resource Management*, 18(12), 2128–2146.

Taljaard, C. C., Ward, M. J., & Muller, C. J. (2015). Board diversity and financial performance: A graphical time-series approach. *South African Journal of Economic and Management Sciences*, 18(3), 425–447.

Thomas, D. A. (2004). Diversity as strategy. *Harvard Business Review*, September. https://hbr.org/2004/09/diversity-as-strategy.

Thomas-Hunt, M. C., & Phillips, K. W. (2004). When what you know is not enough: Expertise and gender dynamics in task groups. *Personality and Social Psychology Bulletin*, 30(12), 1585–1598.

Torchia, M., Calabrò, A., & Morner, M. (2015). Board of directors' diversity, creativity, and cognitive conflict. *International Studies of Management & Organization* 45(1), 6–24.

Tuggle, C. S., Schnatterly, K., & Johnson, R. A. (2010). Attention patterns in the boardroom: How board composition and processes affect discussion of entrepreneurial issues. *The Academy of Management Journal*, 53(3), 550–571.

Waldersee, R., & Griffiths, A. (2004). Implementing change: Matching implementation methods and change type. *Leadership & Organization Development Journal*, 25(5), 424–434.

Wasserman, I. C., Gallegos, P. V., & Ferdman, B. M. (2008). Dancing with resistance: Leadership challenges in fostering a culture of inclusion. In K. M. Thomas (ed.), *Diversity resistance in organizations* (pp. 175–200). Taylor & Francis.

Weitzner, D., & Peridis, T. (2011). Corporate governance as part of the strategic process: Rethinking the role of the board. *Journal of Business Ethics*, 102(1), 33–42.

Winters, M.-F. (2014). From diversity to inclusion: An inclusion equation. In B. M. Ferdman & B. Deane (eds), *Diversity at work: The practice of inclusion* (pp. 205–228). Jossey-Bass.

9 Conclusion

Key Lessons and Future Directions

Introduction

In this concluding chapter we review the key learnings from developing the leadership-in-governance conceptual framework and applying it to the case studies featured in this book. As we have shown in this book the leadership in governance framework is based on the entity model of the corporation which serves to unleash the potential of the corporate form to generate value over time (Watson, 2022). It also provides a way for boards to balance the interests of shareholders as owners of shares in the company, with the interests of stakeholders of the company. By requiring a focus on the company itself, the entity model also legitimises boards adopting a long term perspective that extends beyond current shareholders.

At the heart of this conceptual framework is *the integrative approach* to the research process that it actively promotes. The main features and benefits of this integrative approach are highlighted in this chapter in the hope that it will encourage other researchers to explore and further refine this approach. Fundamentally, this integrative approach promotes greater engagement and cross-fertilisation within multi-disciplinary teams, and between researchers and practitioners.

Looking ahead to how leadership in corporate governance research can profitably develop in the future, we advocate that *diversification* is a key imperative. This imperative encompasses diversification in research methods, diversification in leadership theorisation, diversification in knowledge sources, diversification of governance concerns and issues, diversification in governance leadership, diversification in stakeholder engagement, and diversification in governance technologies.

Notwithstanding the diversification imperative that we advocate, we close the book by arguing that it is vital that leadership in governance researchers and practitioners work together to find practical ways for organisations, industries, communities and governments to foster shared and compelling purpose that can guide communal action in tackling the very real and urgent global challenges that we all need to address.

DOI: 10.4324/9781003054191-9

Our Key Learnings

The primary objective of this book has been to integrate and cross-fertilise the research and practice of leadership and corporate governance. We have argued that leadership is core to governing an organisation. Leadership, regardless of whether it is good, mediocre or outright bad, is inherent to the governance of every organisation. Institutionalised structures and legal rules provide only a general definition of the director's principal roles. Within these customary prescribed roles, directors through the quality of their leadership significantly influence the effectiveness of corporate governance and the achievement of the organisation's purpose and goals.

The combination of legal perspectives and behavioural perspectives is vital in better understanding and promoting better leadership in governance. These perspectives have traditionally been working in splendid isolation in separate 'camps' emphasising their relative pertinence and superiority (Yar Hamidi & Gabrielsson, 2014) but they should not indeed be separated. We need to transcend our long-held penchant for dualistic explanations and instead focus on appreciating the power of the continuum. Hence the subtitle of our book: *An Integrative Approach*.

The genesis of our multi-disciplinary research team was described in the introductory chapter. While we were initially challenged by the different ways in which we saw as being the key drivers of and constraints upon corporate governance as well as the different language that we brought to our discussions, we began to relish the fresh insights and deeper understanding that was generated when we worked more closely as a team. We strongly recommend the creation of more multi-disciplinary research teams to examine and promote leadership in governance processes and practices. In addition to law, corporate governance and leadership, it would make sense in the short term at least to include scholars from anthropology, economics, linguistics, psychology, sociology and potentially in the longer term from the arts, the humanities and the sciences.

The book prompts the reader to recognise that there are no clear-cut right answers in leadership in governance and it is important to understand that certain behaviours align with governance processes to achieve different organisational objectives. By presenting and discussing extensive case studies of real organisations and contemporary governance issues, the book has provided a prism through which the reader has been given an opportunity to contemplate how directors' beliefs and behaviours (leadership) and structural frameworks (governance), jointly impact organisational practices and performance. In a nutshell, it considers *what* leadership in governance is, *why* it is important, and offers practical approaches on *how* it is developed and practised.

One of our key learnings from the case analyses is that the board provides an even more important source of leadership in organisations and comes from a wider range of sources than we recognised before we engaged in this research. This leadership is not only exerted within the board but also with the executive team members and throughout the entire organisation. The strong board-management relationship was well exemplified in the Bank of New Zealand Diversity Initiatives case study featured in Chapter 8. Board leadership is not only exerted through direct engagement with executives, managers and employees but also through indirect mediated interaction. This observation further underlined the importance of the entity model of the corporation that underpins our work.

Leadership is expressed in all facets of the board's work and is not only confined to their future looking generative and strategic work but also to the ways in which the board carries out its fundamental fiduciary duties (Chait et al., 2005). What the board pays attention to, how it pays attention to this and what happens when the organisation does not follow through and execute sends the strongest leadership signals about what is really important to the organisation and stakeholders. This was most especially revealed in the contrasting fortunes in the cases of Lombard Finance and Diligent that were presented in Chapter 4 which highlighted the board's role in providing organisational oversight and monitoring. In particular these case studies highlighted the moral domain of informal accountability that board members navigate in striving to exercise responsible leadership in governance. The big questions that boards need to continually ask is *who* are we responsible to? For *what* are we responsible?

The effectiveness of board leadership is most obviously demonstrated in transitions in corporate control. In Chapter 6 we featured two contrasting case studies—Auckland International Airport and Aldridge Energy—in which the former board's leadership was found to be lacking in the unsuccessful takeover attempt by an overseas financial institution and the latter successfully led the initial public offering in state-owned energy company. In both of these cases we saw how the board's leadership needs to extend well beyond the organisation to existing and potential shareholders combined with other stakeholder groups.

Another key learning from the book was how much we learned simply by talking with those who are directly engaged in governance work. Our interviews with both executive and non-executive directors broadened our appreciation of the range and scope of governance work and the dedication that is shown by many who engage in this work. The openness, creativity and collective commitment that was shown by the Air New Zealand directors in determining three very different CEO succession processes in our first case study (featured in Chapter 7) set the tone for our case studies throughout the research project. We got a genuine sense from many of the directors that we spoke with that they were well ahead of the research agenda in the academic realm because they are working and trying to respond to such a rapidly changing and dynamic field. It raised an important question for us: in this environment what should be the role of the leadership in governance researcher?

We believe that our integrative approach should actively involve both practitioners and researchers to work together to blend research and development in corporate governance in an ongoing virtuous cycle. In this way we can shorten knowledge creation and dissemination cycles and promote a culture of experimentation in which professional boundaries are broken down and permeated. Scholars should be encouraged to take a different approach to researching governance, proposing that corporate governance offers a specific and focused context within which to explore leadership impact. We also need to support practitioners wanting to develop a leadership approach to governing informed by a deeper understanding of how different leadership and governance interactions influence board effectiveness and enterprise performance.

Our final lesson was that the case study can act as a vital means for promoting the research development of corporate governance. In deciding at an early stage to make case studies a key output, we were able to garner support from our study participants who were anxious to participate because they saw the value of creating case studies that could inform our teaching work. We also recognised that case studies were perceived as being highly invaluable not only for those who participate in our courses but also practitioners who were keen to learn best practice in such governance challenges as CEO succession, diversity initiatives and value creation. We were delighted to receive requests for case studies from a variety of organisations and the enthusiastic response to the master classes that featured these cases. While case studies are generally highly valued in academic circles, within practitioner circles they are still given a high premium. Our challenge in the future is how to innovate the format and delivery of case study in a highly inter-mediated world.

Future Directions for Leadership in Governance Research

While our experience in writing this book has underlined to us the importance of taking an *integrative approach* to the way in which we research and teach leadership in corporate governance, as we look ahead, we recognise the need to take a *diversifying approach* to what we choose to research and teach. Below we highlight several lines of inquiry which we believe we need to diversify in order to ensure that our research remains relevant, insightful and impactful.

Diversifying Research Methods

In our study we endeavoured to integrate both primary data collected through in-depth retrospective interviews with directors and executives as well as secondary data which combined both quantitative and qualitative data. In being able to conduct these interviews we did find a way to at least partially break into the black box of corporate governance (Eraković &

Overall, 2010). However, it is readily evident that we need to find ways to collect observational data that captures in-the-moment leadership dynamics if we are to fulfil the promise of the leadership in governance approach.

Recognising how hard it is to gain access to board meetings we applaud the pioneering work that has been done in direct observation of boards in action (Bezemer et al., 2018; Nicholson et al., 2017; Veltrop et al., 2021). We also note that most of this work has been done within not-for-profit sector organisations and are keen to see similar work done in publicly listed and privately-owned organisations. We also recognise the power of conducting longitudinal research work at multiple levels within the organisation to track the evolution and differential impact of leadership in governance over a sufficiently lengthy period of time.

Diversifying Leadership Theories

The leadership in governance approach paves the way for the application of an array of leadership theories to examine corporate governance. Recognising that in contrast to the corporate governance field, leadership studies is particularly susceptible to novelty as witnessed in the explosion of 'adjective' leadership ideas and so prudence is advisable, it has been pleasing to see a number of leadership theories being brought into examine board leadership including authentic leadership (Guerrero et al., 2015), ethical leadership (Aubé et al., 2021), responsible leadership (Maak, 2007; Pless, 2007; Waldman & Balven, 2014) and leadership identity work (Ward, 2020). This work has served to highlight the importance of understanding the influence that the moral virtues of individual board directors have upon the quality of responsible leadership that is exhibited by the board.

We believe that corporate governance research would also benefit from the greater application of collective leadership theories (Denis et al., 2012; Fairhurst et al., 2020; Ospina et al., 2020; Yammarino et al., 2012) to foreground the inter-relational leadership dynamics within boards and between boards and their stakeholders and highlight the inherently collective nature and impact of leadership in governance. The following collective leadership theories would likely be most pertinent: complexity leadership (Uhl-Bien & Arena, 2017), leadership-in-practice (Raelin, 2016), shared leadership (Uhl-Bien and Arena, 2017) and team leadership (Day et al., 2006; Nolan, 2015). There is also ample scope for leadership in governance to draw on critical leadership perspectives (Alvesson & Spicer, 2012).

Diversifying Knowledge Bases

There has been some debate regarding the extent to which corporate governance knowledge and practices are converging or diverging throughout the world (Ahmad & Omar, 2016; Witt & Stahl, 2016). With the growing ascendency of capital markets, many have predicted global convergence towards a uniform Anglo-Saxon system of corporate governance. However, Clarke (2007) has sagely noted the persistence of the rich institutional diversity that has survived and is indeed valued reflects the history of individual nations. More importantly, 'they signify that nations are animated and distinguished by cultural forces rooted in the past' (Clarke, 2007, p. 9). We take the view that in view of the growing complexity of global challenges that we are facing it is important that we can learn from and draw upon a diverse knowledge base of corporate governance that has stood the test of time.

In this regard, Aotearoa[1] New Zealand is blessed to have developed two different governance models based on culturally distinctive knowledge forms: a variant of the Anglo-Saxon model introduced into the country by settlers and a Māori governance model based on indigenous knowledge. A number of commentators have noted that Māori governance is well-suited to promoting responsible leadership in governance by virtue of its in-built stakeholder, balanced perspective and long-term views. For example, Spiller et al. (2011b) have noted that the relational wisdom approach of Māori which is underpinned by an ethic of kaitiakitanga or stewardship which emphasises the interconnectedness of life in a woven universe, holds the potential to enrich and further humanise our understanding of business and encouraging truly reciprocal relationships. Spiller et al. (2011a) have shown though four Māori business case studies how this relational well-being approach which puts care at the heart of its values can create spiritual, cultural, social, environmental and economic well-being.

An increasing number of non-Māori (or Pākehā) organisations, including Air New Zealand, have taken an explicit interest in actively learning from Māori governance practices, partially in ensuring that their organisations are properly honouring the Te Tiriti o Waitangi,[2] but also because of the intrinsic benefits that this approach can bring to reforming their governance practices so that they can be properly guided by the environmental, social and governance (ESG) reporting framework.

Diversifying Board Concerns and Issues

In this book we have analysed leadership in governance case studies that have examined a range of governance issues from monitoring and oversight; investor strategies; corporate control; value creation; promoting diversity and inclusion and CEO succession. All of these issues have been pertinent to corporate governance for at least a decade and some for very much longer. But what of the plethora of global issues that have gripped organisations in the past three years? The corporate response to the global COVID pandemic and the continued threat of future pandemics has dominated many company agendas. Ljiljana and Susan have been involved in a research project that has examined the lived experiences of New

Zealand CEOs, board chairs and directors in handling the crisis (Benson-Rea et al., 2021). This issue has faced stiff competition from formulating the corporate response to Climate Change and the drive towards carbon neutrality reinforced by ESG and triple-bottom line reporting frameworks. All this while ensuring that the cyber-security risk mitigation strategies are put in place and are one step ahead of cyber criminals.

How do we as leadership in governance researchers, let alone corporate directors, keep pace with these burgeoning challenges in a way that our research can still resonate with any degree of relevance with practice? Moreover, what was once a speciality field known as crisis governance that had been drawn on in relatively rare moments has now moved centre stage as the dominant modus operandi for many companies. How do leadership in governance practices need to change and adapt in order to support this approach to governance? Although there has been some growing attention paid to the grand challenges in leadership studies, we sadly agree with Dennis Tourish's observation that 'mainstream leadership theories are of little help, since an environment of radical uncertainty means that leaders have less information, expertise and resources to guide them than is often assumed' (Tourish, 2020, p. 262). What do we do to turn this around? One crucial response is to reduce our publishing cycles. The publication of a special issue of *Leadership* journal on 'Pandemic Leadership' within three months of the formally declared outbreak of COVID-19 is an impressive step forward in this regard.

Diversifying Governance Leadership

One response towards addressing the increasing diversity and complexity of governance issues has been to diversify board membership. In addition to doing this because it is the right thing to do and is long overdue, another guiding idea is that boards need to draw on the best talent from all constituencies and that these constituencies need to be better understood and worked with to develop the most responsive strategies to these issues. While the central focus has been on promoting gender representation on boards through government mandates or self-driven (as described in our Bank of New Zealand case study) there is growing momentum to promote broader diversity including ethnic and generational diversity.

Researchers have played a critical role in identifying the barriers that have impeded diversity and how they can be overcome (Aluchna & Aras, 2018). We have an important opportunity to investigate the impact that diversifying board membership is having on how leadership is being practised within boards and between boards and between boards and their key stakeholders (Magnanelli & Pirolo, 2020). Specifically, in more diverse boards how are issues identified, selected and prioritised? How is performance measured and rewarded? How are conflicts managed and decisions made? Which stakeholders are engaged with and how are they engaged with? What has been the impact on the employees? (Biswas et al., 2021).

We have made an initial contribution to this work by applying our leadership-in-governance framework to a study of four women who were independent board chairs and two who were deputy chairs (Cikaliuk et al., 2018). We concluded that, while these chairs were enacting effective shared leadership with board members, their CEOs and external stakeholders, a concerted system-wide effort needs to be made in identification, development, appointment and retention of women board chairs.

Diversifying Stakeholder Engagement

The fundamental objective of Responsible Leadership is to enhance the interest of others both within the organisation, and those connected with and affected by the organisation. Without the support of these stakeholders the organisation might cease to exist (Freeman & Reed, 1983). Traditionally, primary stakeholders in a typical corporation were recognised as being its investors, employees, customers and suppliers but more recently with the growing complexity of global issues our recognition of stakeholder salience has been widened to include regulators, creditors, unions, professional associations, community, iwi and interest groups as well as the broader citizenry under a broader shift away from 'shareholder capitalism' to 'stakeholder capitalism' (Schwab, 2021).

In recognition of the complex network of stakeholder relationships and the need to genuinely address the full gamut of social, economic, environmental and cultural challenges we all share in common, Jackson et al. (2022) have argued that responsible leadership is best not seen as a distinctive theory of leadership but rather as a particular orientation of leadership. They outline a series of five re-orientations along the following dimensions that are highly pertinent to boards in researching responsible leadership in governance: a shift away from studying leadership behaviour towards studying decisions, actions and outcomes; a shift away from a pre-occupation with leader(s) and followers towards leader(s) and stakeholders (those internal and external to the organisation); a shift away from a short-term focus towards a long-term focus; and a shift away from place-agnostic approach towards a place-centric approach; away from individualistic (and heroic) approaches to leading towards collaborative approaches with a strong emphasis placed upon stewardship.

Diversifying Technologies

The final line of inquiry that leadership in governance researchers need to actively consider and address in their research is the disruption created by the rapidly increasing digitisation of governance processes (Wolfe, 2020). The availability of 'big data' will not only create new market niches but it will also have a profound impact on the way boards work. For example, as compliance becomes automated, compliance and data logs will become a source of oversight for audit committees. Board portals are promising to provide directors with better and more timely data to support their internal and external scanning work. Artificial Intelligence has the potential to assist and indeed take over a number of corporate governance processes (Hilb, 2020). Torre et al. (2020) argue that board members will need to significantly develop their artificial intelligence (AI) leadership capability by guiding the company's AI operational capability and innovation and by supervising AI governance capability (i.e. data management, AI security ad business ecosystem leadership).

The field of leadership studies has paid all too scant attention to researching and developing responsible virtual leadership processes which have become a central concern with the rapid escalation throughout the world of remote and hybrid working. The field is even more poorly placed in its examination of the leadership implication of big data, artificial intelligence and cyber-security. The responsible leadership of digital governance is an urgent research and development priority. The field of corporate governance is comparatively better placed. For example, Åberg et al. (2017) have created a useful framework that identifies several timely board practices with the potential to improve the way boards strategise under conditions of increasing digitalisation. Taking a knowledge management perspective, Bankewitz et al. (2016) predict that digitalisation will influence boards in two main ways. First, boards in the future will primarily consist of virtual networks of people where the need for monitoring management is diminished and shared leadership becomes more prominent. Second, boards will work according to a dynamic board agenda based on emerging organisational threats and opportunities.

In Closing

Notwithstanding the diversification imperatives that we have outlined above, it is vital that leadership in governance researchers and practitioners ensure that they find a way to create a unity of purpose. It is vital that we work together to find practical and meaningful ways for organisations, industries, communities and governments to foster a shared compelling purpose that can guide communal action in tackling the very real and urgent global challenges that we all need to address (Kempster & Jackson, 2021).

It is, therefore, essential that responsible leadership in governance research orients its scholarship to address the enormous challenges that face society, the environment, and indeed humanity. We hope that the responsible leadership in governance framework and the integrated approach that has been applied to a range of governance issues in different corporate contexts in this book will serve to open up new lines of inquiry and guide future studies aimed at improving and enlightening the practice of corporate governance for the betterment of all.

Kia kaha, kia māia, kia manawanui—be strong, be brave, be steadfast.

Notes

1 Māori name for New Zealand.
2 Māori name for Treaty of Waitangi, the founding document of New Zealand.

References

Åberg, C., Kazemargi, N., & Bankewitz, M. (2017). Strategists on the board in a digital era. *Business and Management Research*, 6(2), 40–51.

Ahmad, S., & Omar, R. (2016). Basic corporate governance models: A systematic review. *International Journal of Law and Management*, 58(10), 73–107.

Aluchna, M., & Aras, G. (2018). *Women on corporate boards: An international perspective*. Routledge.

Alvesson, M., & Spicer, A. (2012). Critical leadership studies: The case for critical performativity. *Human Relations*, 65(3), 367–390.

Aubé, C., Francouer, C., Sponem, S., & Séguin, M. (2021). Ethical leadership and corporate board effectiveness: The role of team reflexivity and environmental dynamics. *Group Dynamics: Theory, Research and Practice*, 25(4), 288–302.

Bankewitz, M., Åberg, C., & Teuchert, C. (2016). Digitalization and boards of directors: A new era of corporate governance. *Business and Management Research*, 5(2), 58–69.

Benson-Rea, M., Eraković, L., & Watson, S. (2021). Covid-19 governance challenges: The board's role in Covid-19 crisis management. In K. Husted & R. Sinkovics (eds), *Management perspectives on the Covid-19 crisis: Lessons from New Zealand*, Edward Elgar, forthcoming.

Bezemer, P. J., Nicholson, G., & Pugliese, A. (2018). The influence of board chairs on director engagement: A case-based exploration of boardroom decision-making. *Corporate Governance: An International Review*, 26(3), 219–234.

Biswas, P. K., Roberts, H., & Stainvack, K. (2021). Does women's board representation affect non-managerial gender inequality? *Human Resource Management*, 60(4), 1–22.

Chait, R. P., Ryan, W. P., & Taylor, B. E. (2005). *Governance as leadership: Reframing the work of nonprofit boards*. John Wiley & Sons.

Cikaliuk, M., Eraković, L., Jackson, B., Noonan, C., & Watson, S. (2018). Leadership in governance: Women board chairs. In L. Devnew, M. Janzen Le Ber, M. Torchia & R. Burke (eds), *More women on boards: An international perspective* (pp. 269–283). Information Age Publishing.

Clarke, T. (2007). *International corporate governance: A comparative approach*. Routledge.

Coulson-Thomas, C. (2019). Board leadership, crisis governance and governance in crisis. *Effective Executive*, 22(3), 42–58.

Day, D., Gronn, P., & Salas, E. (2006). Leadership in team-based organizations: On the threshold of a new era. *The Leadership Quarterly*, 17(3), 211–216.

Denis, J. L., Langley, A., & Sergi, V. (2012). Leadership in the plural. *The Academy of Management Annals*, 6(1), 211–283.

Eraković, L., & Jackson, B. (2012). Promoting leadership in governance and governance in leadership. In A. Davila, M. Elvira, J. Ramirez & L. Zapata-Cantu (eds), *Understanding organizations in complex, emergent and uncertain environments* (pp. 68–83). Palgrave Macmillan.

Eraković, L., & Overall, J. (2010). Opening the 'black box': Challenging traditional governance theorems. *Journal of Management & Organization*, 16(2), 250–265.

Fairhurst, G., Jackson, B., Foldy, E., & Ospina, S. (2020). Studying collective leadership: The road ahead. *Human Relations*, 73(4), 598–614.

Filatotchev, I., & Boyd, B. K. (2009). Taking stock of corporate governance research while looking to the future. *Corporate Governance: An International Review*, 17(3), 257–265.

Freeman, R., & Reed, D. (1983). Stockholders and stakeholders: A new perspective on corporate governance, *California Management Review*, 25(3), 88–106.

Gabrielsson, J., Khlif, W., & Yamak, S. (eds). (2019). *Research handbook on boards of directors*. Edward Elgar.

Guerrero, S., Laplame, M-E., & Séguin, M. (2015). Board chair authentic leadership and nonexecutives' motivation and commitment. *Journal of Leadership and Organisation Studies*, 22(1), 88–101.

Hilb, M. (2020). Toward artificial governance? The role of artificial intelligence in shaping the future of corporate governance. *Journal of Management and Governance*, 24(4), 854–870.

Jackson, B., Kempster, S., Liyanage, C., Shang, S., & Sun, P. (2022). Responsible leadership: From theory building to impact mobilisation? In D. Schedlitzki, M. Larsson, B. Carroll & M. Bligh (eds), *Sage handbook of leadership* (2nd ed.; pp. 240–262). Sage.

Kempster, S., & Jackson, B. (2021). Leadership for what, why, for whom and where?: A responsibility perspective. *Journal of Change Management*, 21(1), 45–65.

Maak, T. (2007). Responsible leadership, stakeholder engagement, and the emergence of social capital. *Journal of Business Ethics*, 74(4), 329–343.

Magnanelli, B., & Pirolo, L. (2020). *Corporate governance and diversity in boardrooms: Empirical insights into firm performance*. Palgrave Macmillan.

Nicholson, G., Pugliese, A., & Bezemer, P.-J. (2017). Habitual accountability routines in the boardroom: How boards balance control and collaboration. *Accounting, Auditing & Accountability Journal*, 30(2), 222–246.

Nolan, R. (2015). *Executive team leadership in the global economic and competitive environment*. Routledge.

Ospina, S., Foldy, E., Fairhurst, G., & Jackson, B. (2020). Collective dimensions of leadership: Connecting theory and method, *Human Relations*, 73(4), 441–463.

Pless, N. M. (2007). Understanding responsible leadership: Roles identity and motivational drivers. *Journal of Business Ethics*, 74(4), 437–456.

Raelin, J. A. (2016). Imagine there are no leaders: Reframing leadership as collaborative agency. *Leadership*, 12(2), 131–158.

Schwab, K. (2021). *Stakeholder capitalism*. John Wiley.

Spiller, C., Eraković, L., Henare, M., & Pio, E. (2011a). Relational well-being and wealth: Māori businesses and an ethic of care. *Journal of Business Ethics*, 98(1), 153–169.

Spiller, C., Pio, E., Eraković, L., & Henare, M. (2011b). Wise up: Creating organizational wisdom through an ethic of Kaitikitanga. *Journal of Business Ethics*, 104 (2), 223–235.

Steckler, E., & Clark, C. (2017). Authenticity and corporate governance. *Journal of Business Ethics*, 155, 951–963.

Torre, F., Teigland, R., & Engstam, L. (2020). AI leadership and the future of corporate governance: Changing demands for board competence. In A. Larsson & R. Teigland (eds), *The digital transformation of labor* (pp. 116–146). Routledge.

Tourish, D. (2020). Introduction to the Special Issue: Why the coronavirus is also a crisis of leadership. *Leadership*, 16(3), 261–272.

Uhl-Bien, M., & Arena, M. (2017). Complexity leadership: Enabling people and organizations for adaptability. *Organizational Dynamics*, 46(1), 9–20.

Veltrop, D. B., Bezemer, P.-J., Nicholson, G., & Pugliese, A. (2021). Too unsafe to monitor? How board–CEO cognitive conflict and chair leadership shape outside director monitoring. *Academy of Management Journal*, 64(1), 207–234.

Waldman, D., & Balven, R. M. (2014). Responsible leadership: Theoretical issues and research directions. *Academy of Management Perspectives*, 28(3), 224–234.

Ward, C. (2020). Identity dynamics and board dynamics: A discursive account of board member identity work. PhD thesis, University of Auckland.

Watson, S. (2022). *The making of the modern company*. Bloomsbury.

Witt, M., & Stahl, G. (2016). Foundations of responsible leadership: Western versus executive responsibility orientations toward key stakeholders. *Journal of Business Ethics*, 136(3), 623–638.

Wolfe, J. (2020). *Disruption in the boardroom: Leading corporate governance and oversight into an evolving digital future*. Apress.

Yammarino, F. J., Salas, E., Serban, A., Shirreffs, K., & Shuffler, M. L. (2012). Collectivistic leadership approaches: Putting the 'we' in leadership science and practice. *Industrial and Organizational Psychology*, 5(4), 382–402.

Yar Hamidi, D., & Gabrielsson, J. (2014). Developments and trends in research on board leadership: A systematic literature review. *International Journal of Business Governance and Ethics*, 9(3), 243–268.

Index

Page numbers followed by 'n' refer to notes.